NATURAL RESOURCES AND SUSTAINABLE DEVELOPMENT

NATURAL RESOURCES AND SUSTAINABLE DEVELOPMENT

PROF B.K. PANDA
DR SUKANTA SARKAR

KALPAZ

ISBN: 978-93-5128-125-2
Price : ₹ 1090/-

First Published, 2015

Published by

Kalpaz Publications
C-30, Satyawati Nagar,
Delhi-110052
Ph. : 9212142040
E-mail: kalpaz@hotmail.com

Laser Typesetting : Abhishek Mandal, Delhi
Printed at : G. Print Process, Delhi

Cataloging in Publication Data—DK

Courtesy: D.K. Agencies (P) Ltd. <docinfo@dkagencies.com>

Natural resources and sustainable development /
Prof B.K. Panda, Dr Sukanta Sarkar.

pages cm

Contributed articles.

Includes bibliographical references (pages)
and index.

ISBN 9789351281252

1. Natural resources—Environmental aspects—India. 2. Natural resources—India—Management. 3. Sustainable development—India. I. Panda, B. K., editor. II. Sarkar, Sukanta, editor.

DDC 333.70954 23

Contents

Preface

Natural resources are materials and components (something that can be used) that can be found within the environment. Natural resources occur naturally within environments that exist relatively undisturbed by humanity, in a natural form. Natural resources can be thought of as natural capital assets, distinct from physical and human capital in that they are not created by human activity. Natural resource is often characterised by amounts of biodiversity and geodiversity existent in various ecosystems. Natural resources are useful materials from the Earth, such as coal, oil, natural gas, and trees. People use natural resources as raw materials to manufacture or create a range of modern conveniences. Water and food provide humans with sustenance and energy, for example, and fossil fuels generate heat as well as energy for transportation and industrial production. Natural resources are the raw materials supplied by nature. Everything produced, used and thrown away originates from natural resources. People cannot create natural resources.

We desire to express our heartiest thank to Prof A. Rahman, Department of Agriculture, International University of Business Agriculture and Technology, Dhaka, Bangladesh who despite his busy schedule and hectic academic engagements, all the time encouraged and supported us. We have also beholden to Dr N.G. Pendse, Department of Economics, Rani Durgabati University, Jabalpur who's erudite and scholarly tidbits for preparing such a vast work are still fresh in our mind. We also thanks to

Dr Pradeep Kumar Pandey, Centre of Judicial Studies, Dibrugarh University, Assam; Dr Suman Kalan Chaudhury, Department of Business Administration, Berhampur University, Odisha; Dr Rakesh Joshi, Department of Economics, Saurashtra University, Gujarat; Dr D. Pulla Rao, Department of Economics, Andhra University; Dr Vibhuti Patel, Professor cum Director, Centre for Study of Social Exclusion and Inclusive Policy, SNDT Women's University, Mumbai; Dr Wakar Amin, Department of Social Work, University of Kashmir, J & K; Dr Shazia Manzoor, Assistant Professor Department of Social Work, University of Kashmir, J & K; Dr Pallab Kanti Ghoshal, Department of Commerce, Netaji Subhas College, Udaipur, for their valuable suggestions and moral support.

We are heartily grateful to Prof R. Prasad, Prof Ashish Kumar Shivastava and Prof L.S. Nigam, Pandit Ravishankar Shukla University, Raipur, Chhattisgarh who always encouraged us to carry on this constructive work. Further, we express our heartily thankfulness to each and every person who directly/ indirectly helped usin preparing this work.

It is hoped that this book will be very useful society in general and it is students of Natural Science in particular. Comments and suggestions are most welcomed.

Prof B.K. Panda
Dr Sukanta Sarkar

List of Contributors

Ajaz Ahmad Rather: Lecturer Jammu and Kashmir Government, Jammu and Kashmir, J & K.

Alson Rasool: PhD Research Scholar, Department of History, University of Kashmir, Srinagar, Jammu and Kashmir.

Cliff Dkhar: Library and Information Professional, IIM Shillong, Meghalaya.

Dr A.I. Singh: Associate Professor of Economics, D.N. Govt. College, Itanagar, Arunachal Pradesh.

Dr B.K. Panda: Professor, PG Department of Economics, Berhampur University, Odisha.

Dr Bijay Raji: Assistant Professor in Political Science, D. N. Govt. College, Itanagar, Arunachal Pradesh.

Dr D. Pulla Rao: Professor, Department of Economics, Andhra University, Visakhapatnam, Andhra Pradesh, India.

Dr M. S. Rawat: Professor, Department of Geography, Nagaland University, Lumami Zunheboto, Nagaland.

Dr Manaswini Patra: Librarian I/C, Berhampur University, Odisha.

Dr Mohammad Afsar Alam: Assistant Professor and Head, Department of Geography, Adi-Keih College of Arts and Social Sciences, Eritrea, N.E. Africa.

Dr N.G. Pendse: Professor, Department of Economics, Rani Durgabati University, Jabalpur, Madhya Pradesh.

Dr P. Prabhuswamy: Population Research Centre, Research Analyst, Institute for Social and Economic Change, Nagarabhavi, Bangalore, Karnataka.

Dr P.K. Pandey: Assistant Professor, Centre of Juridical Studies, Dibrugarh University, Assam.

Dr R.L. Dave: Professor, Shri Vaishnav College of Commerce, Gumasta Nagar, Indore, Madhya Pradesh.

Dr Rakesh Joshi: Associate Professor, Department of Economics, Saurashtra University, Rajkot, Gujarat.

Dr Ras Bihari Prasad Singh: Professor, Department of Geography, Patna University, Patna, Bihar.

Dr S.K. Chaudhury: Faculty Member, Department of Business Administration, Berhampur University, Odisha.

Dr Sudhir Kumar Jena: Librarian, IIM Shillong, Meghalaya.

Dr Sukanta Sarkar: Assistant Professor, Faculty of Management Studies, Icfai University, Agartala, Tripura.

Dr Vimal Kishor: Assistant Professor, Department of Education, School of Professional Studies, Sikkim University (A Central University), Gangtok, Sikkim.

Ishfaq Ahmad Malik: Ph.D Research Scholar, CCAS, University of Kashmir, Srinagar, J & K.

Jyoti Walia: Assistant Professor, Jupiter College of Education, V.P.O. Mairi, Teh. Amb, Distt. Una, Himachal Pradesh.

Priyanka Kukreja: Research Scholar in SOS in Economics, Pt. Ravishankar Shukla University, Raipur, Chhattisgarh.

Prof Rohini Prasad: Dean of Social Science, Pt. Ravi Shannkar Shukla University, Raipur, Chhattisgarh.

Rajesh Raushan: Doctoral Fellow, Population Research Centre, Institute for Social and Economic Change, Bangalore, Karnataka.

Sanjay Maheshwari: Assistant Professor, Vishisht School of Management, R.S. Shukla Marg, Pologround, Indore, Madhya Pradesh.

Shanti Bhushan Kumari: Research Scholar, Department of Geography, Patna University, Patna, Bihar.

Abbreviations

CBNRM	:	Community-Based Natural Resource Management
CCAs	:	Community Conserved Areas
CGWB	:	Central Ground Water Board
CPRs	:	Common Property Resources
FAO	:	Food and Agriculture Organisation
GDP	:	Gross Domestic Product
GIM	:	Green India Mission
ICT	:	Information and Communication Technologies
ILL	:	Inter Library Loan
INRM	:	Integrated Natural Resource Management
KSPCB	:	Karnataka State Pollution Control Board
MAP	:	Medicinal and Aromatic Plants
MoEF	:	Ministry of Environment and Forests
MTP	:	Medical Termination of Pregnancy
NDC	:	National Development Council
NEP	:	National Environment Policy
NNRMS	:	National Natural Resources Management System
NR	:	Natural Resources
NRCP	:	National River Conservation Plan
NSDP	:	Net State Domestic Products
OPAC	:	On-line Public Access Catalogue
RGS	:	Rubber Growers Society
RPSs	:	Rubber Producers Societies
SAARC	:	South Asian Association for Regional Cooperation
SPM	:	Suspended Particulate Matter
STB	:	Scheduled Tribes (Recognition of Forest Rights) Bill
STs	:	Scheduled Tribes

TFDPC : Tripura Forest Development and Plantation Corporation
TRPC : Tripura Rehabilitation Plantation Corporation
UNCED : United Nations Conference for the Environment and Development
WAM : Web Access Management
WBRAP : World Bank Aided Rubber Project
WCED : World Commission on Environment and Development
WDPSCA : Watershed Development Project in Shifting Cultivation Areas

1

Deforestation and Development: Causes, Trends, Effects and Government Initiatives

Dr S.K.Chaudhury *and* ***Dr Sukanta Sarkar***

"We need to revise our economic thinking to give full value to our natural resources. This revised economics will stabilise both the theory and the practice of free-market capitalism. It will provide business and public policy with a powerful new tool for economic development, profitability, and the promotion of the public good."

—Paul Hawken

Introduction

Forest and human are connected from the primitive stages. Forests can be found in all regions capable of sustaining tree growth, at altitudes up to the tree line, except where natural fire frequency or other disturbance is too high, or where the environment has been altered by human activity. Forests sometimes contain many tree species only within a small area or relatively few species over large areas. Forests are often home to many animal and plant species, and biomass per unit area is high compared to other vegetation communities. Today, ecologically significant old-growth forests are protected from harvest and represent new values in modern forest management. Old-growth forests can be compared to similar but harvested forests, and conclusions can be reached about the effect of harvest on soils, plant and animal life, the rate of tree growth, and many other parts of a forest's ecology. This kind of research can help improve forest management approaches aimed at supplying wood reliably to the economy while guaranteeing a healthy ecosystem for future harvest and enjoyment.

Forest products are used in our daily lives. All the activities directly or indirectly involve forests. Some are easy to figure out - fruits, paper and wood from trees, and so on. The chief economic product of forests is timber, but the economic benefits, in terms of climate control, pollution abatement, and wildlife maintenance, have rarely been calculated. The economic importance of non-timber forest products is increasing. The forest is vital as a watershed. Because of the thick humus layer, loose soil, and soil-retaining powers of the trees' long roots, forests are vitally important for preserving adequate water supplies. Over the past 50 years, about half the world's original forest cover has been lost, the most significant cause for that being humans beings' unsystematic use of its resources. Forests are complex ecosystems that are important to the carbon and water cycles that sustain life on earth. When they are degraded, it can set off a devastating chain of events both locally and around the world.

What is Deforestation?

Deforestation is the removal of a forest or stand of trees where the land is thereafter converted to a non-forest use. It refers to the cutting, clearing, and removal of rainforest or related ecosystems into less bio-diverse ecosystems such as pasture, cropland, or plantations. It is clearing Earth's forests on a massive scale, often resulting in damage to the quality of the land. Forests still cover about 30 per cent of the world's land area, but swaths the size of Panama is lost each and every year. Most definitions describe deforestation as long-term or permanent conversion of land from forest to non-forest. In the Marrakesh Accord, deforestation is defined as 'the direct human-induced conversion of forested land to non-forested land'. The Food and Agriculture

Organisation defines deforestation as 'the conversion of forest to another land use or the long-term reduction of the tree canopy cover below the minimum 10 per cent threshold.'

Causes of Deforestation

According to the United Nations Framework Convention on Climate Change secretariat, the overwhelming direct cause of deforestation is agriculture. Subsistence farming is responsible for 48 per cent of deforestation; commercial agriculture is responsible for 32 per cent of deforestation; logging is responsible for 14 per cent of deforestation and fuel wood removals make up five per cent of deforestation. Forests are cut down for many reasons, but most of them are related to money or to people's need to provide for their families. The biggest driver of deforestation is agriculture. Farmers cut forests to provide more room for planting crops or grasing livestock.

Common methods of deforestation are burning trees and clear cutting, which is the controversial practice of complete removal of a given tract of forest. Burning can be done quickly, in vast swaths of land for plantation use, or more slowly with the slash-and-burn technique. People have been deforesting the Earth for thousands of years, primarily to clear land for crops or livestock. Although tropical forests are largely confined to developing countries, they aren't just meeting local or national needs; economic globalisation means that the needs and wants of the global population are bearing down on them as well. Direct causes of deforestation are agricultural expansion, wood extraction, and infrastructure expansion such as road building and urbanisation.

Logging trees in a forest to harvest timber for wood, products or fuel, is a primary driver of deforestation. Logging affects the environment in several ways. Hydroelectric dams are quite controversial because while they help to power communities, they contribute to deforestation. Damming opponents believe that the building of such structures not only has a negative environmental impact, but it also opens up the area to loggers and more roads. Fires, both accidental and intended, destroy acres of forest very quickly. Areas affected by logging are more susceptible to fires due to the number of dried, dead trees. Milder winters and extended are warm seasons due to global warm also fuel fires. Mining also results in deforestation. Digging a coal, diamond or gold mine requires the removal of all forest cover, not just for the mines but also for trucks and equipment. Shifting cultivation is considered to be another cause for deforestation. In fact shifting cultivation has occurred due to poor fertility of the soil. In this cultivation a small patch of tropical forests is cleared, vegetation, destroyed and burned. Crops are grown as long as the soil is productive, after which the cultivation is abandoned, and a cultivations move on to fresh patch of land.

Deforestation: Global Perspectives

Deforestation is a complex problem. A recent study by the Food and Agriculture Organisation (FAO) reported that during the decade from 1980 to 1990, the world's tropical forests were reduced by an average of 15.4 million hectares per year (0.8 per cent annual rate of deforestation). The area of land cleared during the decade is equivalent to nearly three times the size of France. In Africa, the statistics are striking: an estimated 90 per cent of the entire continent's population uses fuelwood for cooking, and in Sub-Saharan Africa, firewood and brush supply approximately 52 per cent of all energy sources. Commercial logging only accounts for at most one-quarter of the global deforestation problem, so focusing only on the logging industry is an inadequate solution.

Brazil's natural assets are legendary. The country is home to the largest rain forest biome in the world, the Amazon, containing by far the largest portion of remaining rain forest. The legal Amazon covers 60 per cent of the Brazilian territory, with some 21 million inhabitants, or about 12 per cent of the population, nearly 70 per cent of who live in cities and towns. Brazil has the largest freshwater reservoir in the world, with the Amazon region alone containing up to one fifth of the world's freshwater. In the Amazon, the use of satellite data has helped the government slash deforestation by 80 per cent since 2003-04 by allowing police to pinpoint illegal activity in the vast forest, which is bigger than Western Europe. But the 5,800 km^2 in 2012-13 was a 28 per cent increase on the record-low in the previous year. Brazil has demanded funding from rich nation's to cut deforestation and has been sensitive to criticism of its effort to develop and improve the living standards of its 200 million people. In 2009, the then President Luiz Inácio Lula da Silva said: *"I don't want any gringo asking us to let an Amazon resident die of hunger under a tree. We want to preserve, but they will have to pay the price for this preservation because we never destroyed our forest like they mowed theirs down a century ago."* About three-quarters of Brazil's emissions come from rainforest clearing, as trees are burned or felled and rot, making the nation the world's sixth biggest emitter of the carbon dioxide. The new global satellite study shows that Indonesia, despite being just a quarter of the size of Brazil, now destroys about the same area of forest.

Brazil says the rate of deforestation in the Amazon increased by 28 per cent between August 2012 and July 2013, after years of decline. The government is working to reverse this "crime", Environment Minister Izabella Teixeira said. Activists have blamed the increase in destruction on a controversial reform to Brazil's forest protection law. Last year Brazil reported the lowest rate of deforestation in the Amazon since monitoring began. The provisional statistics from August 2012 to last July suggest that the area suffering deforestation was 5,843 sq km (2,255 sq miles), compared to 4,571 sq km (1,765 sq miles) in the previous 12 months. The 28 per cent rise interrupts a period of declining deforestation which began in 2009. However, it still remains the second lowest annual figure for forest loss in absolute terms.The worst year on record was 2004, when 27,000 sq km of forest was destroyed.

Satellite images of Africa's Congo Basin reveal that deforestation has fallen by about a third since 2000. Sprawling across the heart of Africa, the Congo Basin rainforest is second only to the Amazon in size. It covers nearly 2 million sq km (800,000 sq miles). But from 2000 to 2010, the rate of deforestation had slowed. Fewer than 2,000 sq km (700 sq miles) of rainforest were lost every year. The world's second largest rainforest is losing 2,000 square km. According to the United Nations Food and Agriculture Organisation, Central Africa lost approximately 91,000 km^2 to deforestation in the 10 years between 1990 and

2000. The size of the region's forests was estimated at 24,03,000 km^2 in 2000. In West and Central African countries, degradation of forests has already transformed some areas into savanna grasslands or degraded savannas. Once blanketed with forests, West Africa has been skinned alive over the last decade. Guinea's rainforests have been reduced by 80 per cent, while Liberia has sold logging rights to over half its forests. Within the next few years Sierra Leone is on track to be completely deforested.

Deforestation in the rainforests of West Africa reduces rainfall over the rest of the forest. The forests of West Africa and the Congo Basin are the second largest in the world after the Amazon rainforest. They are important not only as a habitat for a vast and diverse ecosystem but also as a carbon sink, removing a large proportion of the CO_2 in the Earth's atmosphere and slowing down climate change. For many years deforestation has been occurring widely in Africa, with tree canopies being removed in favour of agriculture, plantations and other non-forest uses. Most of the deforestation in the Congo is caused by local subsistence activities by poor farmers and villagers who rely on forest lands for agriculture and fuelwood collection. Slash-and-burn is commonly used for clearing forest. Typically, poor farmers and colonists gains access to forest lands by following logging roads, although in the past few years civil strife has driven many Central Africans deep into the rainforest to escape the widespread violence. The Congo Basin has some of the world's richest mineral deposits. Mining operations are poorly monitored and financial returns are prioritised over social impacts and the long-term health effects — much less to the environmental impact. The biggest drivers of deforestation in the Congo rainforest over the past 20 years have been small-scale subsistence agriculture, clearing for charcoal and fuelwood, urban expansion, and mining. Industrial logging has been the biggest driver of forest degradation. However it's important not to understate the impact of logging in the region. For decades, the dynamics of tropical deforestation in sub-Saharan Africa (SSA) have defied easy explanation. The rates of deforestation have been lower than elsewhere in the tropics, and the driving forces evident in other places, government new land settlement schemes and industrialised agriculture, have largely been absent in SSA.

Deforestation is the permanent destruction of forests in order to make the land available for other uses. An estimated 18 million acres (7.3 million hectares) of forest are lost each year, according to the United Nations' Food and Agriculture Organisation. Deforestation occurs around the world, though tropical rainforests are particularly targeted. Countries with significant deforestation currently or in the recent past include Brazil, Indonesia, Thailand, the Democratic Republic of Congo and other parts of Africa, and parts of Eastern Europe, according to GRID-Arendal, a United Nations Environment Programme collaborating centre. Forests cover 31 per cent of the land area on our planet. They produce vital oxygen and provide homes for people and wildlife. Many of the world's most threatened and endangered animals live in forests, and 1.6 billion people rely on benefits forests offer, including food, fresh water, clothing, traditional medicine and shelter. Deforestation is a particular concern in tropical rainforests because these forests are home to much of the world's biodiversity.

Deforestation has emerged as one of the major concerns of the world community as significant environmental impacts are attributed to it. The plainly observed association between population increase and deforestation in most of the developing countries has deepened the concern on deforestation. Forests are crucial for the well being of humanity. They provide foundations for life on earth through ecological functions by regulating the climate and water resources and by serving as habitats for plants and animals. Forests also provide a variety of essential goods such as wood for domestic and exports markets and recreational opportunities.

Deforestation in India

Deforestation and forest degradation in the Himalayas are a major concern for social scientists and policy-makers because of the large common property externalities involved at both the global and the local levels. At the global level, the Himalayan range is one of the most unstable and fragile mountain areas in the world. At a more local level, the alpine zone of the Himalayas is home to populations who rely mainly on agriculture and livestock rearing for their livelihood. Their livelihoods rely strongly on the forests adjoining their villages. Firewood, timber, fodder and leaf-litter for livestock are collected from these forests. About 60 per cent of the population is engaged in agriculture. The agriculture land is fragmented into uneconomic parcels and overused. Growing population, widespread poverty, limited employment opportunities in agricultural and industrial sector has resulted in heavy pressure on forests, primarily due to unsustainable extraction of fuel wood and over-grasing resulting in forest degradation.

India is witnessing a rising demand for forest-based products. This is causing deforestation and encroachment into forest protected areas, which leads to a severe loss of natural resources. Increasing competition for water among various sectors, including agriculture, industry, domestic, drinking, energy generation and others, is causing this precious natural resource to dry up. Increasing pollution is leading to the destruction of the habitat of wildlife that lives in waterways. India has the tenth largest forest coverage in the world. It is the world's fifth largest carbon emitter, accounting for five per cent of global greenhouse gases, according to the Indian government. Deforestation and forest degradation through agricultural expansion, conversion to pasture land, infrastructure development, logging and fires account for nearly 20 per cent of emissions, says the United Nations. This is more than transportation sector and second only to the energy sector.

For a long time, India has been a major emerging economy that typically has had less area covered by forests compared to some of its emerging market peers. Currently, India's forests account for 12 per cent of the country's total land mass. Approximately 45 per cent of India's land is degraded primarily due to deforestation, unsustainable agricultural practices, mining and excessive groundwater extraction. More than 2/3rds of this can be regenerated. India has the 10th largest forest cover in the world at 68 million hectares. The government's National Action Plan on climate change involves expanding forest cover from the current 23 per cent to 33 per cent of India's territory, and to afforest six million hectares of degraded forest land.

Effects of Deforestation

Deforestation is considered to be one of the contributing factors to global climate change. Trees absorb greenhouse gases and carbon emissions. They produce oxygen and perpetuate the water cycle by releasing water vapour into the atmosphere. Without trees, forest lands can quickly become barren land. Deforestation is indeed a serious issue, and there will be no exaggeration in saying that since 1990 the jungle areas have been declining at a fast pace. India once had 14.8 billion acres of land that was forested, but now has dwindled to just 8.6 billion acres. Forests are chopped basically for two reasons, basic necessities and maintaining the lifestyle. It is true that reason for cutting down of trees is justified to an extent, but, while rasing people do not realise that they are diminishing the existence of flora and fauna, and becoming egocentric. Forests are biosphere's vital part for controlling atmospheric carbon dioxide by utilising it for photosynthesis. However, people are clearing the forests for monetary reasons, which have led to an increase of carbon dioxide levels in the atmosphere. Many nature and wildlife lovers have started taking efforts to save the various wild organisms on the verge of annihilation and the world from running out if its verdant vegetation.

The effects of deforestation can be devastating. It can lose the land of its natural aesthetic. In coming years, dangerous consequences will be visible. Deforestation can damage to the environment, usually stemming from its ability to cause land erosion. When an area is cleared, the soil under the surface is essentially stripped of the roots that provided it structural integrity and support. Deforestation and forest degradation can cause biodiversity to decline. When forest cover is removed, wildlife is deprived of habitat and becomes more vulnerable to hunting. As a result of deforestation, trees no longer evaporate groundwater, which can cause the local climate to be much drier. Millions of people rely directly on forests, through small-scale agriculture, hunting and gathering, and by harvesting forest products such as rubber. Deforestation continues to pose severe social problems, sometimes leading to violent conflict.

Construction of roads through the forests leads to division of habitation of animals, birds and other species. Once the roads are put to use, they pose a barrier for free movement of wildlife. Most people assume that global warming is caused by burning oil and gas. But in fact between 25 and 30 per cent of the greenhouse gases released into the atmosphere each year (1.6 billion tonnes) is caused by deforestation. Some indigenous people's way of life and survival are threatened by the loss of forests. Fewer trees results an insecure future for forests workers. Deforestation can results to watersheds that are no longer able to sustain and regulate water flows from rivers to steams. The stress of environmental change may make some species more susceptible to the effect of insects, pollution and diseases.

Government Initiatives

Monitoring of forests has gained vital recognition in the international scenario due to realisation of its role in carbon sequestration, biodiversity and global warming. Through advancement of remote sensing and GIS technology it is possible to monitor and analyse gross and net changes in forest ecosystems. While the socio-economic pressures on the country's forests are tremendous, the Indian government has been keenly interested in finding solutions for preserving forests and biodiversity. Thanks to an extensive compensation afforestation programme launched in 2011, India will soon be greener by 10 million hectares of regenerated lands over the next 10 years. Called the Green India Mission (GIM), this large-scale, tree-planting initiative also ensures that any diversion of public forests for non-forestry purposes is compensated. In order to create a balance between forests and recent development, India is enacting laws and amendments to ensure that pristine forests are preserved and protected. The government is also trying to involve people in becoming awareness of the priceless forest ecosystems and how to save its resources.

But environmental group Greenpeace India said while it welcomed the move to address emissions cuts from deforestation, the country's forests faced serious challenges from industrial activities such as mining as well as the building of roads, railways and dams. India has always been interested in market mechanisms to address emissions cuts and climate change, but previous examples of such financial reward schemes show that they do not work. If forest must be removed to create cropland, we need to think about what are the shapes and distributions of deforestation that will be least damaging to the adjacent forests and national parks.

Conclusion

The destruction of natural forests because of cutting trees, logging, making space for cattle grasing, mining, extraction of oil, building dams and population expansion is known as deforestation. As per the reports of Natural Conservancy, logging accounts for 32 million acres of earth's natural forests every year. Deforestation is considered to be one of the contributing factors to global climate change. Trees absorb greenhouse gases and carbon emissions. They produce oxygen and perpetuate the water cycle by releasing water vapour into the atmosphere. The effects of deforestation can be devastating. It can lose the land of its natural aesthetic. In coming years, dangerous consequences will be visible. Deforestation can damage to the environment, usually stemming from its ability to cause land erosion. Monitoring of forests has gained vital recognition in the international scenario due to realisation of its role in carbon sequestration, biodiversity and global warming.

References

1. 5 Major Causes of Deforestation in India, Retrieved from http://www.preservearticles.com/2012030625160/5-major-causes-of-deforestation-in-india.html
2. Brazil says Amazon deforestation rose 28% in a year (2013), Retrieved from http://www.bbc.com/news/world-latin-america-24950487
3. C. Sudhakar Reddy, Kalloli Dutta and C. S. Jha, Analysing the gross and net deforestation rates in India, Retrieved from http://www.currentscience.ac.in/Volumes/105/11/1492.pdf
4. Causes and Consequences of Deforestation on the Wildlife of India, Retrieved from http://livinggreenmag.com/2013/03/18/

mother-nature/causes-and-consequences-of-deforestation-on-the-wildlife-of-india/

5. Causes of deforestation: direct causes, Retrieved from http://earthobservatory.nasa.gov/Features/Deforestation/deforestation_update3.php
6. Damian Carrington (2013), Amazon deforestation increased by one-third in past year, Retrieved from http://www.theguardian.com/environment/2013/nov/15/amazon-deforestation-increased-one-third
7. Debra Ronca, How deforestation works, Retrieved from http://science.howstuffworks.com/environmental/green-science/deforestation1.htm
8. Deforestation (2014), Retrieved from http://en.wikipedia.org/wiki/Deforestation
9. Deforestation (2014), Retrieved from http://environment.nationalgeographic.com/environment/global-warming/deforestation-overview/
10. Deforestation (2014), Retrieved from http://kids. mongabay.com/lesson_plans/lisa_algee/deforestation.html
11. Deforestation causes global warming (2006), Retrieved from http://www.fao.org/Newsroom/en/news/2006/1000385/index.html
12. Deforestation in Congo rainforest, Retrieved fron http://rainforests.mongabay.com/congo/deforestation. html#.VFdWpDtQHFw
13. Deforestation in Sub-Saharan Africa, Retrieved from http://web.mit.edu/africantech/www/articles/Deforestation.htm
14. Deforestation in the green heart of Africa, Retrieved from http://wwf.panda.org/what_we_do/where_we_work/congo_ basin_forests/problems/deforestation/
15. Deforestation reduces rainfall in Africa, Retrieved from http://phys.org/news/2011-09-deforestation-rainfall-africa.html
16. Deforestation, afforestation, reforestation on Grow-Trees.com, Retrieved from http://www.grow-trees.com/why_trees/about_deforestation.aspx
17. Deforestation, Retrieved from http://wwf.panda.org/about_our_earth/about_forests/deforestation/
18. Deforestation: cause sand effects on ecological balance, Retrieved from http://readanddigest.com/deforestation-causes-and-effects-on-ecological-balance/

19. Deforestation: Major environmental problem, Retrieved from http://www.civilserviceindia.com/current-affairs/deforestation.html
20. Deforestation: overview, Retrieved from http://www.world wildlife.org/threats/deforestation
21. Dilip C. Nath and Dimacha Dwibrang Mwchahary,
22. Environmental problems in India, Retrieved from http://wwf.panda.org/who_we_are/wwf_offices/india/india_ environ mental_problems/
23. Forest (2014). Retrieved from http://en.wikipedia.org/wiki/Forest
24. Green India: The worlds most populous country combats deforestation, Retrieved from http://www.unep.org/forests/Portals/142/docs/our_vision/Green_India.pdf
25. Importance of forests (2014), Retrieved from http://wwf.panda.org/about_our_earth/about_forests/importance/
26. Importance of Forests (2014). Retrieve from http://www.info please.com/encyclopedia/science/forest-the-importance-forests.html
27. Importance of old growth forests (2014), Retrieved from http://www.dnr.state.mn.us/forests_types/oldgrowth/importance.html
28. Jean-Marie Baland , Pranab Bardhan , Sanghamitra Das and Dilip Mookherjee (2009), Forest Degradation in the Himalayas: Determinants and Policy Options, Retrieved from http://www.isid.ac.in/~pu/conference/dec_09_conf/Papers/Dilip Mookherjee.pdf
29. Jessie Szalay (2013), Deforestation : facts, causes and affects, Retrieved from http://www.livescience.com/27692-defore station.html
30. Malick Diarrassouba and Inoussa Boubacar, Deforestation in Sub-Saharan Africa, Retrieved from http://ageconsearch.umn.edu/bitstream/46799/2/Malick%20&% 20Inoussa.pdf
31. N. H. Ravindranath, Nalin Srivastava, Indu K. Murthy, Sumedha Malaviya, Madhushree Munsi and Nitasha Sharma, Deforestation and forest degradation in India – implications for REDD+, Retrieved from http://admin. indiaenviron mentportal.org.in/files/file/REDD%2B.pdf
32. Nita Bhalla (2014), India drafts policy to cut carbon emissions from deforestation, Retrieved from http://in.reuters.com/article/2014/05/03/india-environment-deforestation-carbon-idINKBN0DJ05D20140503

33. Population Increase and Deforestation: A Study in Kokrajhar District of Assam, India, International Journal of Scientific and Research Publications, Volume 2, Issue 10, October 2012, Retrieved from http://www.ijsrp.org/research-paper-1012/ijsrp-p1051.pdf
34. Puja Mondal, Deforestation in India: Causes and Consequences of Deforestation in India, Retrieved from http://www.yourarticlelibrary.com/environment/deforestation/deforestation-in-india-causes-and-consequences-of-deforestation-in-india/30096/
35. Rebecca Morelle, Deforestation in Africa's Congo Basin rainforest slows, Retrieved from http://www.bbc.co.uk/news/science-environment-23382526
36. Sergio Margulis (2003), Causes of Deforestation of the Brazilian Amazon, Retrieved from https://openknowledge. worldbank.org/bitstream/handle/10986/15060/277150PAPER0 wbwp0no 1022.pdf?sequence=1
37. T.K. Rudal, The national determinants of deforestation in sub-Saharan Africa, Retrieved from http://rstb. royalsociety publishing.org/content/368/1625/20120405
38. The Effects of Industry on the Deforestation in India - See more at: http://www.isfoundation.com/news/effects-industry-deforestation-india#sthash.VXL24BNu.dpuf
39. Tropical deforestation and forest degradation: A case study from India, Retrieved from http://www.fao.org/docrep/article/wfc/xii/0250-a1.htm
40. http://www.brainyquote.com/quotes/keywords/natural_resources.html

2

Exploitation of Natural Resources and Environment in Arunachal Pradesh: An Empirical Study

Dr Bijay Raji

"Our livelihood is intimately tied to the food we eat, water we drink and places where we recreate. That's why we have to promote responsibility and conservation when it comes to our natural resources."

—Mark Udall

Introduction

The adverse impacts of unscientific exploitation of common property resources are from research of *'Hardin's tragedy of the common'*. Under what circumstances will villagers co-operate to supply themselves with goods and services that they all need but could not provide for themselves individually? In what circumstances are those who face a potential 'tragedy of the commons' able to organise a system of rules by which the tragedy is averted? Many writers on collective action and common property consider that these circumstances are very limited. A long line of collective action theorists has argued that people placed in a situation in which they could all benefit from co-operation will be unlikely to co-operate in the absence of an external enforcer of agreements. An equally long line of theorists on property rights has argued that common property resources are bound to be over-exploited as demand rises. The only solution is private enclosure, according to some theorists, or state regulation, according to others. In Robert Smith's words, 'it is by treating a resource as a common property that we become locked in its inexorable destruction'.

Ruin is the destination towards which all men rush, each pursuing his own best interest in a society that believes in the freedom of the commons' (Hardin, 1968). Hardin finds the only viable solution in 'mutual coercion, mutually agreed upon', by which restrained access can be enforced. He takes for granted that this must be done through the state apparatus, in other words, by an authority external to those directly affected by the commons. Just as the Prisoners' Dilemma assumes that each participant has no information about the other's choice, so Hardin's parable assumes that the individual has no information about the aggregate state of the commons and its nearness to the point of collapse. This assumption permits Hardin to have the herder make a decision just prior to collapse that is against his own self-interest—to add another animal thereby precipitating the collapse, with the consequence that he, as well as the others, loses all. At issue is die amount of information people have about the larger situation in which they operate (Kimber, 1983). Similarly, just as the Prisoners' Dilemma says nothing about how the calculations are affected by different absolute values of the payoff, so Hardin's parable does not distinguish between commons where the resource is vital for die individuals' survival, and those where it is not. It is more likely that Hardin's relentless logic will operate where the village council is constituted entirely by the villagers for themselves and does not derive its authority from the state (Robert, 1987).

Environmental degradation has added new problems more particularly, in the developing countries. India which is a developing country is facing environmental problems because of the negative effects of a developing economy and from conditions of poverty and underdevelopment. Development can take place at the cost of environment only until a point. In fact, development without concern for environment can only be short-term development. In the long-run, it can only be anti-development and can go on only at the cost of enormous human suffering, increased poverty and oppression. India is facing with the need for accelerating the pace of development for alleviation of poverty which is to a great extent responsible for many of our environmental problems. If the entire picture of environmental degradation is looked at from the Indian perspective. The outcome of the creation of the Community Conserved Areas (CCAs) has already begun to be reflected in improved conservation of forests along with the enhanced flow of associated environmental services, reduced hunting, and livelihoods for local communities by way of sale of many NTFPs including traditional medicines and wild edibles. The conservation conscious villagers have been patrolling their CCAs to deter illegal poaching, hunting and felling of trees. Plantation of economically rewarding MAP (Medicinal and Aromatic Plants) species within the CCAs would further help in reducing poverty, arrest loss of RET (rare, endangered and threatened) species and increase in the forest canopy. To point out some of the wide ranging adverse ecological, economic and social impact of this menace:

1. Loss of valuable timber resources.
2. Degradation of diverse habitats and catchment areas (e.g. of water).
3. Death of new recruits resulting in reduced natural regeneration and reduction in forest cover.
4. Decline in carbon sink reserves and increase in percentage of CO_2 in the atmosphere.
5. Change in the microclimate with unhealthy living conditions.
6. Increase in soil erosion thereby affecting productivity of soils and production capacity.
7. Health problems leading to disease.
8. Loss of livelihood for forest dependent (e.g. tribal people and the rural poor) communities.

Human related (anthropogenic) causes result from human activity as well as unscientific methods of forest management. These activities can be intentional or unintentional, for example:

1. Grasers and gatherers of various forest products initiate small fires to obtain good grasing grass in the next season, as well as to facilitate gathering of minor forest produce, this may turn into huge and uncontrolled forest fire.
2. The centuries old practice of shifting cultivation called *Jhum* (especially in the North-Eastern region of India) involves intentional burning of slashed forests.
3. The use of fires by villagers to ward off wild animals.
4. Fires lit intentionally by people living around forests or visiting these areas for recreation.
5. Fires started accidentally by careless visitors to forests who discard cigarette and bidi butts, etc.

Climate change involves the interaction of several systems with many variables that must be collectively considered. Natural climate changes have occurred throughout earth's history. Large scale natural events as abrupt as those associated with human environment impacts are known to have occurred in the past. It is now held that human activities are a major factor affecting climate as one of the components of the environment. Climate in turn affects natural vegetation and agriculture. Only during the past few decades have the scale, intensity and permanence of human impacts on the environment been recognised and begun to be understood. The need to establish the pattern and causes of recent climate change to which human activities have contributed is the main force behind the increasing scientific interest in environmental change. The human induced changes are superimposed on natural changes. The future course of natural climate change may in some cases exacerbate human induced change in other cases such changes may neutralise the human effects (Beniston, 2000). It is essential, therefore, to view current and future climate change and have a sound knowledge of all the natural and human induced agents of climate change.

Climate change is one of the most important global environmental challenges that affect all the natural ecosystems of the world. Due to the fragile environment, mountain ecosystems are the most vulnerable to the impact of climate change. Mountains have been recognised as important ecosystems by the convention on Biological Diversity. Arunachal

Pradesh is predominantly a mountainous state and is home of many endemic, endangered and threatened species, as well as to the indigenous people, who are dependent on its biological resources. Climate change will not only threaten the biodiversity, but also affect the socio-economic condition of the indigenous people of the state. Various activities like habitat loss, deforestation, clear felling and overexploitation amplify the impact of climate change on biodiversity. Therefore, some management initiatives should be taken for mitigating climate change. Also, more research work needs to be carried out in Arunachal Pradesh to monitor the trend of climate change and susceptibility of biodiversity.

The imperative of environmental planning for the hill areas has been ultimately acknowledged in the Seventh Plan. The approach paper to the Seventh Plan sets the tone by under-scoring the point in these words: *"Hill area development programme should emphasise harmonisation of socio-economic growth with eco-restoration, eco-preservation and eco-development. This implies co-ordination of ecological aspects while formulating policies, programme and schemes. The basic life support system should be strengthened for optimal and long term human activities recognising the complementarily of the hills and the plains"* (Govt. of India, 1980-85). Due to several decades of non-sustainable land use practices and highly erosive monsoon rains, deforestation and accelerated soil erosion are proceeding rapidly throughout the district. The majority of these non-farming activities involve low productive and low paying work. Trends with respect to the state of natural resources combined with the paucity of options for high-return non-agricultural employment make the prognosis for the future of the area, and of the families that live there, worrying.

The outcome of the destruction and degradation of common property resources (CPRs) have adverse impact not only on the ecological stability but also on livelihood pattern of the rural people who depend heavily on it for meeting their numerous necessary requirements. Moreover, the environmental stressed migration, drying tanks, irregular monsoon, and soil erosion are glaring instances of the decline and degradation of the CPRs in India. Similarly, the livestock farming which the key activity is sustained by CPRs is largely affected due to the decline of these resources. In order to reduce the degradation and depletion of forest resources, Government of India drastically changed its policy from state property regime to community-based forest resource management in late 1980s. The failure of state property regime promoted Government to declare a new and people oriented national forest policy in 1988, in which the participation of the people was encouraged and ensured property rights them over forests.

Common property resources are those resources, which are accessible to the whole community to which no individual has exclusive property rights (Jodha, 1986). Apart from these, the use of these resources by the users are subtractive and having the characteristic of a public good such as indivisibility. Adhering to the definition of Jodha, the resources falling under this category of CPRs in India are protected forests, community forests, village pastures, waste lands, waste dumping places, watershed drainages, grasing land (*gauchar*), village ponds, canals, tanks, wells, streams, rivulets, and river beds. However, CPRs are regarded as an important resource base for the rural economy in many of the developing and underdeveloped countries till today because of their significant economic contributions to the sustenance of rural livelihood (Jodha, 1986). This paper attempts to examine the adverse impacts of unscientific exploitation of common property resources in Arunachal Pradesh on the basis of practical experiences of the indigenous communities.

Methods and Materials

Study Area

The West Siang District, one of 17 district of Arunachal Pradesh located in the central part of Arunachal Pradesh extends between 93 57' to 95 23' East longitude and 27 69' to 29 20' North latitude. It is bounded on the North by China. It is the home-land of various tribes. Of all tribal groups of West Siang district, the Galos rank first in population. Donyi-Poloism is the main religion of the tribes in the district. Total population of this district as per 2011 is 112272 consisting 58589 males and 53683 females. The sex ratio is 916 and population density is 13.

The percentage decadal growth rate of population for 2001-2011 is 8.04. The literacy rate is 67.62 per cent 73.89 per cent for males and 60.76 per cent for females. Out of the six sub-divisions, Likabali sub-division is our study area. This sub-division has three circles: Likabali, Kanku and Gensi. This is the only sub-division where we see three types of physiography viz. Plain land, foot hill and high maintain area. We select one village of each circle.

Data Sources and Tools for Data Collection

The present study was mainly empirical in nature. The data which was used and incorporated in the paper was collected from primary as well as secondary sources. Final data collection was made with the aid of structured and pre-tested questionnaires on the basis of stratified random sampling technique from the respondents of the sampled villages. The questionnaires sought to gather information regarding community forest, private forest, socio-economic and ecological impacts on local communities, environmental and socio-cultural problems, basic needs crises, deprived status reduced accessibility, soil erosion, soil fertility, loss of habitat, water resources, meeting the challenges of resource depletion, factors aggravating damage, adaptation to the changing situation of CPRs.

Sampled Villages for Survey

One village of each circle, which contained more population, was selected for survey and 50 families were selected through random sampling technique without replacement to fill up the pre-designed questionnaire through direct interaction with respondents from each village. Total respondents of three villages of three circles were 150 (50 3 = 150) on the basis of male: female = 3:2. Here only three villages under three circles (one village under one circle) were considered for survey. The respondents of age group (31-60) years were selected as this age group is particularly more responsible to earn the livelihood for their family. The village survey was taken in the month from April to August, 2012.

Analysis of the Data

The data thus collected from all the households of the sampled villages were analysed village-wise. A number of tables were

Table-1: Forest Cover in West Siang and Arunachal Pradesh (Area in Sq. Km)

State / District	*Geographical Area*	*Forest cover*				*Change*
		Very Dense	*Moderately Dense*	*Open Forest*	*Total Forest*	
West Siang	2,172	110 (5.06)	664 (30.57)	453 (20.85)	1,227 (56.49)	12
Arunachal Pradesh	83,743	13,907 (16.60)	39,604 (47.29)	14,508 (17.32)	68,019 (81.22)	-26

Source: Statistical Abstract of Arunachal Pradesh, 1998; **N.B.**: Figure within parenthesis indicates percentage calculated by the researcher.

used to facilitate for easy understanding. Simple numerical calculations were used to analyse the data for writing the report of the study.

Results and Discussion

Degradation of Surrounding Environment

Degradation of surrounding forests, trees and CPRs and rigid forest laws have adversely affected food accessibility, livelihood options and quality of life of local communities in many areas. Such degradation has often caused periodic phases of hunger and malnutrition in absence of supportive means of livelihood for acquiring basic essentials of life. Forest plantations no longer provide the rich bio-diversity available earlier in natural forests. CPRs, in which groups of local people have co-equal use rights, such as community pastures, community forests, waste lands, village ponds, rivers etc., have declined at a rapid pace. In a study of 82 villages (Jodha: 1991), such resources declined since 1950-52 by at least 30 per cent and in some cases more than 50 per cent leading to immense hardship of those communities dependent on them. Such phenomena has led to diminished role of local natural resources which have traditionally constituted invaluable asset-base for meeting basic needs and livelihood requirements of local communities. Let us see the forest cover in the district compared with the state shown in Table-1.

Findings

In comparison to the state, the district has positive growth of forest but the state has negative growth of forest as a whole. Only 5.06 per cent of the district is under very dense forest in comparison to 16.60 per cent of the state. For moderate dense forest, the district has 30.57 per cent while the state has 47.29 per cent. In case of open forest the district has 20.85 per cent while the state has 17.32 per cent. The percentage of total forest in the district is 56.49 where as the state has 81.22 per cent of its total area as total forest.

Findings

In Table-2, we see that 1.4 per cent, 2.5 per cent and 2.14 per cent of Average Community Forest had decreased in 2012

Table-2: Category-wise Natural Resource Assessment (Hectare=2.471 acres/10,000 sq. metres of land)

Study Area	*In 2012*				*In 2002*				*Increasing/Decreasing*		
	Av. Community Forest	*Av. Private Forest per HH*	*Av. Private Land per HH*	*Water Body in the Circle*	*Av. Community Forest*	*Av. Private Forest per HH*	*Av. Private Land per HH*	*Water Body in the Circle*	*Av. Community Forest*	*Av. Private Forest per HH*	*Av. Private Land per HH*
Likabali	5000	9	3	4.4	4030	8	3.5	4.4	-970	1.0	-0.5
Kanku	8000	5	4	6.3	7800	4.5	4.5	6.3	-200	0.5	-0.5
Gensi	7000	6.5	7	5.4	6850	5.5	8	5.4	-150	1.0	-1.0

Source: Field Study, 2012; **N.B.**: Natural Resource Assessment is on the basis of discussion with Forest Ranger and villagers but it is subject to error. HH= Household.

compared to 2002 in Likabali, Kanku and Gensi respectively. It indicated on the basis of interview that the Community Forest had encroached for conversion of agricultural land, construction of road, government and private building etc. Average Private Forest per household had increased by 11.11 per cent, 10 per cent and 15.38 per cent in Likabali, Kanku and Gensi respectively. It signified a positive signal for bio-diversity. The villagers had started to grow more trees like horticulture type or whose hood was valuable in their private land under their management. It was due to profit seeking motivation. Now the villagers had started to understand the value of trees for their day to day requirement of life and bio-diversity.

Average private land per household decreased in 2012 on the basis of 2002. On the basis of response of the respondents, we came to know that some household had divided into two or three small family and thereby the lands were divided among the family concerned. 16.67 per cent, 12.5 per cent and 14.28 per cent of average private landholding per household decreased in Likabali, Kanku and Gensi respectively. Land for water body had not changed but the quantum of water had reduced by more than 20 per cent with the span of 10 years as per opinion of the respondents.

Socio-economic and Ecological Impacts

The human disturbances mentioned above lead to socio-economic and ecological impacts on local communities of which the major ones are listed below:

1. Loss of habitat and local eco-system adversely affected.
2. Food, fuel, fodder, wood crises with no alternative in sight.
3. Deprived socio-economic and legal status in an exploitative framework.
4. Reduced accessibility and increased deprivation.

Environmental and Socio-cultural Problems

The recent debates and developments with regard to the draft National Environment Policy (NEP), 2004 and the Scheduled Tribes (Recognition of Forest Rights) Bill (STB), 2005 are illustrative in different ways of the manner in which social concerns are dealt with in environmental policy and legislation in India. Yet, while the pros and cons of specific policies and legislations have been central to the academic debates on the environment, very little attempt has been made to trace the changes in environmental policy-making and the way social concerns have been problematised. The ecological balance favouring the complete hydrological cycle has been seriously upset over vast areas due to ignorance or lack of appreciation of methods of conserving and managing natural vegetation (whether a forest, grass land or mixed type) and of clearing the vegetation for cultivation. This misuse and destruction of plants cover combined with great increase in human and livestock population has created intense competition for natural resources, in many cases residual, as between forestry, grasing and crop production. In the continued absence of conservation and correctly integrated land use system, overall habitat deterioration has become very widespread.

Our specific focus with regard to social concerns is a community right to resources – a concern that is central to many of the debates on natural resource management. Three arguments are put forth: (i) that while the environment has at one level assumed a non-negotiable presence in policy, social concerns are only highlighted to the extent that they are deemed not to be environmentally destructive, (ii) that the discursive terrain through which social concerns are deemed harmful is overly simplistic and in need of re-examination and (iii) that the changing nature of environmental discourse can only be understood within the wider shifts in development policy. Although there are many who would claim that the environment itself receives an inadequate attention in development policy, a contention that is at least partly true, we are concerned here with how emerging policies and legislations tackle social concerns given the socially constructed nature of the environment.

It has been undisputedly accepted that shifting cultivation creates environment and socio-cultural problems. The growth in the number of members per *jhumia* family and in the number of *jhumia* families cannot be absorbed in settled and *jhum* cultivation, as a result a consumption gap develops in the hills. The greater food requirements cannot be met out of dwindling yields from smaller plots of land devoted to jhuming with smaller and smaller fallowing periods. The over exploitation of forests of jhuming and for commercial purposes also lead to a deterioration of the condition of the forests. The misuse and destruction of plants cover combined with great increase in human and livestock population has aggravated the problem of eco-system. Ecological damage in the hills, widespread poverty among hill-dwelling tribal, social discontent and the growth of extension has been the fall-out of the development of the hill economy. P.R. Kyndiah, Minister of Tribal Affairs and Development of NER *"underlined the strong association of jhum with community life and traditions as well as with the unique mountain eco-system."*

Basic Needs Crises

Forests are sources of living and livelihood. The diverse functions of a forest are critical to many local communities in traditional economies. Accelerated deforestation has affected livelihoods of local people. The local women are also required to walk longer distances for collection of fuel, fodder, food etc.

Deprived Status

Exploitation, expropriation and threats from outside agencies have increased where some local communities have been forced to forfeit their lands and join the ranks of the landless. In case of constitutional right, of local people they get violated most often and, in practice, they stand to lose in the existing socio-economic and political set-ups, which are repressive, and, most often, work to their disadvantage.

Reduced Accessibility

Large areas of forests have been formally kept virtually out of reach of forest people who may be in a position to manage forests sustainably for subsistence and income (Douglas: 1983). Such action/policies have led to tensions in social control of forests and have become acute. Increased pressure on forests is making for low resilience of forests systems leading to fuel wood and fodder problems for local communities. Social and economic problems of local people are increasing and so also are the areas of conflict. As an illustration, let us consider the case of India.

The colonial laws have led to state-ownership of nearly 97 per cent of India's forest land (*Source*: World Resources, 1994-95, p.103) which limits people's accessibility to forests. Local communities having limited access to forests without ownership rights face increased pressure of livelihood. This leads to tension and conflict between foresters and local communities where the latter's need for forest resources is overlooked and not acknowledged in practice. Such a state of affair in natural resource management calls for better management by redefining access to forest resources and clarifying roles and responsibilities of local communities.

Soil Erosion

High rainfall and undulated topography is always associated with problem of severe soil erosion, which affects the environment adversely. The excessive deforestation caused by excessive cutting down of trees for commercial purpose as well as shifting cultivation are resulting in alarming and frightening signals for human survival. Estimates reveal that nearly 181 M.T. of soil is lost annually as a result of shifting cultivation from north-eastern hill region (Task Force Report on shifting cultivation, 1983). Developments in the hills and its fall out on the ecology have caused soil erosion, landslides, floods and droughts in the plains.

Soil Fertility

Burning of vegetation in the process of shifting cultivation chemically alters the plant nutrient supply from organic form to a mineral form in ash, major portion of which is often lost in course of runoff. The shorter the *jhum* cycle preserves the lower level of soil fertility. Five years *jhum* cycle generates very low level of soil fertility. Thus, *jhum* cultivation becomes uneconomic progressively. This necessitates switching over to settled cultivation.

Loss of Habitat

Loss of habitat due to drastic reduction in forest areas have led to increased socio-economic problems of local communities; diverse functions of forest eco-systems such as watershed properties and micro-climatic regulations have been affected, thereby affecting lives and livelihood of local communities. Forest communities are losing their habitat. Data on habitat defined as 'wild land', 'natural vegetation', 'degree of naturalness' etc. can provide a broad idea of its extent and loss, and, thereby, in absence of actual measure, provide a surrogate measure for loss of habitat of indigenous people who share the same natural habitat as that of bio-diversity.

The extent of deforestation of tropical forest has caused worldwide alarm as tropical forests provide more than 50 per cent of modern medicine. Tropical forests are living museums and laboratories that have yielded only a tiny fraction of their treasures to scientific study. Arunachal Pradesh is, as if, a natural garden of more than 20,000 identified species of medicinal plants and so many still remain unidentified. In course of shifting cultivation remarkable varieties of flora and fauna are disappearing, which need immediate attention for extensive and intensive studies. The type of vegetations destroyed depends upon the length of jhum cycle. A dense forest of long cycle has more tree species than grasses, whereas a forest of short cycle has more number of grasses. About 300 plant species out of native flora in North-Eastern India are used for edible purpose. Of these, over 25 provide tubers/rhisomes etc., which are eaten raw or boiled. Over 50 are consumed as green with their leaves/tender shoots cooked as vegetable; about 170 ripe fruits, which are pulpy and sweet/sub-sweet are eaten raw and many of these are used for pickles/vegetables, when unripe; about 15 have edible seeds are eaten raw or roasted.

Wildlife in the natural situation constitutes the most important component of the ecosystem, which participates affectively in the energy flow and bio-geo-chemical cycling. Animal-plant, plant-plant and animal-animal interactions are the basic milestone of the success of an ecosystem and its productivity. As such, the richness of the ecosystem means the capacity of hold high species diversity but deforestation has threatened the very fabric of the survival of wildlife and the ecosystem in the region. This area is the habitat of as many as 55 major mammalian species of which 17 are rare or extremely rare. 21

rare species of extremely rare birds are found in this region and there are innumerable species of insects. As such, there are different species of wildlifes found in this region. Almost all of them are dared as protection species under the Protection Act of 1972. Like flora, other forest resources are also disappearing and become rare.

Arunachal Pradesh is a home to myriad life forms coexisting in diverse ecological situations in their pristine glory. The state is today known for its rich bio-diversity. Floristically, there are more than 5000 species of flowering plants, 600 species of orchids, 89 species of bamboos, 18 species of canes, 400 species of ferns, 24 species of gymnosperms and an equally high number of unexplored algae, fungi, lichens, bryophytes, and micro-organisms inhabiting the state. Faunistically, the state is also rich in having more than 100 species of mammals, 650 birds, 83 reptiles, 130 fishes and 7 non-human primates and innumerable species of insects, micro-organisms and other life forms. The rich bio-diversity both of flora and fauna have contributed to its recognition as one of the 25 *"Bio-diversity Hotspots"* in the world. The human pursuit for development has led to environmental degradation to such an extent that it has become almost irreversible loss of forests and other natural resources thereby threatening the very survival of mankind. A number of plant and animal species have either become extinct or come under rare, threatened or endangered category (*Arunachal Times*, 5th June, 2010). Man inhabits two worlds: one is the natural world of plants and animals, soil, air and water which preceded him by billions of years and of which he is a part. The other is the world of social institutions and artifacts he builds for himself, using his tools and engines, his science and dreams to fashion the environment obedient to human purpose and directions. It is absolutely necessary that there should be a complete harmony and balance between the two worlds of man (*Arunachal Times*, 5th June, 2010).

Water Resources

There is ample of water resources in North-Eastern Hill Region. Almost 10 per cent of the total rainfall of the country is received in this region. Soil erosion and deforestation favour in less retention of water under ground and more runoff water causing flood in the plains. This causes great loss to human and animal lives as well as crops. Now-a-days, supply of drinking water has become serious problem in every town in the hill region.

Meeting the Challenges of Resource Depletion

For local communities, depletion of forests and CPRs through human intervention, have resulted in disturbance or breakdown of their support base and has led to immense hardship especially because of limited substitution possibilities available for alternative sources of livelihoods. There are also those local communities, whose traditional access and rights have been denied to such local resources thus paving way for their increased impoverishment. However, on the brighter side, there are many cases where local communities have accepted the challenge of natural resources depletion and are participating at local levels, either by themselves, or in collaboration with developmental agencies, to organise themselves for regenerating trees, forests and water bodies while conserving and preserving the existing ones.

Factors Aggravating Damage

Such interventions/policies/actions adversely affect the lives and livelihoods of local communities. Their ability to participate fully in sustainable development practices on their lands becomes limited as a result of multiple factors which are of economic, social and historical nature. Their position is aggravated by the following factors, such as,

1. Lack of effective communication between intervening agencies and local communities/groups.
2. Lack of awareness about their rights and privileges.
3. Inadequate compensation received and rehabilitation problems.
4. Denial of forest rights.
5. Falling production, payment and nationalisation of minor forest produces (MFPs).
6. Diversion of MFPs to industries.

7. Exploitation by government agencies and contractors in marketing of MFPs.
8. Lack of programmes to regenerate sources of MFPs (Chambers, Saxena and Shah: 1991).

(*Source*: Discussion with the villagers in the surveyed area)

Adaptation to the Changing Situation of CPRs

The negative impact or other side effects of formal reforms, market integration, the top-down development intervention, etc., is not to minimise their positive gains. The major underlying forces, which are more numerous as well as more effective than the simple increase in the number of people to accelerate degradation of community-level environmental resources, force the rural people to adapt themselves in the changing scenario. We can venture to indicate possible approaches to address the consequences of these underlying forces on CPRs and the process of demographic changes. We should see that how the rural people individually or as a group has responded to the changes. Accordingly, the net consequences of degradation of CPRs and depletion of social capital are reflected through the situation summarised in the Table-3. The Table-3 presents the features of community approach and behaviour in the context of the depleted state of CPRs. Since the rural community is more differentiated and has individualised its approaches to CPRs, the adjustments of rich and poor people to the CPRs change show considerable differences, though the key circumstances underlying their responses are broadly common. For instance, the decline of social arrangements to manage CPRs induces the rich and the poor to grab CPRs land; it also encourages the poor to overextract the resources of common property without obligation or incurring private cost in the process. Similarly, the public policies, while legalising encroachments on CPR lands with minimum penalties and creating patronage or subsidy based incentives, include both rich and poor though in different degrees to privatise CPRs with no fear and cost. The loss of social capital at the community level is the single most important factor in the case of both poor and rich. Since community has no control over local resources without owning them.

Table-3: People's Adaptations to Changing Situation of CPRs

Measures adopted by Different Groups in the face of Decline in Area, Productivity and Management Systems of CPRs		
Rural Rich	*Rural Poor*	*Rural Community (General)*
Withdrawal from CPRs as users of products (opportunity cost of labour higher than CPR product value)	**Using of CPRs** as an important source of sustenance complementarily of CPR-cropland-based activities	**Acceptance of CPRs as open access resources**: no collective efforts to enforce users obligations, regulations
Increased reliance on alternative options -Own biomass supplies (stall feeding, etc.) -Non-renewable/external resources(e.g. replacing thorn fencing with stone fencing, local wooden tools with iron tools)	**Acceptance of interior options** -Opportunity cost of labour lower than value of products of degraded CPRs -No other private cost of resource use	**Selective approach to specific CPR units:** Despite general neglect of CPRs, concern for some productive units. -Limited exceptions where collective arrangements still survive.

(Contd.)

(Contd. Table 3)

Rural Rich	*Rural Poor*	*Rural Community (General)*
Private squeeze on CPRs as assets -Grabbing CPR lands -Preventing others using seasonal CPRs (private crop lands during off-season)	**Measures reflecting desperation** -Premature harvesting of CPR products -Removal of roots/base of products -Over-crowding and over-exploitation of CPRs -Use of hitherto unusable inferior products	**Focus on "other' uses of CPRs** -Focused item in seeking government subsidy/relief, in running factional quarrels, in populist programmes, etc. -Community responds only to external directions, does not plan own activities
Approach to CPR Management -Indifference to decline of CPRs -Act as influential local party to non-functioning legal system administrative superstructure for community resources	**Approach to CPR Management** -No capacity to organise users -Extraction without obligation	**Party to non-operating legal and administrative measures** -acceptance of external impositions without protest, etc. -Loss of "social capital" ability to act jointly

Source: Field Study, 2012; Table adapted from Jodha, 2002 and fitted in the Study Area.

Table-4: Decline of Area of CPR Land in the Study Area on the basis of Response

Village Under Study	*Opinion of the Respondents*	*CPR Land, 2012 (ha)*	*CPR area as Percentage of village area*		
			2002	*2012*	*Decline*
Likabali	Construction of Road, Govt. building, Common vacant place, Encroachment for agricultural operation for being unemployment and House construction due to population growth	1750	75	60	20
Kanku	Do	1350	85	75	11.76
Gensi	Do	1800	85	80	5.88

Source: Field Survey, 2012. CPR land considered here on the basis of opinion of the respondents is subject to error.

Under the circumstances as shown in the table, rehabilitation and sustainable use of CPR and rebuilding of social capital are quite difficult tasks, especially when the policy implication and present process of economic transformation are not congenial for them. A strong policy support in terms of a legal framework to encourage user groups; transfer of control of local resources to local communities and provision for investment in CPRs, which are presently so depleted that no community would be able to rehabilitate them on their own (Jodha, 1992).

However, despite the need for user group-based collective action as well as policy and funding support from the state, the divided local communities may not have the capacity to respond to new opportunities and take up new responsibilities. The need for catalytic role of NGOs and other volunteer agencies to mobilise rural communities and help in their capacity building to undertake new responsibilities (Poffenberger *et al.* 1996). The information presented in this chapter hopefully may help the community mobilisers to understand the process by which rural communities were disempowered and their collective stakes in natural resources disintegrated. This in turn can help evolve the strategies to change the situation. A few NGOs in India have already incorporated such insights in their work plans.

Findings

On the basis of response of 150 respondents of three (3) villages, one village of each circle, the average degradation of CPRs of each village is shown in Table-4. As per opinion of the respondents, the CPRs are degrading due to construction of road, Govt. building and encroachment for agricultural operation for being unemployment, house construction due to population growth. The Government is very much conscious for holistic development of this area especially road communication due to China's frequent claim on Arunachal Pradesh. Area of CPRs has declined 20 per cent in Likabali, 11.76 per cent in Kanku and 5.88 per cent in Gensi.

Conclusions

Presently, tribal indigenous lifestyle, including mode of economy, societal status, culture, polity as well, are intrinsically linked with and transformed according to the overall changes in the ecological base of their present habitats. Though no less impressive is the pattern of their spatial distribution. In addition, unprecedented increase in population among tribes also generates environmental degradation in such tribal habitats of the district. So, increasing tribal population results into a tremendous stress on the natural environment of the tribes in those areas which again reduces the capacities of local environment to provide adequate support to the tribal people and the others. Thus, the problem of physical survival of the tribal people of the district under such circumstances crops up inviting attention of the authority by and large. It is evident that, tribal assimilation into peasant mode of production is a very slow process though its consequences may be detrimental due to the fact that slow rate of change in tribal economy, leading to the transformation of tribal mode of production again led to the destruction of physical environment in the end.

References

1. Agarwal, S. K. (2004): Global Warming and Climate Change: Past, Present and Future, A.P.H. Publishing Corporation, New Delhi, p. 364.
2. Beniston, M. (Ed), (2000): Environmental Change in Mountain and Uplands, Urnold and Oxford University Press, p. 172.
3. Dawes, R. 1975: Formal models of dilemmas in social decision-making, in Kaplan, M. and Swartz, S. (Eds), Human Judgement and Decision Processes, New York, Academic Press.
4. Ghosh, P.(2011): "Agents of Climate Change", Envis Bulletin, Himalayan Ecology, Vol. 19, Almora, pp. 37-38.
5. Jodha, N.S. (1986): "Common Property Resources and the Rural Poor in dry regions of India", Economic and Political Weekly Vol. XXI, No. 27.
6. Jodha, N.S. (2002): "Decline of Rural Commons: Role of Population Growth and Public Policies" in Marothia, D.K. (ed.), Institutionalising Pool Resources, Concept Publishing Company, New Delhi, pp. 33-52.
7. Jodha, N.S. (1991): Common Property Resources, a growing crisis, Gatekeeper Series, Sustainable Agriculture Programme, IIED. London.

8. Jodha, N. S. (1992): Rural Common Property Resources: A Missing Dimension of Development Strategies. World Bank: Discussion Paper No. 169. Washington D. C.: The World Bank.
9. Johns, M (2000): Ovenbird (Raleigh: North Carolina Wildlife Resources Commission), available at http://www.ncwildlife.org/pg07_Wildlife Species Con/ Profiles/ovenbird.pdf.
10. Hardin, G. (1968): The tragedy of the commons, *Science*, Vol. 162, December.
11. Kimber, R. 1983: 'The tragedy of the commons reappraised', Department of Politics, University of Keele, mimeo.
12. Poffenberger, M. and M.B. McGean (eds) (1996): Village Voices, Forest Choices: Pioneering India's Forest Management in 21st Century, New Delhi: Oxford University Press.
13. Wade, Robert (1987): "The management of common property resources: collective action as an alternative to privatisation or state regulation", Cambridge Journal of Economics 1987, 11, 95-106.
14. Arunachal Times, 5th June, 2010, the daily news paper.
15. Read more at http://www.brainyquote.com/quotes/keywords/natural_resources.html#pLm5MVEvSuzRiSj5.99

3

Impact of Shifting Cultivation on Environment in North-East India and Its Sustainability

Dr A.I. Singh

"For far too long the world's poorest people have seen no benefit from the vast natural resources in their own backyards. It is time to end the injustice where ordinary people are silent witnesses, left to suffer without basic services, as the profits from their countries' assets are hidden and plundered by corrupt regimes."

—Nick Clegg

Introduction

The North Eastern Region of India consists of seven states, namely, Assam, Arunachal Pradesh, Meghalaya, Mizoram, Manipur, Tripura and Nagaland. Large sections of the people in the region are Tibeto-Mongoloid origin speaking variety of languages. The hills constitute about 70 per cent of the total land area, where shifting agriculture, locally called jhum is the chief land use (Ramakrishna, 1996). The Brahmaputra and the Barak Valley in Assam is the largest valley land where settled agriculture is confined. The region covers 7.76 per cent of the geographical area of the country. The ethnical, linguistics and cultural diversities of the region make it a mini-modal for

Table-1: Decadal Variation of Population in North Eastern Region (in percentage)

State	*Decadal Growth of Population (per cent)*		*Change in the Growth Rate*	*Average Annual Exponential Growth*	
	1971-81	*1981-91*		*1971-81*	*1981-91*
Arunachal Pradesh	+35.83	+36.83	+1.68	3.04	3.06
Assam	+36.05	+24.24	-11.81	2.12	2.12
Manipur	+32.46	+29.29	-3.17	2.83	2.51
Meghalaya	+32.04	+32.86	+0.82	2.80	2.76
Mizoram	48.55	+39.70	-8.85	3.99	3.29
Nagaland	+50.05	+56.08	+6.03	4.09	4.50
Tripura	+31.92	+34.30	+2.38	2.79	2.90
N.E. Region	+33.90	+36.30			
All India	+24.66	+23.85	-0.87	2.22	2.11

Source: Census of India 1991, Series-i, Paper-2 of 1992.

* Computed figures

representing the country as a whole. There are hundreds of different tribes in the region differing linguistically and culturally.

The entire region is more or less geographically isolated from the rest of the country. The only gateway to rest of India for all the seven states is Guwahati, the capital city of Assam. The whole of the region is almost surrounded by international borders with Bangladesh, China and Myanmar. The long stretch of border areas not only creates occasional sense of insecurity but also disrupts the inter-regional communication link. The road communication along the border areas through hilly terrain has become difficult and many places are still inaccessible to vehicular traffic. This has heavily affected the economy of the border areas of every states of the north-eastern region (Barua 1990).

Demographical Features

The growth rate of population is much larger in all the states of NER as compared to the all India average. While some states like Assam, Tripura and to some extent Meghalaya and Mizoram have experienced a large scale influx of people from neighbouring countries like Bangladesh and Nepal, the other states are characterised by much higher birth rate than death rate (Lekhi and Choudhury, 1994). As a result the decadal variation in the states of NER seems to be very high as compared to all India average. The decadal variation of the states of the region is shown in Table-1.

The Table-1 confirms the high rate of decennial variations in the NER as compared to the country as awhole. The all India trend shows decline in the variation from 1971- 81 to 1981-91, the north-eastern states individually or the region as a whole showed an increasing trend during the period. While the average annual exponential growth rate shows that in both the decades 1971-81 and 1981-91 in almost all the states of N.E. region the growth rate becomes higher than all India average. This trend will surely have an impact on the socio-economic condition of the region.

Method of Shifting Cultivation

The forest farmer in the humid tropics has practiced for centuries the method of shifting agriculture or popularly known in India as *jhum* (Ramakrishnan, 1996). This is the simplest method of cultivation available to the tribal population living in the hilly region. There is no other alternative way of cultivating the land in the hill areas. The shifting cultivation is the natural way of life to the tribal people in the hill areas. In fact, man-nature relationship of a community is reflected in its mode of resource use across ideological axis. At a given level of ideology man's material requirements and his perception of nature and natural phenomena determines his interaction with nature and characterises ideal type of the mode of resource use. At this level, ideology acts as determinant variable of mode of resource use and is external to the system. The ideological base of a community, for example, governs production relations forces of production and exploitation of natural resources as well (Gadgil and Guha, 1992). Use of land resources for shifting cultivation by the different tribes is, however, not indiscriminate, rather it follows certain norms even at ideological level.

The system of shifting cultivation involves a number of operations. First, forest bushes are cut up to the stump level in the months of December-January and small trees and bamboos are felled. Short tree stumps and large tree boles are left intact. The under ground organs of different species are not disturbed. Next, the stumps are allowed to dry, after which they are set on fire. After the burning is completed, the land is cleared and digging stick and seeds of different crops as required are scattered into the holes before the onset of the rains. The cultivation is confined to the area close to the village. After the every crop season of two, the area is left for 25 or 30 years and the cultivator moves to another area to slash and burn and cultivate (Lekhi and Choudhury, 1994). This laborious process often completed by the men from two or three families. Such a joint effort is one of the essential ingredients of a well-knit social organisation. This effort along with the process of allotment of sites for jhum by the village head man who is incharge of overall control of the village community helps to promote kinship among the members of the village (Ramakrishnan, 1996). However, the system of allotment of lands differs from tribes to tribes.

Paddy is the main crop in jhuming. Among the other crops cultivated are maize, millet, sweet potatoes, leafy vegetables etc. Each family chooses its own cropping pattern according to what it consumes and in quantities enough to meet its own needs. The crops are all rainfed and harvesting starts from August. The paddy grown in jhum fields matures earlier than the paddy grown in plain (Lekhi and Choudhury, 1994).

Factors in Favour of Jhuming

1. *Land tenure system in Tribal areas:* Communal system of landownership is most suitable for shifting cultivations. Unless there is private ownership of land or cooperative farming, permanent cultivation in the existing economic order is difficult under communal ownership.

2. *Law of Inheritance:* It makes separation from joint family early. As there is not much immovable property to inherit, no adult member is required to cling to the family poverty. Because of the free gift of labour under shifting cultivation, a married young man is assisted by the co-villagers to construct separate dwelling house. Villagers also give a young couple some share in the *jhum* land for cultivation.

3. *Religious Belief:* Many religious customs, ceremonies and festivals amongst the tribal people are linked with shifting cultivation. There are special ceremonies at the time of clearance of *Jhum* land, harvesting of products; even in case of illness spirit gods are to satisfy in Jhum fields. When jhumming is replaced the rural people must have some alternative mass ceremonies. It is noticeable amongst the Garos converted to Christianity, that althougth they have changed their religion, their habits associated with jhumming still prevails.

4. *Hill top Dwelling:* Because of their age-old preference to have dwelling house on the hill tops, it will be difficult to have such suitable hill top near the valley area suitable for permanent cultivation.

5. *Mixed Cropping:* Mixed cropping gives the jhumias their daily requirements of food grains and vegetables, in addition to providing insurance against shortage of one crop by another crop. If only one crop is grown under settled farming, the jhumias will have to depend for their requirements on outsiders. But in the

absence of marketing facilities it will be difficult for the jhumias to get their requirements easily.

6. *Food Habits:* Jhumias have special attachment to the rice varieties and vegetable grown in jhum land. Encouraging permanent cultivation will have to be associated with change of taste.

7. *Crop Production:* As *Jhum* cultivation is undertaken by whole village in a compact plot of land and as each homestead gets its requirement within the compact block, it becomes easier in the consolidated field to protect crop from wild animals (e.g. Elephant, monkey, boars, wild buffaloes) and fires compared to scattered permanent plots in hilly terrain.

8. *Capital Investment:* Jhuming requires very little capital. If land and human labour is available, cultivation is possible. In permanent cultivation, a pair of bullocks, irrigation, land preparation by manual labour becomes essential.

In spirit of all these favourable factors for jhum cultivation, because of the pressure of population and progressive deterioration of soil in the hill slopes, it has become invariably difficult to get suitable jhum land on hill slopes. Extension of jhum cultivation in steep slopes will aggravate the problems of soil erosion and the agricultural prospect in hill and plains wil be jeopardized. Hence jhuming as practiced now cannot continue owing mainly to the absence of suitable land. Some alternative to jhuming either by field rotation or improved system of jhuming or by combinations of both settled farming and jhuming must be found out.

Jhum Cycle

In shifting agriculture, cultivator in a particular area for one or two years and then moving into other areas and again returning to the first area for cultivation completes a 'cycle'. The cycle includes the number of years an area is under cultivation plus the years the area is kept under forest fallow. Previously the fallow period was 25 years to 30 years, but it has now come down to four to five years (Dhar, 1995). Long cycles were possible earlier because population pressures were not heavy and land availability did not limit the cycle. In NER, the average size of a jhum plot varies from 1.0 to 2.5 ha. The average family consists of two adults and three to four children (Ramakrishnan, 1996).

Agriculture and Environment and Concern for Sustainability

Beyond upland and other less favoured regions, the role of agriculture in the sustainability of rural population and as a means of protection the environment has receded in the face of post-war farm policies. Agriculture has escaped the mandatory environmental controls applied to other economic sectors, such as the authorisation of pollution sources, application of a polluter-pays principle, pollution taxes and so on. Today, such measures are increasingly mooted as means to control modern agriculture, but wide spread changes to landscapes to ecosystem and to natural resources have occurred already. Indeed agricultural modernisation has been predicted upon processes that are inherently damaging to the environment, such as the increasing use of chemical additives, biological and genetic transformation, tree clearance, land drainage and use of heavy machinery (Nature Conservancy Council, 1984). Popular and scientific concern for the environmental effects of agriculture has been slow to emerge. The broad consensus over post-war agricultural development along with a long established belief that agriculture is a "natural" rural activity has had pervasive effect upon European attitude. Initially, the scale and implications of change brought out by agricultural modernisation took environmentalists and policy-makers by surprise. Today, the environmental impact of intensive agriculture is a major issue in all European countries (Buller, 1992).

The agricultural change and its impact on environment is a growing concern for all the countries of the world, developed or underdeveloped. The remarkable success of green revolution technology in increasing agricultural productivity and improving the food security situation in Asia is hardly debated. It also catalysed investments in agricultural research, institutional development, infrastructure improvement and above all, in extensive development of irrigation facilities. These benefits also marked the damage to living environment, physical properties of the natural resources stocks, especially the soil and water and human and animal health caused by indiscriminate use of synthetic pesticides and fertilizers. These concerns have led tone initiatives and policy commitments towards sustainable development which basically shifts the emphasis from inputs like seeds and chemical fertilizers to resource management (A.P.O. Reports, 1997).

In fact, there are at least three classes of argument one could make to justify a claim that economic activity should be sustainable. The first argument is a moral one. We, the present generation, have main obligations to those generations which will come after us. The second type of argument is ecological one. Suppose you believe that ecological diversity is an important objective in its own right. Then economic activity that threatens to reduce such diversity is intrinsically undesirable. The third approach to justifying a sustainability goal is an economic one. To develop an economic case, one should need to argue either that sustainable economic behaviour is more efficient than non-sustainable behaviour or that sustainable behaviour is that which maximises inter-temporal social behaviour (Perman *et. al.*, 1996).

Concern for Sustainable Shifting Agriculture in N.E. Region

The major advantage of the shifting cultivation to the hill people is that it provides a very easy method for the preparation of land for cultivation. Weeds and jungles can be easily cleared by slash and burn process and yield can be obtained within a short period of time. However, the most important evil effect of shifting cultivation is that destruction of forest in the hill area causes heavy soil erosion due to rainfall. Moreover, loss of the top soil in the hill areas to the extent of 22 per cent of the total soil due to jhuming causes a serious fall in the fertility of the soil and thus it creates a serious problem for the tribal people (Dhar, 1995). In fact, the major problems associated with jhum in the NER are the drastic shortening of the jhum cycle to four to five years during recent years. The important cause for shortening of the cycle is the rapid increase in the tribal population and consequent reduction in the availability of land for cultivation. The obvious effect of shortening of the cycle can be grouped into two classes: (i) Economic effects, and (ii) Environmental effects.

Table-2: Monetary Input-Output under Different Jhum Cycles in N-E Region (Rs./hect./yrs.)

	Jhum Cycle		
	30 Years Gap	*10 Years Gap*	*5 Years Gap*
Input	2616	1830	896
Output	5586	3354	1690
Net gain/loss	2970	1524	794
Output/Input	2.13	1.83	1.88

Source: Ramakrishnan: 1996:25.

As a result of the reduction in the "jhum cycle" has adversely affected economic yield with gradual decline in yield over a period of time when short cycles are imposed (Ramakrishnan, 1996). The Table-2 compares the monetary output/input analysis of the jhum under different cycles in the north-eastern region.

The reduction in overall economic return is very obvious, when cost is calculated on the basis of prevailing market rates. The decrease in economic return under short cycle of jhum is related to reduced soil fertility and increased weed potential of the site. Another most important effect of the shifting cultivation is that it leads to environmental degradation and disturbs the fragile ecosystems in the north-eastern region. This occurs as a result of the destruction caused to the surrounding natural vegetation. The environmental imbalance has resulted uneven spread of monsoon rainfall leading to the problem of draught and excessive rainfall resulting flood in the region. In Meghalaya, unabated jhuming has turned the once thick evergreen forest belt of Cherrapunji, a place which used to record the highest rainfall in the world into a dry brown scar. The jhuming practice has caused extensive climatic changes in the state and destroyed rare flora and fauna (Dhar, 1995). The Cherrapunji ecosystem that now stands desertified due to deforestation inflicted sometime in the distant past no refused to recover its original state. Linked with this drastic loss in biological diversity is the human suffering which now is immense. Water is a scarce commodity during the dry months in this high rainfall spot of the world, a contender for being the driest spot on earth along

Table-3: Change in Forest Cover (1991 and 1993) Assessment (Sq. Kms.)

State	*1991 Assessment*			*1993 Assessment*			*Total Change in 1993 assessment*
	D.F.	*O.F*	*Total*	*D.F.*	*O.F*	*Total*	
Arunachal Pradesh	54542	14215	68757	54510	14151	68662	-96
Assam	15842	8908	24751	15998	8510	24508	-243
Manipur	5309	12376	17685	5307	12314	17621	-64
Meghalaya	3305	12570	15875	3305	12464	15769	-106
Mizoram	4279	14574	18853	4238	14459	18697	-156
Nagaland	3351	10790	14321	3487	10861	14348	+27
Tripura	1825	3710	5535	1819	3719	5538	+3
Total	88633	77144	165777	88664	76478	165142	-635

Note: D.F.: Dense Forest, O.F.: Open Forest

Source: Basic Statistics of N.E. Region, 1995, North Eastern Council.

Table-4: Loss/Gain in the forest covers in 1993 assessment as compared to 1991 assessment in the N.E. States (sq. km.)

State	*Loss due to*			*Gain due to*			*Net (+) Gain (-) Loss*
	Shifting cultivation	*Other reason*	*Total loss*	*Regeneration in abandoned shifting cultivation*	*Other reason*	*Total gain*	
Arunachal Pradesh	70	26	96	-	-	-	-96
Assam	165	190	355	104	8	112	-143
Manipur	28	36	64	-	-	-	-64
Meghalaya	110	2	112	6	-	6	-106
Mizoram	256	-	256	100	-	100	-156
Nagaland	63	-	63	90	-	90	+27
Tripura	10	27	37	15	25	40	+3
Total	702	281	983	315	33	348	-635

Note: net loss in forest cover in the N.E. States = 983 " 348 = 635 sq. km.

Source: Govt. India, Forest Survey of India (Ministry of Environment and Forest), 1993.

with the nearby Mousengram in the Khasi Hill of Meghalaya. The tribal who is traditionally bound to the forests has been forced to seek other avenues for survival (Ramakrishnan, 1996). A relative scenario of change in forest cover in the N.E. Region is depicted in Table-3 and Table-4.

The Table-3 and Table-4 depicted a detailed picture of forest coverage in the NER. From Table-3, (it is found that the total loss of forest area in the NER between 1991 and 1993 was 635 sq. km. from the loss and gain accounts. Table-4 indicates that loss due to shifting cultivation accounted to 702 sq. km., while the total loss becomes 983 sq. km. Due to regeneration and other reasons gains amounted to 348 sq. km., totalling a net loss of 635 sq. km. The principal reason for loss of forest area seems to be the practice of shifting cultivation. The net loss due to shifting cultivation during the period was 387 (702-315) sq. km.

Conclusion and Suggestions

Govt. and other agencies have undertaken various measures for controlling shifting cultivation in desired directions. The North Eastern Council and the Indian Council of Agricultural Research has been effectively involved to find way out to solve the problem. From Fifth Plan onwards different programmes have also been undertaken in this direction. In the Environment report submitted by the Union Environment Ministry to the United Nations in 1992 has mentioned about the practice of jhum cultivation among the tribal people of the North-East India. The report reasoned out why the old practice became enviable and damaging and also states that the increasing population and decreasing availability of land led to the fall in the jhum cycle affecting the cultivation process.

Although various attempts have already been made by the State Government and various other agencies in weaning the north-east tribals into modern scientific cultivation but most of these attempts have failed to achieve desired results. A field study of the Department of Sociological Anthropology of the North Eastern Hill University, Shillong in 1994 showed that the tribal hardly used the subsidy given to them for starting a settled way of cultivation. In some cases they sold the land allotted to them, and went back to their old life. The study pointed out thatjhuming is an ancient socio-economic tradition that the tribes likes to cling to. However, tribal resistance to change alone is not the only reason rather lack of whole hearted effort on the part of government agencies is also responsible for such failure. Field surveys in Garo hills of Meghalaya show that some areas selected for terrace cultivation as part of the anti-jhuming efforts were unsuitable for food crops. Seeds were often not supplied on time and proper infrastructural facilities required in this connection are also not provided in the resettlement colonies. Such half-hearted official endeavours will hardly stop jhuming silent march in the NER (Dhar, 1995). The fact that recently jhum around Cherrapunji is banned by the village council is a positive indication of transformation. What needed is an area-oriented approach of planning and more patience on the part of the Government agencies and NGO's. These will help in making the painful switch to settle agricultural existences. The universities of the region must also come forward in arranging area oriented specific short term motivational programme on the issue.

References

1. Barua, P.C., (1990): Development Planning of North East India, Mittal Publications, New Delhi.
2. Buller, J. Henry, (1992): "Agricultural Change and the Environment in Western Europe" in Keith Haggart (Ed), Agricultural change, Environment and Economy, pp. 68-70.
3. Dhar, P.K., (1995): The Economy of Assam (including Economy of N.E. India), Kalyani Publishers, New Delhi.
4. Dutta, P.C. and Mandal, R.K. (2011): Globalisation, Growth and Inequality in North East India, Kalpaz Publications, New Delhi.
5. Gadgil, M. and Guha, R, (1992): The Fissure Land; an Ecological History of India, Oxford University Press, Delhi.
6. Goswami, P.C. (1980): "Problem of Jhum control" in Mathew, T (ed), Tribal Economy of the North-Eastern Region, Spectrum Pub. Gauhati pp. 55-57.
7. Lekhi, R.K. and Choudhury, R.K. (1994): Economy of India Including Assam and North East, Kalyani Publishers, Kolkata.
8. Perman R., Ma Yue and Mcgilvray J. (1996): Natural Resource and Environmental Economics, Longman, London and New York.

10. Ramakrishnan, P.S. (1996): Shifting Agriculture and Sustainable Development, UNESCO and the Parthenon Publishing Group.
11. Read more at http://www.brainyquote.com/quotes/keywords/natural_resources.html#pLm5MVEvSuzRiSj5.99

4

Natural Resources of India: An Overview

Dr N.G. Pendse *and* ***Dr Sukanta Sarkar***

"Some global hazards are insidious. They stem from pressure on energy supplies, food, water and other natural resources. And they will be aggravated as the population rises to a projected nine billion by mid-century, and by the effects of climate change. An 'ecological shock' could irreversibly degrade our environment."

—Martin Rees

Introduction

Nature refers to the phenomena of the physical world, and also to life in general. It ranges in scale from the subatomic to the cosmic. Within the various uses of the word today, nature often refers to geology and wildlife. Earth has evolved through geological and biological processes that have left traces of the original conditions. The outer surface is divided into several gradually migrating tectonic plates. The atmosphere of the Earth serves as a key factor in sustaining the planetary ecosystem. The first form of life to develop on the Earth was microbes, and they remained the only form of life on the planet until about a billion years ago when multi-cellular organisms began to appear.

Biodiversity is the degree of variation of life. Biodiversity is most commonly used to replace the more clearly defined and long established terms, species diversity and species richness. Biologists most often define biodiversity as the totality of genes, species, and ecosystems of a region. Biodiversity is not evenly distributed; rather it varies greatly across the globe as well as within regions. Among other factors, the diversity of all living things (biota) depends on temperature, precipitation, altitude, soils, geography and the presence of other species. A biodiversity hotspot is a region with a high level of endemic species that is under threat from humans. Biodiversity is the result of 3.5 billion years of evolution. Biodiversity's relevance to human health is becoming an international political issue, as scientific evidence builds on the global health implications of biodiversity loss. The growing demand and lack of drinkable water on the planet presents an additional challenge to the future of human health. Many industrial materials derive directly from biological sources. These include building materials, fibers, dyes, rubber and oil. Biodiversity is also important to the security of resources such as water, timber, paper, fiber, and food.

What are Natural Resources?

Natural resources are materials and components that can be found within the environment. They occur naturally within environments that exist relatively undisturbed by humanity, in a natural form. It can be thought of as natural capital assets, distinct from physical and human capital in that they are not created by human activity. It is often characterised by amounts of biodiversity and geodiversity existent in various ecosystems. Natural resources are derived from the environment. Some natural resources such as sunlight and air can be found everywhere, and are known as ubiquitous resources.

Natural resources are useful materials from the Earth, such as coal, oil, natural gas, and trees. People use natural resources as raw materials to manufacture or create a range of modern conveniences. Water and food provide humans with sustenance and energy, for example, and fossil fuels generate heat as well as energy for transportation and industrial production. They are the raw materials supplied by nature. Everything produced, used and thrown away originates from natural resources. People cannot create natural resources.

Significance of Natural Resources

There is no direct link between the availability of natural resources and the level of economic development. There are many countries which are rich in natural resources but still they are underdeveloped. In fact, for the economic development of a country, optimum exploitation of natural resources is more important than their availability. They are very important to the economy of a community. Different communities around the world use the natural resources around them to make their lives better. Coal has many uses. Coal is burned in some of our power plants to produce electricity. The electricity is used by factories to power machinery and in homes for light and heat. Another very important natural resource that comes from deep inside the earth is oil. Oil is used to make gasoline. Oil is also used to fuel airplanes, and ships, power machinery, and heat homes.

Types of Natural Resources

Natural resources are often classified into renewable and non-renewable resources. Renewable resources are generally living resources (fish, coffee, and forests, for example), which can restock (renew) themselves if they are not overharvested. Renewable resources can restock themselves and be used indefinitely if they are used sustainably. Once renewable resources are consumed at a rate that exceeds their natural rate of replacement, the standing stock will diminish and eventually run out. The rate of sustainable use of a renewable resource is determined by the replacement rate and amount of standing stock of that particular resource. Non-living renewable natural resources include soil, as well as water, wind, tides and solar radiation. Resources can also be classified on the basis of their origin as biotic and abiotic. Biotic resources are derived from animals and plants. Abiotic resources are derived from the non-living world e.g. land, water, and air. Mineral and power resources are also abiotic resources some are derived from nature. Both extraction of the basic resource and refining it into a purer, directly usable form, are generally considered natural-resource activities, even though the latter may not necessarily occur near the former.

Natural Resources in India

The Indian landmass contains a multitude of both types of resource and its economy, especially in rural areas, is heavily dependent on their consumption or export. Due to overconsumption, such as uncontrolled logging or overfishing, many valuable natural resources are rapidly being depleted. India's land area includes regions with high rainfall to dry deserts, coastline to Alpine regions. Around 21 per cent of the total geographical area consists of Forests. India has a long history in fishing and aquaculture. India has rich marine and inland water resources. It has an 8129 km long coastline. Inland fishery is carried out in Rivers, Reservoirs and Lakes. In Indian rivers more than 400 species of fish are found and many species are economically important.

Coal mining in India started in 1774 through East India Company in the Raniganj Coalfield along the western bank of Damodar River in the Indian State of West Bengal. Growth of the Indian coal mining started when steam locomotives were introduced in 1853. India had about 125 million metric tonne of proven oil reserves as April 2010 or 5.62 billion barrels as per EIA estimate for 2009, which is the second-largest amount in the Asia-Pacific region behind China. Most of India's crude oil reserves are located in the western coast (Mumbai High) and in the northeastern parts of the country, although considerable undeveloped reserves are also located in the offshore Bay of Bengal and in the state of Rajasthan. As per the Ministry of Petroleum, Government of India, India has 1,437 billion cubic metres of confirmed natural gas reserves as of April 2010. A huge mass of India's natural gas production comes from the western offshore regions, particularly the Mumbai High complex. The onshore fields in Assam, Andhra Pradesh, and Gujarat states are also major producers of natural gas. Oil is being explored in India at many places of Assam and Gujarat. Digboi, Dimapur, Naharkatia, Kasimpur, Palliaria, Rudrapur, Shivsagar, Mourn (All in Assam) and Bay of Khambhat, Ankaleshwar and Kalol

(All in Gujarat) are the important places of oil exploration in India.

Major resources of Copper are available at Rajasthan, Madhya Pradesh and Jharkhand. As on 2010, India had 1.56 billion tonnes of Copper ore. India is one of the 20 major Copper producers. India is the World's fourth largest Zinc reserve as in 2013. Hindustan Zinc Limited is the main producer of Zinc in India. Most of the resources are available in Rajasthan. Minor amount of resources are available in Andhra Pradesh, Madhya Pradesh, Bihar and Maharashtra states. India is the World's third biggest exporter of Iron ore as in 2013. Major amount of Hematite is found in Odisha, Jharkhand, Chhattisgarh, Karnataka and Goa. Minor amount of Hematite is found in Andhra Pradesh, Assam, Bihar, Maharashtra, Madhya Pradesh, Meghalaya, Rajasthan and Uttar Pradesh.

The total reserves of iron-ore in the country are about 14,630 million tonnes of haematite and 10,619 million tonnes of magnetite. Haematite iron is mainly found in Chhattisgarh, Jharkhand, Odisha, Goa and Karnataka. India ranks third in the world after China and USA in the realm of coal production. The main centres of coal in India are the West Bengal, Bihar, Madhya Pradesh, Maharashtra, Odisha and Andhra Pradesh. Bulk of the coal production comes from Bengal-Jharkhand coalfields. Bauxite is a main source of metal like aluminium. The total resources of bauxite as per United Nations Framework Classification (UNFC) in the country were placed at 3,290 million tonnes as on April 1, 2005. The areas of bauxite deposits in India are: Andhra Pradesh, Jharkhand, Goa, Gujarat, Jammu & Kashmir, Karnataka, Kerala, Chhattisgarh, Maharashtra, Odisha, Rajasthan, Tamil Nadu and Uttar Pradesh. Major reserves are concentrated in the East Coast bauxite deposits of Odisha and Andhra Pradesh.

India possesses only a limited gold reserve. There are only three main gold mine regions—Kolar Goldfield, Kolar district and Hutti Goldfield in Raichur district (both in Karnataka) and Ramgiri Goldfield in Anantpur district (Andhra Pradesh). As per UNEC the total reserves of diamond is estimated at around

4582 thousand carats which are mostly available in Panna (Madhya Pradesh), Rammallakota of Kurnur district of Andhra Pradesh and also in the Basin of Krishna River. The total resources of manganese ore in the country are placed at 379 million tonnes. Its maximum deposit is found in Karnataka, Odisha, Madhya Pradesh, Maharashtra and Goa also possess relatively larger deposits of manganese. As per IJNFC, the total resources of chromite as on 1st April, 2005 were 213 million tonnes. As per UNFC, India has got 74 million tonnes deposits of barytes as on April 1, 2005 which are mostly available in Mangampet of Cuddapah district of Andhra Pradesh.

Ministry of Mines is responsible for survey and exploration of all minerals, other than natural gases, petroleum and atomic minerals.The Ministry of Environment and Forests (MoEF) is the nodal agency in the administrative structure of the Central Government for planning, promotion, co-ordination and overseeing the implementation of India's environmental and forestry policies and programmes. Ministry of Water Resources is responsible for laying down guidelines and programmes for the development and regulation of the country's water resources. National Natural Resources Management System (NNRMS) is a national level inter-agency system for integrated natural resources management in the country. The Forest Department of Chhattisgarh is engaged in planning, implementation, monitoring and evaluation of forestry, and environmental programmes in the state. The National River Conservation Plan (NRCP) by the Ministry of Environment and Forests aims at preventing pollution of rivers and improving water quality. The Forest Department is responsible for the management of forests and wildlife in the state of Rajasthan. The Central Ground Water Board (CGWB), a subordinate office of the Ministry of Water Resources, is the National Apex Agency entrusted with the responsibilities of providing scientific inputs for management, exploration, monitoring, assessment, augmentation and regulation of ground water resources of the country.

Degradation of Natural Resource

Many aspects of natural resource and environmental management cut across regions: increasing beneficiary and community participation, developing and sharing environmental friendly technologies, fostering environmental policies, and promoting rural finance to encourage off-farm income-generating activities and microenterprise to help take the pressure off natural resources. Degradation of natural resources is a serious problem in eastern and southern Africa: the region suffers from deforestation, loss of soil fertility, soil compaction, water scarcity and overgrazing. A major concern is land and water degradation, caused largely by the spread of desertification and the growing scarcity of arable land surface, groundwater and rangeland. As the growing population turns to wooded lands for its cooking fuel, timber and expanding agriculture, the resulting depletion of forests is compounding the problem.

Environmental degradation is the deterioration of the environment through depletion of resources such as air, water and soil; the destruction of ecosystems and the extinction of wildlife. It is defined as any change or disturbance to the environment perceived to be deleterious or undesirable. One major component of environmental degradation is the depletion of the resource of fresh water on Earth. Climate change affects the Earth's water supply in a large number of ways. It is predicted that the mean global temperature will rise in the coming years due to a number of forces affecting the climate. The issue of the depletion of fresh water can be met by increased efforts in water management.

Natural Resource Management

Natural Resource Management are more important, it shows the management of natural resources such as land, water, soil, plants and animals, with a particular focus on how management affects the quality of life for both present and future generations. It deals with managing the way in which people and natural landscapes interact. Natural resource management specifically focuses on a scientific and technical understanding of resources and ecology and the life-supporting capacity of those resources. The community-based natural resource management approach combines conservation objectives with the generation of economic benefits for rural communities. The three key assumptions being that: locals are better placed to conserve natural resources, people will conserve a resource only if benefits exceed the costs of conservation, and people will conserve a resource that is linked directly to their quality of life. Integrated natural resource management is a process of managing natural resources in a systematic way, which includes multiple aspects of natural resource use (biophysical, socio-political, and economic) meet production goals of producers and other direct users (e.g., food security, profitability, risk aversion) as well as goals of the wider community (e.g., poverty alleviation, welfare of future generations, environmental conservation).

Conclusion

Natural resources are useful materials from the Earth, such as coal, oil, natural gas, and trees. People use natural resources as raw materials to manufacture or create a range of modern conveniences. They are often classified into renewable and non-renewable resources. Renewable resources are generally living resources (fish, coffee, and forests, for example), which can restock (renew) themselves if they are not overharvested. Environmental degradation is the deterioration of the environment through depletion of resources such as air, water and soil; the destruction of ecosystems and the extinction of wildlifc. It is defined as any change or disturbance to the environment perceived to be deleterious or undesirable. The Indian landmass contains a multitude of both types of resource and its economy, especially in rural areas, is heavily dependent on their consumption or export. Around 21 per cent of the total geographical area consists of Forests. India has a long history in fishing and aquaculture. It has rich marine and inland water resources. It has an 8129 km long coastline. Inland fishery is carried out in Rivers, Reservoirs and Lakes. In Indian rivers more than 400 species of fish are found and many species are economically important.

References

1. Biodiversity (2014), Retrieved from http://en.wikipedia.org/wiki/Biodiversity
2. Environment and Natural Resource Management, Retrieved from http://www.ifad.org/pub/enviorn/EnvironENG.pdf

3. Environmental degradation (2014), Retrieved from http://en.wikipedia.org/wiki/Environmental_degradation
4. Lesson: Our Natural Resources, Retrieved from http://www.deq.state.or.us/lq/pubs/docs/sw/curriculum/RRPart0201.pdf
5. Natural resource management (2014), Retrieved from http://en.wikipedia.org/wiki/Natural_resource_management
6. Natural resources (2014), Retrieved from http://en.wikipedia.org/wiki/Natural_resource
7. Natural resources helps communities to grow, Retrieved from http://www.studyzone.org/testprep/ss5/b/comnatresl.cfm
8. Natural resources in India, Retrieved from http://en.wikipedia.org/wiki/Natural_resources_of_India
9. Natural resources, Retrieved from http://india.gov.in/topics/environment-forest/natural-resources
10. Natural Resources, Retrieved from http://www.epa.gov/osw/education/quest/pdfs/unit1/chap1/u1_natresources.pdf
11. Natural resources: Definitions, trade patterns and globalization, Retrieved from http://www.wto.org/english/res_e/booksp_e/anrep_e/wtr10-2b_e.pdf
12. Smriti Chand, What are the Different Types of Natural Resources Produced in India? Retrieved from http://www.yourarticle library.com/economics/what-are-the-different-types-of-natural-resources-produced-in-india/2683/
13. Read more at http://www.brainyquote.com/quotes/keywords/natural_resources.html#pLm5MVEvSuzRiSj5.99

5

The Socio-Economic Problems of Minorities in Raipur City

Priyanka Kukreja *and* ***Prof Rohini Prasad***

"Environmental activism against the resource industry is widespread all over the world, but at the same time we have to realise that these are basic materials on which civilisation depends. We need to tap natural resources in a sustainable manner."

—Anil Agarwal

Introduction

The Constitution of India uses the word 'minority' or its plural form in some Articles – 29 to 30 and 350A to 350B – but does not define it anywhere. Article 29 has the word "minorities" in its marginal heading but speaks of "any sections of citizens.... having a distinct language, script or culture." This may be a whole community generally seen as: a minority or a group within a majority community. Article 30 speaks specifically of two categories of minorities – religious and linguistic. The remaining two Articles – 350A and 350B relate to linguistic minorities only.[1] Article 29 and 30 deal with cultural and educational rights of minorities: Article 29 provides that: (a) any section of the citizens residing in the territory of India or any part thereof having a distinct language, script or culture of its own shall have the right to conserve the same, and (b) no citizen shall be denied admission into any educational institution maintained by the State or receiving aid out of State funds on grounds only of religion, race, caste, language or any of them.[2]

Article 30 is a minority-specific provision that protects the right of minorities to establish and administer educational institutions. It provides that *"all minorities, whether based on religion or language, shall have the right to establish and administer educational institutions of their choice"*. Clause (1-A) of the article 30, which was inserted by the Constitution (Forty-fourth Amendment) Act, 1978 provides that *"in making any law providing for the compulsory acquisition of any property of an educational institution established and administered by a minority, referred to in clause (1), the State shall ensure that the amount fixed by or determined under such law for the acquisition of such property is such as would not restrict or abrogate the right guaranteed under that clause"*.[3] Article 30 further provides that *"the State shall not, in granting aid to educational institutions, discriminate against any educational institution on the ground that it is under the management of a minority, whether based on religion and language"*.[4]

Chhattisgarh State Minorities Commission

Chhattisgarh government, Tribal, Scheduled Caste, Backward Classes and Minorities Welfare Department Order No. / D -1932 / 2717 / Ajak / 2001 dated 12-7-2001, including the Chairman of the State Minorities Commission have formed a 3-member state. Chhattisgarh State Minorities Commission Act, 1996 Section 3 (2) In exercise of the powers conferred by the Chhattisgarh government, Tribal and Scheduled Caste Development Department by following commands Section 4 (1) provision of the chairman and members of the three-year period have been appointed: Chhattisgarh government, Tribal and Scheduled Caste Development Department Order Number / F - 17/2007/25-1 / Ajak on December 7, 2010 by the Honorable Mr. Chhattisgarh State Minorities Commission member Cladiys lamp post of president has been ordered to work and Sl. order. F 3-8/ 09/1 / a Dinanak May 23, 2011, have been given the status of Minister of State. (Appendix-02)[1] Chhattisgarh government,

Tribal and Scheduled Caste Development Department Order Number / F -17/2007/25-1 / Ajak on December 15, 2010 by Hon'ble Shri Sardar Dilip Singh Hora has been appointed a member of the Chhattisgarh State Minorities Commission.[5]

Review of Literature

Adalberto[6], Rurhuks. T[7] Brown Hanae[8] has researched the ability of local civil rights movement to influence the development of local war on poverty programme. The impact of larger global context on the experiences of Asian and Pacific Islander in the US is traced special attention towards the discrimination in education and prejudices against gays and their exploitation in the workplace.

Distifano, Anthony Eric[9] and Hakali[10] Lehmann[11] using qualitative interviews and participant observation Distifano experienced violence between lesbian, gay, bisexual transgender in Japan providing formative data indicating violence. Eric argues in his paper about the transition from dominant minority to dominant majority ethnicity whereas minority domination was common in pre-modern societies. This article begins with conceptual clarification. Lehmann presented special issue of Jewish social studies discussing workshop held at Stanford University about the ambiguity of Jeruselem and other Jewish communities.

Objectives of the Study

(1) To examine the Human Development Index of Minorities in Raipur city.
(2) To examine the public facility available with Minorities.
(3) To examine goal like security, equality, and freedom experience by Minorities.

Hypothesis of the Study

(1) There is positive correlation between provision of minorities in Constitution of India and Socio-Economic problems of Minorities.
(2) Socio-Economic Inequality is evident in society of Minorities.

Research Methodology

For the study of Socio-Economic problems of minorities Muslims and Christian community has been taken. There are

77963 Muslims and 16857 Christians in Raipur city out of which 13951 Muslims in Rural and 64012 Muslims in urban Raipur; and 4721 Christians in Rural and 12136 in Urban Raipur city. Average Sampled Families are calculated and so out of that five per cent sample size is taken that is about 779 Muslim families and 168 Christians are taken. Total sampled Family size of Minorities is 947 families.

Sample Families of Minorities in Raipur City

Sl. No.	*Study Area*	*Muslim*	*Christian*	*Total*
1.	Rural	139	47	186
2.	Urban	640	121	761
3.	Total	779	168	947

Total Sample Families = 947 Families

Finding of the Study

Analysing the variation of illiteracy among minorities in Raipur city, we did the data collection on the rural and urban basis which shows that illiteracy rate is high in Christian community as compare to Muslim community, men in rural Christian are around 24 per cent and in Muslim are around seven per cent only. Where as in urban area the Christian men illiterate were 70 per cent and in Muslim there are zero per cent. Supporting to these datas we found the same status of illiteracy in women also in both the areas. In rural area the illiterate Christian women were again higher in compare to Muslim illiterate women that's around 75 per cent in Christian and 17 per cent in Muslim community. In urban area the children in both the communities were not illiterate this is good sign for the better livelihood of minorities in Raipur city. But still men and women were to some extent found to be illiterate.

100 per cent deliveries are happened to be complicated not fine. Whether it is Christian or Muslim in both the Communities deliveries have been complicated totally. This shows the poor infrastructure of not only human on the health indicator but truly it shows the pathetic and poor infrastructure of health and

medical facilities in Raipur city. It shows the lack of not only modern medical technique, but also better infrastructure health care centre etc. Health is a major indicator of the human development because it is more important than even education and standard of living, which is a pathetic in minor community in Raipur city.

Analysing the housing facilities like drinking water, electricity, toilet facilities, it can say that all are utilised 100 per cent by both the communities in both rural and urban. None of the minority people are living under standard life. On the term of ownership of house we can say that Muslim is living in rented house in more proportion to self owned as compare to Christian. None of the minor has taken the houses under any of the scheme by the government IMR is zero in rural Muslim. Whereas there does exist IMR in rural Christian of about four per cent. Sarcastically there is more percentage of IMR in urban area as compare to rural area in both the community. Although there is much more modern medical facility in urban area as compare to rural area. On terms of hygienic status also we all are certain about cleanliness in urban as compare to rural areas still it is a strange to know that IMR is more in urban area in both the community. MMR again is zero in rural Muslim and 44 per cent in rural Christian, which is a strange detail for us to know the socio-economic status of minorities in Raipur city in rural area. In urban area we have an acceptable datas of IMR and MMR that's much more in Muslim community as compare to Christian. MMR is almost three times in Muslim community than Christian community in Raipur city.

The detail of land holding by Muslim and Christian community in rural and urban areas is on the basis of square per meter and acres. The land holding in rural area on the sq.m basis is same in both the communities. The landholding on the acre basis is much more in Christian community in rural area as compare to Muslim community. The rate of employment of Christian community is higher in self control and of Muslim community is higher in government service. It is around 50 per cent in Muslim community and 43 per cent in Christian community. Followed by least in private sector of Muslim community are around six per cent and 11 per cent in government service in Christian community.

Conclusion

The demography of minority communities, their rural-urban distribution, sex composition, literacy and educational status, marital status and livelihood patterns do indicate the lifestyle of the people. Pattern of landholdings, sources of income and health status narrate their quality of life. Today, socio-economic changes are taking place rapidly in the country affecting the majority as well minority communities, due to diversification of economic pursuits, urbanisation, westernisation of education, inter-caste marriages etc. The detail of landholding by Muslim and Christian community in rural and urban area as on the basis of square per meter and acres. The landholding in rural area on the sq.m basis was same in both the communities. The landholding on the acre basis was much more in Christian community in rural area as compare to Muslim community. To conclude the socio-economic status of minorities on the HDI basis we found that the condition of Health and Literacy and standard of living was not apt enough in Raipur city in both rural and urban areas, and socio-economic status on terms of financial basis and demographic profile also was on an average.

References

1. www.minorities/oxforddefinition.com
2. P.S. Krishnan, *"Understanding the backward classes of Muslim society"*, Economic and Political Weekly, August 21-27, 2010, Vol. xlv, no. 34.
3. Kamlesh Kumar Wadhva, *"Minorities safeguards in India"*, Thomson Press provision and their implication, Delhi 1975, pp. 2 and 22.
4. Joseph Keenan, *"Hoarding warns against Christians sharing faith in Chhattisgarh"*, Christian Today India, Thursday, 16 July, 2009, 16:54 (IST).
5. Kamlesh Kumar Wadhva, *"Minorities safeguards in India"*, Thomson Press provision and their implication, Delhi 1975, pp. 2 and 22.

6. Adalbert, *"Spaces of mobilization: Asian American struggle for social justice"*, Social Justice, 2008, 35, pp. 1-17.
7. Rhuks T, *"Minority Rights issues in Nigeria"*, International Journal on Minority and group rights, 2009, 16, pp. 53-65.
8. Brown, Hunae, *"Repression, Mobilation and social policy : the Virginia Civil rights movement and war on poverty"*.
9. Distefano, Anthony, *"Intimate partner Violence among sexual minorities in Japan exploring perception and experiences"*, Journal of Homosexuality, February 2, 2009, pp. 121-146.
10. Eric and Hoklai, "Dominant ethnicity: From Minority to Majority" Nation and Nationalism, October 14, Vol. 4, 2008, pp. 734-767.
11. Lehman, Matthias B, *"Introduction: sephard identities"*, Jewish social studies, 2008, 15, 1, fall 1-9.
12. Read more at http://www.brainyquote.com/quotes/keywords/natural_resources.html#pLm5MVEvSuzRiSj5.99

6

Economic Performance and Prospects of South Asian Economies

Ishfaq Ahmad Malik *and* ***Ajaz Ahmad Rather***

"When elected officials abandon our environment and ruin our natural resources, public health is endangered. I know the importance of providing a clean environment for our children; I have attended more than one funeral for a child who has died from an asthma attack."

—Gwen Moore

Introduction

South Asia is a region of 1.3 billion populations or one-fifth of the world's population that comprises Afghanistan, Pakistan, India, Bangladesh, Sri Lanka, Bhutan and Maldives. These countries are members of South Asian Association for Regional Cooperation. The region accounts nearly three per cent of world's GDP and one per cent of world's total exports and main exporting items are cotton, sugar, manufacturing, information technology and textiles. Poverty concentration is largest and ranks of human development indicators are lowest of this region. Some common characteristics of developing countries are present in this region like low per capita income, low standard of living, high population growth rate, unemployment problems, imperfect market, etc.

The interdependence of economic growth and structural transformation is emphasised by a number of empirical studies carried out by Kuznets, Chenery, Clark and Fisher. According to these studies as economy grows, employment and production shift from agriculture to manufacturing sector and ultimately to the service sector. Production leads such a sectoral shift followed by employment. Nonetheless such a conceived classical pattern seems not to be adhered by most of the developing countries in their economic transformations over time. Most developing countries follow heterogeneous and diverging transformation paths that deviate from the classical pattern that was followed by the developed countries. Over the past four decades the fast growth East as well as South East Asian economies have been close to the classical model of structural transformation, other developing counters, like those of Sub-Saharan Africa have faltered to follow the pattern in principle. The fast growth in the former has been associated with successful and dynamic economic transformation with a progressive dwindling role for agriculture and rise of industry and services sector.

Growth and Structural Change

Table 1 portrays growth of GDP and PCY, and size of population for the year 2013 for respective SAARC members. It reveals that most of the member countries have large population and high population growth rate. The annual population rate is 2.2 per cent, while as population growth in rest of the world is 1.6 per cent. Consequently, South Asian economies growth is strangled by population explosion, like population density of Bangladesh is 1,007 people per sq/km, due to which nowadays they are facing food security problem, lower capital intensity of production, low labour productivity, income inequality and lower savings and investment are major issues.

The per capita income is highest in Maldives (6567) followed by Sri Lanka (2923) and Bhutan (2399). Afghanistan is having the least per capita income (687) amongst all South Asian countries. There is almost the same per capita income in India (1489) and Pakistan (1257). Additionally the average growth of GDP for the year 2013 of South Asian countries has been notable,

Table 1: Major Economic Indicators

Countries	*GDP Billion US$*	*GDP Growth*	*Per Capita income US$*	*Per Capita GDP Growth*	*Population Growth*
Afghanistan	20.49	3.3	687	2.5	4.1
Bangladesh	116.35	6.0	752	4.7	1.7
Bhutan	1.77	5.2	2399	5.1	3.0
India	1841.70	4.9	1489	3.5	1.8
Maldives	2.22	3.7	6567	3.6	2.6
Nepal	18.96	3.6	690	3.3	2.1
Pakistan	225.14	3.6	1257	1.5	2.5
Sri Lanka	59.42	7.3	2923	6.2	1.3

Source: World Bank Database.

Table 2: Sectoral Contribution

Country	*Agriculture*			*Industrial*			*Service*		
	2011	*2012*	*2013*	*2011*	*2012*	*2013*	*2011*	*2012*	*2013*
Afghanistan	-7.9	31.5	1.6	9.8	7.2	2.5	12.7	7.3	4.3
Bangladesh	5.1	3.1	2.2	8.2	8.9	9.0	6.2	6.0	5.7
Bhutan	1.6	2.9	2.6	8.0	3.5	5.0	13.7	8.0	3.8
India	5.0	-1.4	4.6	7.8	1.0	0.7	6.6	7.0	6.9
Maldives	1.1	-0.0	1.7	12.1	1.2	-1.2	5.8	1.4	4.7
Nepal	4.5	5.0	1.3	4.3	3.0	1.6	3.4	4.5	6.0
Pakistan	2.0	3.5	3.3	4.7	2.7	3.5	3.9	5.3	3.7
Sri Lanka	1.4	5.2	4.7	10.4	10.3	9.9	8.6	4.6	6.4

Source: World Bank Database.

though great diversity among the economies of the region. However, smaller countries in terms of GDP like Sri Lanka and Bangladesh have achieved remarkable growth rate, while as India's growth rate is 4.9 per cent and Bhutan 5.2 per cent.

The high growth rate of GDP of South Asian region is due to growing industrial and service sectors. Table 2 shows sectoral growth rate of this region, that service sector is growing than agricultural and industrial sectors. To some extent growth rate of all three sectors are same in the South Asian countries. Almost all the countries of the region experienced a declines trend in the growth of their agriculture sector except India and Sri Lanka. The good whether monsoon in 2013 increased growth rate of agriculture by 4.6 per cent, which increased food grain to 263.2 million tons. Similarly, whether the conditions in Sri Lanka are helps for increased growth rate of agriculture at 4.7 per cent.

The growth rate of industrial sector has increased tremendously in Sri Lanka, Bangladesh and Bhutan in 2013. Industrial growth rate of Sri Lanka was 9.9 per cent in 2013 and 10.3 per cent in 2012, due to slower growth in mining and quarrying. Similarly, Bangladesh's industrial growth to some extent remains constant, 8.9 per cent in 2012 to 9.0 per cent 2013, due to good performance of small scale industries and construction. Economic growth of Bhutan decreases 5.2 per cent in 2013 from 6.5 per cent in 2012. The retard largely reflects policy measures adopted in 2012 to alleviate growing shortages of Indian rupee reserves. The measures entailed credit and import restriction, especially in import-heavy activities like construction and transport that requires large rupee payments.

The service sector has shown an increase in its growth rate in all economies of this region except Bhutan and Pakistan. In India, service sector contributes more than half in GDP, which is growing at 6.9 per cent in 2013. The growth rate of service sector in Bangladesh declined from 6.0 per cent in 2012 to 5.7 per cent in 2013; this was mainly due to stagnant imports and often strikes. The growth rate of service sector decreases from 8.0 per cent to 3.8 per cent due to reduction in transport and communication from 10.3 per cent to 5.2 per cent, moreover less domestic investment on retail trade, restaurants and hotels are also responsible factors. Subsequently, weak growth in service sector was caused mainly by hold-up in telecommunication. This countered improvement in finance and insurance that reflected little more than commercial banks profit from their high investment in government securities.

The experience of development economies shows that the process of economic development brings about a systematic pattern of structural changes. According this pattern, the contribution of industrial sector in GDP rises fast in the initial stages of development process, while service sector increases in subsequent stages in addition decline in the share of agricultural sector to GDP. The classical pattern of structural transformation follows the following chain.

A-S-I → A-I-S → I-A-S → I-S-A → S-I-A

Where A is agriculture, S is service sector, I is industrial sector.

While most of the South Asian countries have experienced the structural shortcut as the relative decline in agriculture and increase share of service sector than industrial sector. Most of the South Asian economies were in traditional A-S-I or A-I-S structure where agriculture was dominated and its share in GDP was highest till 1990's, but after that service sector was contributing the largest share to GDP and these countries were therefore in S-I-A type. Despite the fact that there has been structural shift in GDP growth pattern but there has not been any change in occupational structure. Even though more population are engaged with agricultural sector.

Saving and Investment Rates

According to classical and modern economists, capital accumulation has been considered as a strategic factor of growth. Number of studies empirically shows that there exists positive relation investment and growth of GDP. The South Asian economies gross domestic saving and investment in relation to GDP are shown in Table 3. The data shows that the proportion of gross domestic saving in relation to GDP has increased in all the South Asian countries since 1991 to 2013 except Maldives which shows -0.62 in 2013.

Table 3: Gross Domestic Investment and Saving

Country	*Gross Domestic Investment*			*Gross Domestic Saving*		
	1991-2000	*2001-2010*	*2013*	*1991-2000*	*2001-2010*	*2013*
Bangladesh	19.5	24.15	26.56	20.5	27.16	28.15
Bhutan	42.6	51.5	52.6	23	35.5	31.7
India	23.5	31.5	34.7	22.5	32.5	34.7
Maldives	28	26.5	20	22.5	11.8	-0.62
Nepal	23.5	26	31.77	18	28	35.05
Sri Lanka	25	24.5	32.6	20.5	21	28.52

Source: Asian Development Bank.

Table 4: Quality of Life and Social Indicators

Country / Rank	*HDI Value 2012*	*Life Expectancy*	*Mean years of schooling*	*Expected years of schooling*	*GNI per capita (2005 PPP$)*
Sri Lanka (92)	0.715	75	9.3	12.7	5170
Maldives (104)	0.690	77	5.8	12.5	7782
India (136)	0.554	65	4.4	10.7	3285
Bhutan (140)	0.538	67	2.3	12.4	5246
Bangladesh (146)	0.515	69	4.8	8.1	1785
Pakistan (146)	0.515	65	4.9	7.3	2566
Nepal (157)	0.463	69	3.2	8.9	1137
Afghanistan (175)	0.374	49.1	3.1	8.1	1000

Source: UNDP.

Similarly gross domestic investment has increased in all individual countries from 2000 to 2010 and currently 2013 it increased. In year 2013, gross domestic investment was highest in Bhutan 52.6 per cent and during 1991-2000 and 2001-2010 it was 42.6 and 51.5 per cent respectively followed by India and Maldives. These countries are experiencing resource gap due to low saving rate as compared to investment. Moreover all these countries try reducing this gap through foreign resources. There is small gap in Bangladesh, Nepal and Sri Lanka while resource gap is highest in India, Bhutan and Maldives. The diversity in the saving and investment performance explains the economic performance of the economies. But high rate of investment is necessary but not the sufficient condition for accelerating economic growth because growth is also depends upon efficiency. According to investment productivity index, that has been calculated by dividing the growth rate of gross domestic production by the ratio of gross domestic investment to GDP. This index shows that productivity of investment is highest in Bangladesh, Nepal, India and Sri Lanka.

Although saving and investment ratio as a percentage of GDP have increased in almost all South Asian countries while India have also been able to achieve self-reliance in financing investment by their own savings. It shows that there is need of foreign resources in terms of modern technology to enhance productivity which could increase rate of economic growth.

Human Development Index

This development index is a criterion to understand the development of any country. This index determines the standard level of any country, in this index three variables are used like life expectancy, education index and income index.

From the above table, in SAARC members only Sri Lanka falls in high human development index its rank is 92, while India, Maldives and Bhutan are in medium human development index and rest of the countries falls in low human development.

Conclusion

The countries in the south Asian region exhibit similarity and congruence in many characteristics. Their state of development at the regional level in the global context is relatively similar and this is obvious from their socio-economic indicators of development compared with other regions of the world. Nonetheless at the intra-regional level they exhibit diversity in many of their essential features. This diversity is exhibited in geographical size of the countries with some countries relatively well-sized and others quite small. The diversity is further exhibited in the differing size of the population. The size of the economy as well is quite different in the region. Apart from the differences in magnitudes, these economies have differing development experiences as a result of different policies pursued to foster social and economic development.

References

1. Aitken, B., Hanson, G.H. and Harrison (1997). Spillovers, Foreign Investment and Export Behaviour, *Journal of International Economics*, Vol. 43, pp. 103-132.
2. Balassa B. (1986). Policy Responses to Exogenous Shocks in Developing Countries, *American Economic Review*, Vol. 76, No. 2, pp. 75-78.
3. Bandra, J.S. and W. Yu (2003). How Desirable is the South Asian Free Trade Area? A Quantitative Economic Assessment , in D. Greenway (ed.) The World Economy: Global Trade Policy, Oxford UK: Blackwell Publishers.
4. Baysan, T., A. Panagariya and N. Pitigala (2006). Preferential Trading in South Asia, Policy research Working Paper 3813, Washington DC: The World Bank.
5. Charan D Wadhwa (1999). Assessing the SAARC Preferential Trade Arrangement in Eric Gonslaves and Nancy Jetly (ed.). The Dynamics of South Asia, Sage Publications, New Delhi.
6. Debendra K. Das (1995). SAARC: Regional Cooperation and Development, Prospects and Problem. Deep and Deep Publications, New Delhi.
7. Kapila Uma (2006). Indian Economy since Independence, Academic Foundation, pp. 1067.
8. Kumar Nagesh (1995). Liberalisation and Changing Patterns of Foreign Direct Investment, *Economic and Political Weekly*, Vol. 23, No. 22.

9. Mayer, J. and A. Wood (2001). South Asia's Export Structure in a Comparative Perspective, *Oxford Development Studies*, Vol. 29, No. 1, pp. 5-29.
10. Sally, R. And R. Sen (2005).Whiter Trade Policies in Southeast Asia? The Wider Asian and Global Context, *ASEAN Economic Bulletin,* Vol. 22, No. 1, pp. 92-114.
11. UNCTAD, Trade and Development Report, New York, Various Issues.
12. UNCTAD, World Investment Reports, Various Reports.
13. United Nations, International Trade Statistics Yearbook, New Delhi, Various Issues.
14. World Bank, World Development Indicators Database.
15. World Bank, World Development Reports, Oxford University Press, Various Issues.
16. Read more at http://www.brainyquote.com/quotes/keywords/natural_resources.html#pLm5MVEvSuzRiSj5.99

7

Jhum Cultivation to Rubber Plantation: Strategically Progress in Tripura

Prof B.K.Panda *and* ***Sukanta Sarkar***

"The world is using up its natural resources at an alarming rate, and this has caused a permanent shift in their value. We all need to adjust our behavior to this new environment. It would help if we did it quickly."

—Jeremy Grantham

Introduction

Rubber plantation is an important commercial crop in North-east India. Hevea brasiliensis is the most important commercial source of natural rubber. It is a native of the Amazon River basin of South America. It was introduced to tropical Asia in 1876 through Kew Garden in the United Kingdom with the seeds brought from Brazil. Rubber cultivation in India had been traditionally confined to a narrow belt extending from Kanyakumari district of Tamil Nadu in the South to Dakshin Kannada and Kodagu districts of Karnataka in the north and lying in general west of the Western Ghats and parallel to them for approximately 400 km. Later on, it was extended to non-traditional regions including north-east India, hinterlands of coastal Karnataka, Goa, Konkan region of Maharashtra, hinterlands of coastal Andhra Pradesh, Odisha and certain areas of West Bengal.

Rubber plantation is mostly situated on sloping and undulating lands. Rubber plantation can be classified in two ways, immature plantation and mature plantation. Immature plants are those whose ages are less than seven years and if it is more than seven year then it is called as mature plant. The rubber tree is sturdy, quick growing and tall. Rubber trees have a well develop tap root and laterals. The bark on tapping yields latex. The young plants show characteristic growth pattern of alternating period of rapid elongation and consolidated development. The leaves are trifoliate with long stalks. Normal annual leaf fall of mature trees known as wintering occurs during the period of December to February. In North-east India, June/ July is the best season for planting and so all preparations should be completed before that period.

The state of Tripura is situated in the extreme southwest corner of the North Eastern region of India with a geographical area of 10,492 Sq.km. Rubber was introduced in Tripura in 1963 by the Forest Department. With the intervention of the Rubber Board since 1967, rubber got domesticated and coming out of the estates, it has reached to the small grower's yard. In 1976, Tripura Forest Development and Plantation Corporation Limited was set up to bring out more area under rubber cultivation. In 1982, Tripura Rehabilitation Plantation Corporation Ltd. was formed with the main objective of economic rehabilitation for the shifting cultivators and tribal marginal farmers through rubber plantation.

Jhumias of Tripura

Jhum cultivation is a local name for slash and burn agriculture practiced by the tribal groups in the northeastern states of India like Arunachal Pradesh, Meghalaya, Mizoram and Nagaland and also in the districts of Bangladesh like Khagrachari and Sylhet. This system involves clearing a piece of land by setting fire or clear felling and using the area for growing crops of agricultural importance such as upland rice, vegetables or fruits. After a few cycles, the land loses fertility and a new area is chosen. About 45 per cent of tropical agricultural area in the world is under shifting cultivation while one-third of agriculture in South-East Asia constitutes shifting cultivation and 60 per cent of Africa's food is also produced through shifting cultivation. Shifting cultivation has been identified as one of the main human impacts influencing biodiversity in Tripura, Northeast India. Over the last few years a new class of shifting cultivators has emerged that has adopted non-traditional forms of jhuming which have been responsible for the loss of biological diversity in the state. The Planning Commission approved implementation of Scheme of Watershed Development Project in Shifting Cultivation Areas in seven States of North Eastern Region, namely, Arunachal Pradesh, Assam, Manipur, Meghalaya, Mizoram, Nagaland and Tripura with 100 per cent special Central assistance to the States as per directions of National Development Council in 1994-95.

Jhum cultivation is most practiced on the slopes of hills in thickly forested landscapes. The cultivators cut the tree tops to allow sunlight to reach the land. They burn all the trees and grasses for clean and fresh soil. It is believed that this helps to fertilise the land, but can leave it vulnerable to erosion. Later seeds and crops are planted. Plants on the slopes survive the rainy season floods. Looking at all the effects, the government of Mizoram has launched a policy to end Jhum cultivation in the state. At one time jhuming was universally practiced in Tripura. According to Hunter, till about 1830 there was *"little or no plough cultivation"* and as late as 1908, the Imperical Gazetteer reported that *"the nomadic tillage known as Jhum cultivation is almost universal."*

A significant number of persons and families continue to depend on forests and jhum cultivation as their main source of livelihood. J.B. Ganguly's book on the *Problems of Jhumias in Tripura* (1968) showed that in 1961 there were about 25,000 families who were dependent on jhum for their livelihood. By 1978, this number had increased to 46,854 families, of which about 23,292 families were primarily dependent on jhum for their livelihood. By 1987, the estimate was revised to 55,049 families that were more or less dependent on jhum for their survival. Of these, 40,000 were in TTAADC areas. Further, 21,677 families were primarily dependent on jhum, and 33,372 families were partially dependent on jhum for their livelihood. In 1999, according to the Department of Tribal Welfare, 51,265 families were dependent on jhum, and the large majority of them were fully dependent on jhum. The big concentration of jhumia families was in Dhalai and South District. In 2007, the Forest Department completed a first-ever Census enumeration of hard core shifting cultivators and found 27,278 families (or 1,36,000 persons) dependent on jhum. The total count shows a clear decline in the number of jhumia families.

Actual forest area affected by shifting cultivation was highest in Manipur at 77.4 per cent and lowest in Arunachal Pradesh at 12.4 per cent. Nagaland, Mizoram, Tripura followed next while Assam ranked fifth with 74.1 per cent, 68.5 per cent and 62.3 per cent of total forest area respectively. The Tripura government has pleaded for development of traditional slash-and-burn method of agriculture (Jhum) instead of eradicating the practice by resorting to high yielding varities in Northeastern states.

Rubber Plantation in Tripura

India ranks third in terms of production of Natural Rubber in the world after Thailand and Malayasia. Kerala is the largest and Tripura is the second largest producer of natural rubber in the country. In Tripura, rubber plants (Hevea brasiliensis) were introduced for soil and moisture conservation by Forest Department in 1963. Rubber is a tropical crop and grows well in Tripura. The species has proved excellent for permanent settlement of Tribal jhumias.

Although the North Eastern region lies far outside the traditional rubber growing zone, the agro-climatic conditions obtained there are unique in as much as near tropical features are experienced in most parts owing to low elevations, exposure to monsoons and other moderating influences. Encouraged by the positive results obtained from trial plantations undertaken in early 1960s in the then undivided Assam and Tripura, commercial scale plantations were raised by Government Forest and Soil Conservation Departments. Public sector corporations set up later joined rubber planting endeavours on extensive scales. Thus, while in Assam and Tripura, public sector corporations are leading in the rubber plantation sector, their

Table-1: State-wise Share of Area and Production of Rubber in North-Eastern States

States	*2005-06*		*2006-07*	
	Percentage Share of Area	*Percentage Share of Production*	*Percentage Share of Area*	*Percentage Share of Production*
Tripura	5.72	2.03	6.15	2.19
Assam	2.48	0.42	2.58	0.58
Meghalaya	0.85	0.42	0.87	0.47
Nagaland	0.38	0.07	0.4	0.08
Manipur	0.31	0.01	0.3	0.02
Mizoram	0.08	0.01	0.09	0.01
Arunachal Pradesh	0.07	0.01	0.07	0.01
Total	**9.89**	**2.97**	**10.47**	**3.35**

Source: Rubber Board, Guwahati.

counterparts in Meghalaya, Manipur, Mizoram and Arunachal Pradesh are the State Forest and Soil Conservation Departments. Widespread plantings by individual growers are also contributing to fast growth of rubber cultivation in the region.

Table 1 shows that in rubber cultivation and production Tripura is far ahead than the other states in the region. Tripura is able to get first position which is followed by Assam, Meghalaya, Nagaland, Manipur, Mizoram and Arunachal Pradesh.

Table-2: Shows the Year-wise Extension in area of Rubber Plantation

Sl. No.	*Year*	*Area (in Ha.)*
1.	1976-77	574
2.	1981-82	3590
3.	1986-87	10085
4.	1991-92	17860
5.	1996-97	23936
6.	2001-02	30576
7.	2006-07	35760
8.	2007-08	39670
9.	2008-09	46588

Source: Rubber Board, Tripura.

Table 2 indicate that in Tripura rubber plantation is increasing very rapidly from the initial stages when it was introduced.

Rubber has already started influencing the socio-economic profile of rural Tripura. The state government, right from the beginning has been giving great importance to rubber and the Rubber Board has been implementing a variety of programmes for the development of rubber in the state. The state government agencies like Tripura Forest Development and Plantation Corporation Ltd. and Tripura Rehabilitation Plantation Corporation Ltd also have contributed significantly for the rubber plantation development in the state.

Table-3: Shows Agency-wise area brought under Rubber Plantation in 2007-08

Sl. No.	*Name of the agency*	*Area promoted by the agency (ha)*	*Proportional share*
1.	TFDPC Ltd	10744	30.04
2.	TRPC Ltd	6047	16.91
3.	TTADC	1100	3.08
4.	Rubber Board	17869	49.97
	Total	**35760**	**100**

Source: Rubber Board, Tripura.

Rubber Board is providing both technical as well as financial assistance for promotion of rubber cultivation in the state. State Govt. agencies like TFDPC Ltd., TRPC, TTAADC etc. are also doing their own efforts for expansion of rubber cultivation in the state. The Rubber Board, Tripura Forest Development and Plantation Corporation Ltd, Tripura Rehabilitation Plantation Corporation Ltd, Development Unit, North Eastern Council and the state government are working together towards the goal of rehabilitation under the upliftment of the tribals of the state.

The TFDPC is the major producer of rubber in the state and it functions under the administrative control of State Forest Department. TFDPC Ltd. markets rubber in the form of ribbed smoke sheet, cenex, crepe rubber and scrap form. It has taken up the treatment of rubber wood for production of substitute wood to reduce the demand on forests. Treated rubber wood is similar in properties to natural teak wood and is in fashion in western world for its shining white cream colour and better properties. TFDPC implemented, alongside commercial cultivation of rubber, a pilot project for rehabilitation of 100 tribal shifting cultivators through rubber plantation at its Warangbari Plantation Centre in West Tripura under a centrally sponsored scheme. The families worked on payment of wages for establishment of their own plantation with the hope and assurance of a good earning from sale of latex on maturity. Success of this project caught the imagination of the planners and generated some trust and confidence amongst the poor tribes dwelling in the hills and uplands. The Warangbari experience was the precursor to the adoption of a new model for rehabilitation of shifting cultivators and other landless and poor through rubber plantation on uplands considerations of poor productivity and very limited utility till then.

TRPC Ltd. was registered on the 3rd February, 1983 under the Companies Act, 1956 with the objective to economically rehabilitate shifting cultivators (jhumia), tribal landless and small farmers principally through rubber plantation. Tribal Welfare is the administrative department of the corporation. The first phase of TRPC project for creation of 1200 hectares of rubber plantation for 800 shifting cultivators was supported by bank loan under NABARD refinance scheme channeled through a consortium of three banks, State Bank of India, United Bank of India and Tripura Gramin Bank. TRPC received a loan of Rs 173.82 lakh under the World Bank Aided Rubber Project for raising 1000 ha of rubber plantation for tribal small farmers owning unarable uplands; and against that 924 ha of rubber plantation was created for 720 beneficiaries during 1993-94 to 2000-01. TRPC promotes formation of Rubber Producers Societies with beneficiary families as members, one for each plantation centre. TRPC also organises training on rubber cultivation and management including tapping and processing for beneficiaries.

The Rubber Board played a major role in the World Bank Assisted Rubber Project implemented from 1992 with the main objective of expanding and strengthening the rubber plantation sector to increase production of small holdings, improves processing and increase on-farm and off-farm employment. The Rubber Board has devised a novel method of helping small growers to organise themselves at grass-root level and to jointly work to acquire up-to-date know-how in the improvement of productive efficiency, group processing and competitive marketing. These voluntary organisations of growers are known as Rubber Producers Societies. Very recently another type of organisation called Rubber Growers Society, comprising only immature growers, is also taking shape. The RGS members adopt group approach to raise nurseries and supply planting materials, procure and supply farm inputs and acquire modern farming technology.

Table-4 : Shows District Level Rubber Plantation in 2008-09

Sl. No.	*District*	*Mature area (ha)*	*Immature area (ha)*	*Total area (ha))*	*Production (MT)*
1.	West	11089.19	10396.49	21485.68	12238
2.	South	6988.21	9812.11	16800.32	10400
3.	North	2929.45	2394.50	5323.95	2394
4.	Dhalai	2268.55	709.50	2978.05	556
	Total	**23275.40**	**23312.60**	**46588**	**25588**

Source: Rubber Board, Tripura.

Table 4 shows that out of four districts, West Tripura is far ahead in rubber cultivation than the other districts.

Block Plantation Scheme is a rubber-based rehabilitation project intended to wean away tribal Jhumias from shifting cultivation and also achieve the dual goals of eco-restoration and sustainable income for the beneficiaries. The scheme is extended to the Scheduled Caste community of the state. This is a collaborative project of the Rubber Board, and Tribal Welfare Department (SC Welfare Department, Govt. of Tripura). Under this scheme a compact land (block) owned by SC/ST families is identified. The plantation is raised by engaging the SC/ST families as wage earners. The plantation is raised by engaging the SC/ST families as wage earners. The work is done under the direct supervision of the Rubber Board officials. On attaining tappability, the beneficiaries are imparted training in tapping and processing and marketing procedures under the Rubber Producers Society.

Rubber Block Plantation for socio-economic settlement of the 'Jhumias' in Tripura has been considered a great success. An international organisation like World Bank has commended it as outstanding. The scheme has so far adopted about 3000 families along with their 20000 dependents and settled them permanently with 3251 hectares of rubber in 53 different parts of the state. Beneficiaries in 25 colonies (block plantation units) have already begun to sell rubber produced in their units and earn money, as tapping has commenced in their 1992 and subsequent plantations. The most successful story in the rubber cultivation is the establishment of marketing set up. The wide network of rubber dealers, spread over most of the areas, ensures for the growers, the countries best farm gate price of an agriculture commodity. The increased global demand also contributed to price stability. Two other factors, which were of prime effectiveness, are regular market intervention by the Rubber Board- promoted companies and the bargaining capacity built up by the Rubber Producers' Societies.

The people of Tripura have placed rubber plantation in their heart and made it the major source of income within 45 years of inception. It has become a popular crop in Tripura providing a lot of employment opportunities in the rural areas. The major quantity of rubber produced in the State is now transported to other States for consumption. The proposed Rubber Park which is being set up at Bodhjungnagar Industrial area may increase the consumption by providing more value added Rubber goods. It will also provide more employment opportunities to the people of Tripura. Although growth rate of rubber cultivation is higher in this state but it also faces various challenges and difficulties.

Jhumia Rehabilitation

In Tripura, Jhumia rehabilitation is promoted primarily by the Tripura Rehabilitation Plantation Corporation. TRPC was set in the year 1983 with the avowed aim of offering a settled livelihood to the tribal Jhumias of the state. It has chosen rubber plantation as a new means of achieving this goal in view of its adaptability, large employment potential, comparatively shorter gestation period and ecological sustainability. The beneficiaries are engaged as plantation worker during the plantation attains the tapping size. The latex collected by the beneficiaries is purchased by the corporation and is sold in the market after processing. Rubber Board started implementing Group and Block plantation schemes from 1992 and thus a revolution set off. Rubber Board kept on promoting rubber from village to village and a spectacular progress could be achieved. Till 2008-09, Tripura has about 46,588 hectares of rubber plantation. Total production of rubber in the State was 25,588 Mt in 2008-09.

The TFDPC Ltd. is the major producer of rubber in the State and it functions under the administrative control of State Forest Department. The Tripura Rehabilitation Plantation Corporation Ltd. under administrative control of State Tribal Welfare Department is the second largest producer of rubber in the State. TFDPC Ltd. has so far raised 11,578.77 hectares of plantation on forest land over last 26 years. It has so far raised 3177.89 hectares of rubber for settling the tribal jhumias in the private land owned as well as scheduled caste families.

Table 2: Growth of Rubber Plantation under Various Agencies

Name of the agency	*Area promoted by the agency (Ha)*	*Proportional share*
TFDPC Ltd	10,744	30.04
TRPC Ltd	6,047	16.91
TTAADC	1100	3.08
Rubber Board	17,869	49.97
Total	**35,760**	**100**

Source: Rubber Board, Tripura.

Rubber Plantation in Tripura needs no further introduction. The people of Tripura have placed it in their heart and made it the major source of income within 45 years of inception. It has become a popular crop in Tripura providing a lot of employment opportunities in the rural areas. Rubber Board is providing both technical as well as financial assistance for promotion of Rubber cultivation in the state. State Govt. agencies like TFDPC Ltd., TRPC, TTAADC etc. are also doing their own efforts for expansion of rubber cultivation in the State. The major quantity of rubber produced in the State is now transported to other States for consumption. The proposed Rubber Park which is being set up at Bodhjungnagar Industrial area may increase the consumption by producing more value added Rubber goods. It will also provide more employment opportunities to the people of Tripura.

Tripura Forest Improvement and Poverty Alleviation as an externally aided project have started in 2008-09 with funding from Japan Bank of International Co-operation. The project requires to be implemented effectively to increase the level of income and reduce the poverty among the people dependent on forest resources of the State.

Conclusion

Rubber plantation is a new identity of Tripura, not only in North-east India but whole over India. In this state rubber plantation is expanding very rapidly in rural areas. Currently Tripura is able to maintain second position in rubber production just after Kerala. There are many government agencies like Rubber Board, TRPC, TFDPC, and TTAADC which are working for extension of rubber plantation in hilly areas. Out of four districts in Tripura, West Tripura is more ahead in Rubber cultivation and production. Rubber plantation has two types of benefits, firstly, source of income and secondly, fight against deforestation. Rubber Plantation is a new instrument in the hand of government for economic settlement of jhumias in hilly areas.

References

1. M.G. Sathees Chandran Nair and K.G. Satheesh Kumar (Ed), Rubber Growers Companion, 2009, Published by Rubber Board, Kottayam, p. 3.
2. Economic Review of Tripura 2008-09, Government of Tripura, Agartala, p. 128.
3. Ahuja Ram, 2007, "Social Problems in India", Second edition, Rawat Publications, Jaipur, pp. 19-20.
4. Bhattacharya, D.C., 2008, "Sociology", Seventh edition, Vijoya Publishing House, Kolkata, pp. 385-389.
5. Bhowmick, P.K., 2005, "Tribal and Sustainable Development", First edition, Kalpaz Publications, New Delhi, pp. 13-17.
6. Chakravarti, T., 1998, "Economic Participation of Rural Tribal Women of Tripura", First Publication, Tripura State Tribal Cultural Research Institute and Museum, Agartala, pp. 21-24.
7. Dr. Sarkar, B.B., 2007, "Economic Settlement of Tribal Youths in Tripura", First edition, Tripura Research Institute, Agartala, pp. 82-83.

8. Rao, C.N.S., 2009, "Sociology-Principles of Sociology with an Introduction to Social Thought", Sixth revised edition, S. Chand & Company Ltd., New Delhi, pp. 200-202.
9. Sahu. B.S., 2004, "Human Resource Development for Industrial Workers-With Special Reference to Tea Industries", First edition, Mittal Publications, New Delhi, pp. 10-18.
10. Sengupta, S., 2009, "The Tea Labourers of North East India", First edition, Mittal Publication, New Delhi, pp. 115-116.
11. Achintya Kumar Sinha, Prospect of rubber plantation in NE region with special reference to the state of Tripura, Detailed available at http://thetripurafoundation.org/art-rubber-prospect-tripura-and-north-east
12. Aggarwal, Bina, 'Work Participation of Rural Women in Third World', Economic and Political Weekly, Vol. XX, No. 51 and 52, December 21-28, 1985.
13. A. K. Gupta, Shifting Cultivation and Conservation of Biological Diversity in Tripura, Northeast India, Volume 28, Number 4, 605-629http://www.springerlink.com/content/m16w4167061 45187/
14. Banerjee, Nirmala, 'Trend in Women's Employment 1971-81", Economic and Political Weekly, Vol. XXX, No.17, 1995.
15. Bhattacharjee, Gayatri (1988), Refugee Rehabilitation and its Impact an Tripura's Economy, Delhi: Omsons Publications
16. Bhattacharjee, P.R. 'Sociological Aspects of Resource Use Pattern in Tripura: An Analysis in Historical Perspective', Tui (A Quarterly Research Magazine on Tribal Life and Culture), September- November, Vol. III, 1993.
17. Bhattacharjee, P.R. and Ganguli, J.B., 'Relative Economic Status of Social Groups: A Study in Inequality', Journal of North-East Council for Social Science Research, Vol. 17, No. 2, October 1993.
18. Boserup, Ester (1970), Women's Role in Economic Development, London: George Allen and Unwin Ltd.
19. Boyee, J.K.1994, 'Inequality as a cause of environmental degradation', Ecological Economics,11: 169-178.
20. Brief of Special Central Assistance to State Plan Scheme on Watershed Development Project in Shifting Cultivation Area (WDPSCA) (As on March 2009), Detailed available at http:// www.agricoop.nic.in/Nrm/WDPSCA.pdf

21. Chakraborty, C., S. Dutt and P. Katiha, 2005, "Fishery Co-operatives in West Bengal: A Socio-Economic Appraisal'. Environmental and Ecology, 23 (spl-1): 50-57.
22. Chakravarti, Mahadev (1986), The Tribal Areas Autonomous District Council and The Tribal Problems, Agartala: Govt. of Tripura.
23. Chakravarti, Mahadev, Das Gupta, Malabika and Sarkar, Bithi (1987), A Study on the Lushais of Jampui Hills in Tripura, Agartala: Govt. of Tripura.
24. Das Gupta, Malabika, Ed. (1993), Status of Tribal Women in Tripura, Delhi: Vikas Publishing House.
25. D.N. 'Significance of Women's Position in Tribal Society', Economic and Political Weekly, Vol. XXIII, No. 26, June 25, 1988.
26. Economic Review of Tripura 2008-09, Detailed available at http://destripura.nic.in/review20078.pdf
27. Ganguli, J.B., (1968), Economic Problems of the Jhumias of Tripura, Calcutta: Bookland Private Ltd.
28. Ganguli, J.B., 'Pattern of Occupational Structure of Tribal Population of Tripura', Parisankhyan Barta, Vol.1, No.2, 1985. Agartala: Directorate of Statistics and Evaluation, Govt. of Tripura.
29. Hevea brasiliensis (2012), Detailed available at http://en.wikipedia.org/wiki/Hevea_brasiliensis
30. Horam, M. (1977), Social and Cultural life of Nagas, Delhi: B.R. Publishing Corporation.
31. Jhum Cultivation (2012), Detailed available at http://en.wikipedia.org/wiki/Jhum_cultivation
32. Jhum / Shifting Cultivation and Jhumias, Detailed available at http://www.agritripura.in/Agriculture/Pages/jhum.htm
33. Kak, Shakti, 'Rural Women and Labour Force Participation', Social Scientist, Vol.22, Nos. 3-4, 1994.
34. Know Tripura, Detailed available at http://tripura.nic.in/kt3.htm
35. Malabika Dasgupta (1986), Jhumias of Tripura, *Economic and Political Weekly*, Vol XXI, Nos aa and 45, Detailed available athttp://www.jstor.org/discover/10.2307/4376302? uid=3738256 &uid= 2129&uid=2&uid= 70&uid=4&sid=47698756199967
36. Natural Rubber (2012), Detailed available at http://en.wikipedia.org/wiki/Natural_rubber

37. P.S. Chudhuri, Sabyasachi Nath and R. Paliwal, Earthworm population of rubber plantations (Hevea brasiliensis) in Tripura, India, Tropical Ecology 49(2): 225-234, 2008, P.1, Detailed available at http://www.tropecol.com/pdf/open/PDF_49_2/13%20Chaudhuri.pdf
38. Rubber and tea, Detailed available at http://tripura.nic.in/indm4.htm
39. Rubber- plantation in Tripura, Detailed available at http://tfdpc.com/about7.htm
40. Saikia, P.D. and Gogoi, R, 'Women Labour in North-East India', *Yojana*, Vol.25, No.12, 1981.
41. Sarkar, S (2010),Revolution of Jhuias life through Rubber Plantation: A Case of Dhalai District, Tripura, FEPPCAR, Detailed available at http://feppcar.org/69/revolution-of-jhumia%e2%80%99s-life-through-rubber-plantation-a-case-study-of-dhalaidistrict-tripura/#more-69
42. Sen, Biswajit, 'Displacement of Tribals Yojana', Vol. 33, No. 22, 1989.
43. Tripura Forest Development and Plantation Corporation Limited, Detailed available at http://tfdpc.com/
44. The Hindu (Dec 17, 2006), 1 lakh hectares for rubber plantation in Tripura, Detailed available at http://www.hindu.com/2006/12/17/stories/2006121702901200.htm
45. Tripura concerned over jhum cultivation in North-East (2010), Detailed available http://www.sinlung.com/2010/06/tripura-concerned-over-jhum-cultivation.html
46. Tripura urges modernisation of Jhum cultivation (2011), Detailed available at http://www.newkerala.com/news/world/fullnews-177499.html
47. Unni, Jeem, 'Changes in Women's Employment in Rural Areas 1961-82', *Economic and Political Weekly*, Vol. XXIV, No. 17, 1989.
48. Read more at http://www.brainyquote.com/quotes/keywords/natural_resources_2.html#wcdE1MWD1vppEztZ.99

8

Recent Trends in Bihar Sex Ratio: Evidences from Latest Data

Shanti Bhushan Kumari, Rajesh Raushan *and* ***Ras Bihari Prasad Singh***

"From protecting our natural resources to providing maritime security and national defense, the Coast Guard's duties are broad in scope, and the performance of those duties has never been more important."

—**Russ Carnahan**

Introduction

It is widely argued that sex ratio is a powerful indicator of the social development and associated social behaviour of any society throughout the world conveys about the existing and/or ongoing gender relations. An almost equal number of females and males in their population composition in every society have assumed for their balance but is not possible in reality. Internationally, socially as well as economically advanced societies have shown a favourable sex ratio to female, but for many south and Southeast Asian countries this relationship has not been so straightforward (Patel, 2007). The problem of less number of females than males in those countries are making the situation more panic where high degree of discrimination and deprivation endured by females has been responses for their much less number than their male counterparts. It has found that millions of women are missing, particularly in Asia and Africa and noted alarming fact of increasing sex ratio imbalance at an early age in China, India and South Korea than at overall sex ratio (Sen, 1990). In a country like India, where strongly embedded patriarchal mindset does not accept females with full blessings with some exceptions, responses in the poorest of the poor gender relations. Dyson and Moore in the early 80s had clearly added that patriarchy, kinship system, forms of marriage and cultural practices and rituals greatly divide India into the north-south dichotomy of gender relations.

Awareness of gender has become inevitable in recent studies of demographic processes and has studied very widely by many scholars like Visaria (1971), Mitra (1978), Dyson and Moore (1983), Dasgupta (1987), Kishor (1993), Das Gupta and Bhat (1997), Agnihotri (2000), Patel (2007) etc. in various contexts. Their work is a pioneer in strengthening different forms of gender relations in Indian context endured in form of negligence, discrimination and deprivation resulted in the scale of sex ratio, health, nutrition, healthcare, and the poor status of females. It would not be surprising fact that the high masculine sex ratio in India has attracted attention right since the first decennial census of 1881 but first had been pointed out by Visaria (1971) study in the early 70s. An earlier report or most probably first in its nature on the status of women, *'Towards Equality'* put status of women forcefully on the national agenda by arguing that the position of Indian women had declined since 1911 and an increase in neglect of female lives resulted in continuous decline in sex ratio in India over periods (GoI, 1974).

The greater deprivation and poor welfare attitude towards females as opposed of males strongly reflect the existing and continuing discrimination with females in the country as well as in the states. A plethora of studies have burgeoning the evidences of negligence and discrimination with females and its linkages with excessive female death before birth (female foeticide), at birth, during infancy and in childhood (Dasgupta, 1987; Kishor, 1995). Every decennial Indian census figures strongly validate it with other national level macro and many more micro level survey findings, which strengthen less number of females and more prominently less number of female children compared to male children. Visaria (1971), Das Gupta (1987) and Miller (1981) had studied gender discrimination through sex differences in mortality and child survival. While Visaria (1971) postulated sex differentials in mortality as a main cause of high masculine sex ratio, Miller (1981) postulated discrimination in unequal access of basic life sustaining inputs to females resulted into high female mortality than male particularly in juvenile age groups. According to Miller, the neglect of daughters amounted to extended infanticide, which resulted into a low juvenile sex ratio. It can't be surprising that in last 50 years, the child sex ratio has been decreased from 976 per 1000 in 1961 to 919 at the 2011 census (GoI, 2011) is a major evidence in this regard. Here, it is important to add that the emerging cause other than the above mentioned reasons is female foeticide.

This cultural dynamics of 'son preference' and 'daughter dispreference' have led to female foeticide behind the shade of medical termination of pregnancy (MTP) and pre-natal diagnostic techniques (PNDT) which contributed more on sex selective abortions are the underneath reasons. Overwhelmingly, the earlier census results have sparked serious concern about the widespread use of ultrasound and amniocentesis tests to detect the sex of foetus, followed by sex selective abortions (Patel, 2007), this might be continue in practice and is evident with the latest census 2011 results where the child sex ratio has again declined by eight points as against about 927 per 1000 of the 2001 census. Further, discrimination and deprivation on the social and economic scale at later age responsible for their poor status and under enumeration as well as led to the number of missing women (Sen, 1990) have resulted into masculine sex ratio over the periods at national as well as states and regional level in India.

The problem of masculine sex ratio is widely spread over the country and most of the states are experiencing the problem with it, with the exception of few south Indian states and the north-eastern states as well. But it is an apt problem of states in the north and west India where number of females are continuous on the decline. Among the north Indian states, one is Bihar where the declining proportion of females compared to their male counterpart delineates the problem of decreasing sex ratio in the state. The declining proportion of females delineates about the practices of gender discrimination and inequalities in work, education, food allocation, healthcare and fertility choices which responses in their poor status (Pradhan and Arokiasamy, 2010) in the state like Bihar. The problem of declining child sex ratio is more serious than the overall sex ratio within the state. The child sex ratio has declined seven points as against of overall sex ratio by a margin of one point during the last decade. But the problem is much more critical at the district level where decline has reached to around 50 points needs a fresh exploration of the issue at district level in the state of Bihar. In the context, the paper investigates the temporal and pattern of changing sex ratio over the period across the settings and their distribution at district level in Bihar with special consideration of sex ratio at early ages and their possible reasons.

Data Source, Methodology and Limitations

A prominent source of the data for the study is census and Annual Health Survey (hereafter, AHS)[1] data have been used. Census data are best and reliable source on the headcount of females and males and latest 15th round has been conducted in 2011 for the whole country. Although, to analyse temporal variation in sex ratio, census data since 1961 has been used, but to study districts level variation last three round census data i.e., 1991-2011 has been used here. To support the notion of declining female children, AHS data for 2010-11 has been used to observe the persisting discriminatory behaviour since the time of birth. Using AHS data, sex ratio at birth and sex ratio in the age group 0-4 years has been included here.

At global level many countries define sex ratio in terms of males for every 100 females, but in India, the number of females for every 1000 males is considered as sex ratio (hereafter, OSR). Henceforth, throughout the study sex ratio would be understood as so. In case of child sex ratio (CSR), it is considered as the number of girls for every 1000 boys in 0-6 year age groups. For regionalisation within the newly formed state after bifurcation of old Bihar in 2000, river Ganga is used as a demarcation line separate new Bihar in north and south Bihar as it flows from west to east throughout the Bihar. So, northern part of the river Ganga can be understood as 'north Bihar', and south part of the river Ganga as 'south Bihar'.

There are some limitations of the study also. The first and most important limitation is that the study covers only the new Bihar state after bifurcation of old Bihar into Jharkhand and Bihar on 15th November 2000. But for 1961, 1971 and 1981 census data for old Bihar is used. Second, during 1991-2011 periods many districts have also been created in old[2] and new[3] Bihar. So data for those newly formed districts have carved out from the district from which they created for the respective census years. Third, prior to the 1991 census, data of old Bihar has used for Bihar state. Fourth, the primary census abstract (PCA) data has been used for the latest 2011 census.

Bihar's Sex Ratio Profile: 1961-2011

The sex ratio is one of the best illustrations of societal mindset in a country like India, where social realities are hardly embedded in everyone's day to day life practice responses into negligence and discrimination to females and domination over their rights and powers. It is true that women are having a glorious history as they are termed as goddess in India for a long time, but at the other end of the reality, even at early periods the discrimination to women was prevailing in some regions and some communities. But, we don't have much valid and truthful information on the inferior status of that time. However, at present, their poor social, economic and deprived status is much enough to witness their inferior and endured discrimination imposed by their counterparts on them. Still, females are getting less privilege on developmental aspects and they are bound to spend their most of life within the household boundary.

Even at household level they are heavily loaded with household chores like cooking, cleaning, collecting of fuels and water, and carrying children and taking care of the elderly

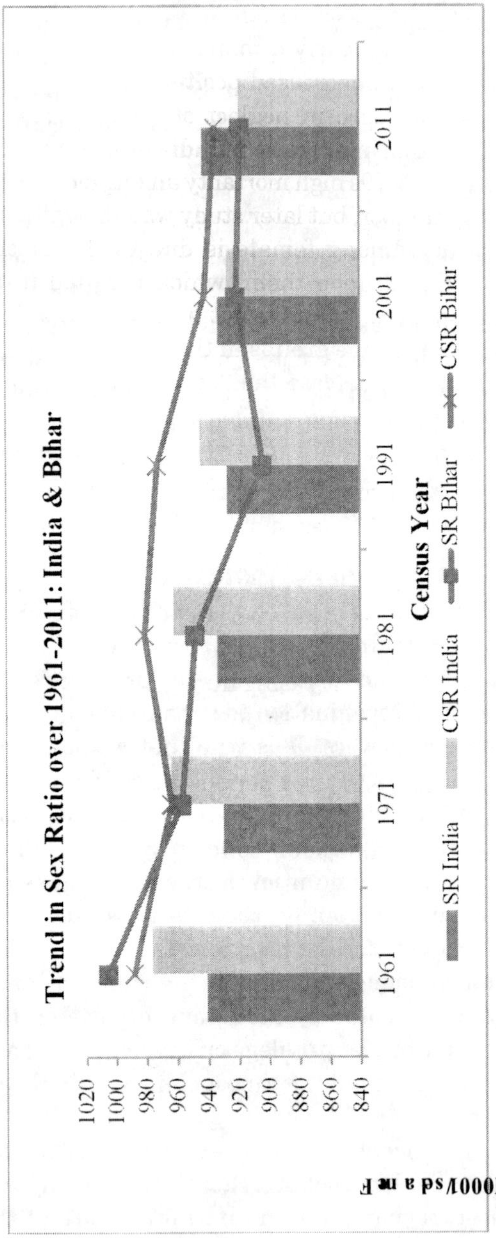

Figure 1: Sex ratio and Child sex ratio for India and Bihar: 1961- 2011.

(Arokiasamy, 2003). So, it would not be surprising to keep with them on their less number than males are bound to reflect into a poor sex ratio. An early committee on the status of women had reported about decreased position of Indian women since 1911 and an increase in neglect of female lives resulted in continuous decline in sex ratio in India over periods (GoI, 1974). Moreover, in early 70s high mortality among females had reasons for their less number, but later study was strengthened that the high mortality among female is due to the discriminatory practices endured upon them, which resulted in continuous decline in numbers and have got a voice with a declining sex ratio across the all age groups in the state.

As the paper analyses the recent trends in declining sex ratio with fresh exploration from 2011 census, it has found that at country level OSR has increased by 10 points at the 2011 census, but the surprising findings is that CSR has again decreased by eight more points and reached to 919 female children for every 1000 male children. Although, in the post - independence era, OSR had declined from 941 in 1951-61 period to 927 during 1981-91 census period (lowest since independence) but afterwards during two consecutive censuses have shown good sign of continuously increasing number of females and recorded 933 for 1991-2001 to 943 during 2001-11. It is a notable point that for the first time after independence, OSR for the country has reached near to 1941-51 periods, figures, but the sex ratio at an early age, i.e., CSR is drastic and embarrassing and has reached to its lowest, is a serious concern and will have adverse demographic consequences in the coming future.

Moving on Bihar, OSR and CSR for the same period, OSR has declined to 918 in 2001-11 of 1005 of 1951-61 periods. On the other end, CSR has reached to its lowest of 935/1000 at 2011census as against of 988/1000 at 1961census. Studies have depicted that the high mortality of female child, under the enumeration of females and migration, etc. contributes to less number of females. If this is true, then why the sex ratio at birth (hereafter, SRB) is much lower in the state is 919 female newborn for every 1000 male newborn. In reality, an increase in continuous deficit of girls at very early ages is an indicative of a strong possibility that traditional methods of neglect of female children are increasingly being replaced by not allowing female children to be born. In the 21st century, we are talking about gender equality and the elimination of gender biases, but the existing situation reflects the opposite side of the picture.

District Level Overall Sex Ratio in Bihar: 1991-2011

It has found that change in CSR is starker than the OSR and for better understanding of the prevailing discrimination and negligence, districts level analysis has been provided for 1981-91 to 2001-11 periods. Looking over the periods, data reveal that change in OSR is positive for 1991-2001 decade, but during 2001-11 periods, it has observed almost near to 2001 figures, although it is one point less than the 2001 census. The evidences support that during the previous to last decade the discrimination might be was less resulted in the addition of more females shown of 15 point increase in OSR and during the last decade is somehow manageable, but can't be depicted as a sign of reducing discrimination and negligence with the females in the state.

Districts differentials in overall sex ratio over 1991-2011 periods in Bihar reveals that during 1991-2001 periods, there was only one district, i.e. Bhojpur, where sex ratio had declined by three points, but during 2001-11, it was the surprising fact that there are 14 districts who have recorded fall in OSR (Table 1). When considering 1991 as base for analysing changing sex ratio in the state, there are eight districts where a fall in sex ratio has been observed. These are the districts where the maximum decline was happening during last ten year period. Considering latest census data reveals that there is huge variation in the declining sex ratio from one point in Banka district to a maximum of 43 points in Siwan district. Analysing 1991-2001, highest positive change of 41 points has been observed in Lakhisarai district situated in south of river Ganga whereas lowest positive change of two points has been found in Samastipur district lying in north of river Ganga. It is Vaishali district only where OSR has remained constant during the period of 1991-2001. One important observation during 1991-2001 has found that as the distance increases from the state capital, variation in OSR decreases.

Table 1: Sex Ratio in Districts of Bihar over Decades: 1991-2011

Districts	*All Age Sex Ratio*			*0-6 Age Sex Ratio*		
	1991	*2001*	*2011*	*1991*	*2001*	*2011*
W. Champaran	878	901	909	963	953	953
E. Champaran	882	897	902	942	937	933
Sheohar *	876	885	893	947	916	929
Sitamarhi	884	892	899	920	924	930
Madhubani	932	942	926	955	939	936
Supaul *	902	920	929	938	925	944
Araria	907	913	921	983	963	957
Kishanganj	933	936	950	990	947	971
Purnia	904	915	921	966	967	954
Katihar	909	919	919	980	966	961
Madhepura	885	915	911	937	927	930
Saharsa	884	910	906	917	912	933
Darbhanga	911	914	911	954	915	931

(Contd.)

(Contd. Table 1)

Districts	All Age Sex Ratio			0-6 Age Sex Ratio		
	1991	*2001*	*2011*	*1991*	*2001*	*2011*
Muzaffarpur	904	920	900	944	928	915
Gopalganj	965	1001	1021	962	964	954
Siwan	1017	1031	988	962	934	940
Saran	963	966	954	961	949	926
Vaishali	920	920	895	944	937	904
Samastipur	926	928	911	942	938	923
Begusarai	897	912	895	958	946	919
Khagaria	869	885	886	944	932	926
Bhagalpur	863	876	880	941	966	938
Banka *	894	908	907	970	965	943
Munger	851	872	876	927	914	922
Lakhisarai *	880	921	902	957	951	920
Sheikhpura *	894	918	930	951	955	940
Nalanda	897	914	922	961	942	931

(Contd.)

(Contd. Table 1)

Districts	*All Age Sex Ratio*			*0-6 Age Sex Ratio*		
	1991	*2001*	*2011*	*1991*	*2001*	*2011*
Patna	867	873	897	939	923	909
Bhojpur	904	902	907	927	940	918
Buxar *	884	899	922	906	925	934
Kaimur (Bhabua) *	883	902	920	917	940	942
Rohtas	893	909	918	962	951	931
Jehanabad	917	926	926	970	915	944
Aurangabad	915	934	937	969	943	960
Gaya	921	938	939	982	968	945
Nawada	936	946	922	972	978	956
Jamui *	904	918	922	973	963	922
Alwar*	922	935	928	964	920	940
BIHAR	**904**	**919**	**918**	**973**	**942**	**935**

* Newly formed districts during 1991-2011.

Further, during 2001-11 period pictures are very different in the state as of the previous one as only 14 districts have shown negative changes in OSR. The surprising fact is that Siwan is the district who had recorded maximum of 1031 females per 1000 males, but during 01-11 periods, maximum decline of 43 points has been found there. It is also notable that during the last census Vaishali had remained on constant of 920 females for every 1000 males, but at the 2011 census, it has recorded a fall of 26 points and reached to 895 females for every 1000 males. On the other hand, maximum increase of 24 points has been observed in Patna followed by Buxar (22 points). The notable point is that both the districts are situated in south Bihar (Table 1).

Distributional pattern of OSR in the state does not have any unique pattern, however, districts in north Bihar shows less fluctuation than that of the district situated in south Bihar during 1991-2001. In a south Bihar district of maximum positive change (41 points) to maximum negative change of three points has been found. Overall, west Bihar is doing better than east Bihar. During the period, boarder districts have a better sex ratio than inner districts with some exceptions (Table 1). But, the latest census reveals a completely different picture than that of the previous one as a state have recorded a decline of only one point in OSR, ranging from a maximum fall in the number of women in north-western Bihar to a maximum increase in the number of women south to south western Bihar and North Eastern Bihar. Looking at regional pattern in north Bihar, from south to north and from central-north Bihar to west and east characteristics of declining sex ratio reduces. Siwan (43 points), Vaishali (26 points) and Muzaffarpur (20points) are the districts where the decline in the sex ratio is more than or near to 20 points. In case of south Bihar, when we move to southwards, the decline in OSR increases, but it is also interesting to add here that it is Jehanabad district situated in south Bihar have found remained constant in OSR during the last decade (Table 1).

District Level Child Sex Ratio in Bihar: 1991-2011

For better understanding and to observe the prevailing scenario towards females, it is better to analyse sex ratio at early ages. In this regards the sex ratio under 0-6 years as a

Table 2: Juvenile Sex Ratio in Bihar: 2010

Status		*No. of Districts*	*Districts*
			Sex Ratio at Birth
Worst	<900*	11	Sitamarhi, Darbhanga, Kaimur (Bhabua), Purnia, Samastipur, Muzaffarpur, Vaishali, Gopalganj, E. Champaran, Sheikhpura, Madhubani
Poor	901-930	14	Nawada, Araria, Khagaria, Patna, Rohtas, Bhojpur, Katihar, BIHAR, Madhepura, Saharsa, Saran, Munger, Lakhisarai, Sheohar, Nalanda
Moderate	931-960	5	Jehanabad, Siwan, Jamui, Begusarai, Bhagalpur
Average	>960	7	Gaya, Kishanganj, Supaul, Banka, Aurangabad, W. Champaran, Buxar
			Sex Ratio in 0-4 Years
Worst	<900	5	Samastipur, Sitamarhi, Munger, Kaimur (Bhabua), Purnia
Poor	901-930	17	Muzaffarpur, Darbhanga, Vaishali, Lakhisarai, Madhubani, Saharsa, Sheikhpura, Sheohar, Patna, Gopalganj, Saran, Bhagalpur, E. Champaran, Rohtas, Bhojpur, Jehanabad, Khagaria
Moderate	931-960	7	BIHAR, Araria, Madhepura, Katihar, Siwan, Begusarai, Nawada, Jamui
Average	>960	8	Nalanda, Supaul, Buxar, Aurangabad, Gaya, Kishanganj, Banka, W. Champaran

* Female/ 1000 Male Children

Author's calculation based on annual Health Survey Data: 2010-11.

CSR in Table 1 and the sex ratio under five years of age as sex ratio in 0-4 years and sex ratio at birth (SRB) has been provided in Table 2. Analysing evidences from census data, few districts were having better CSR were situated in north Bihar at the 1991 census, like Kishanganj (990), Araria (983), Katihar (980) and some like Gaya (982) in south Bihar. However, at 2001 better performing districts were found in south Bihar like Nawda (978), Gaya (968), Bhagalpur (966) and some in north Bihar like as Purnia (967), Katihar (966) districts. At the 2011 census, districts like Kishanganj, Katihar, and Araria are performing almost better than others.

On the other hand, as the major concern is declining in number of female child comparable to a male child, Table 1 clearly depicts that minimum CSR had found in south Bihar as in Buxar (906) in 1991 which turned to north Bihar in Saharsa (912) in 2001 and it shifted to Vaishali (904) at the 2011 census. It is interesting to point out here that at 1991, there was a gap of 84 points in the district having maximum and minimum CSR which reduced to 66 points in 2001 which has noticed to 67 points at the 2011 census. It is noteworthy to point out here that the districts having lowest CSR are near to 900 female children for every 1000 male children as against of highest of above or near to 970 female children for every 1000 male children. Decline in child sex ratio in 0-6 years provides very different picture than that of overall sex ratio in the state. Analysis of data reveals that there was a decline of 31 points in CSR during 1991-2001 periods. During 2001-11, it declined by seven points only. At district level, during 1991-2001 period, Jehanabad (-55), Kishanganj (-44), Alwar (-44), Darbhanga (-40) etc were having high decline have shown increases of 29, 25, 20 and 16 points respectively. Whereas Gaya (-14), Jamui (-10), Begusarai (-13) districts which had declined CSR in 2001 is continually declining and recorder decline from 23, 42 and 27 points respectively. Findings from other sources like Annual Health Survey also reveal the persisting situation across the districts within the state and it can be very clearly point out in Table 2. Considering sex ratio at birth, Table 2 reveals that there are 11 districts performing worst at illustration of the sex ratio of birth were less than 900 females are getting birth as against of every 1000 male births, whereas for 0-4 years there are five districts having number of female child less than 900 for every 1000 male children, however in 0-6 years no any district has found (Table 1 and 2).

Discussion and Conclusion

The issue of low and declining proportion of females is India has remained a long debated issue and in post-independence first time pointed out in the early 70s by Visaria (1971), Natrajan (1972) its work and further 'status of women' report in 1974 depicted about the declining proportion of females than males. Bardhan (1974) mentioned that there are historical, cultural, economical and sociological cause's responses into negligence towards female responses into higher mortality among female child (Visaria, 1971). It arises due to neglect of female child (Sen, 1985) is a remarkable sign of discrimination with females (Miller, 1981) which is directly or indirectly linked with the status of women in Indian society (Dyson and Moore, 1983). It is true that using North-South divide on the status of women criteria, north India has high discrimination with women and women having the poor status of social as well as economic scale than south India. The discrimination and disadvantages endured due to strong patriarchal and patrilineal norms which lead to a strong preference for male child, regulated by social-cultural ethos of the time.

The major components of imbalances in sex ratio have been postulated as sex ratio at birth, sex differentials in mortality, sex differentials in migration and under the enumeration of females. Analysis over 50 years shows that at country level CSR is continuously declining, although OSR in the post-90s shows an increase. The major problem of declining sex ratio is in northern India mostly in Punjab, Haryana, Madhya Pradesh, Rajasthan, Uttar Pradesh and Bihar with some exceptions. Abundant of studies have attributed the decline in child sex ratio to a possible rise in sex ratio at birth owing to the increasing trend in sex selective abortion (Das Gupta and Bhatt, 1997; Sudha and Rajan, 1999). Bhatt (2002) concluded that accelerated fall in CSR after 1981 is largely due to the diffusion of prenatal sex selection techniques in regions with well entrenched gender bias. Further, Arnold *et al* (2002) study using a second wave of national family health survey data found evidences of sex selective abortion considering the use of ultrasound or amniocentesis in India with more prevalent in the north Indian states. A recent study on the adverse consequences of sex selection in India by Kaur (2012), strongly argued that the advent of technologies for sex determination have contributed more to the birth of little girls.

Considering Bihar in the context as the study focus on this only shows the persisting negligence and discrimination in various forms resulted in continuous decline in sex ratio across the ages. Considering OSR analysis suggest that till 1991 there was fast declining in OSR, although thereafter some improvement has noticed, but it is not satisfactory as the latest census 2011 has recorded 918 females for every 1000 males in the state. Considering its position among major states, its position in terms of sex ratio can't be said good as it falls on the states of having worst sex ratio like Haryana, Jammu and Kashmir, Punjab and Uttar Pradesh. Moving on a district level, only three districts have found having OSR more than 950 namely, Gopalganj, Siwan and Saran where as there are 19 districts are having OSR below the state average and even there are 34 districts are below the national average. Drastic feature is that eight districts are having OSR of less than 900 females for 1000 males. Moving on sex ratio at early ages, mainly CSR and SRB, these are the indices depicting more clearly about the ongoing discriminatory practices and poor status of the women in the state. Although to get data to SRB in a country like India is very problematic and district level estimates are much more problematic, but annual health survey data have made it possible to provide district level estimates on SRB, however it is limited to EAG states and Assam only.

The trend in CSR shows a continuous decline in the number of female children in the state and at latest census have recorded 935 female children for every 1000 male children. In the past 50 years CSR in the state has declined by 53 points. Moving on the district level maximum decline has been observed in Jamui, Vaishali, Lakhisarai by more than 30 points, however, there are

18 districts which have recorded a decline in CSR more than state average; moreover sex ratio in 0-4 years provides almost same findings with some exceptions. The clearest picture provides SRB which has reported 919 females new born as against of 1000 males new born. The situation is more pathetic as 11 districts have found having SRB less than 900 and 14 districts are in between 901 to 930 and there are only seven districts having SRB more than 960 as of 2010-11. The prevailing scenario at sex ratio at birth is providing the discriminatory practises like sex determination and sex selective abortion is continuous on their pace within the state.

Although, negligence and discriminatory practices are not new in countries like India and in Bihar also but shifting from traditional mechanisms of discriminatory practices like female infanticide and access to resources to involvement of technological advancement make these practices in other ways of sex selective abortions. Introduction of ultrasound and amniocentesis to monitor high-risk pregnancy led to more on to sex biasness than monitoring for the purpose for what they had introduced. With an increasing number of women under the fold of antenatal care screening, foetal testing has attracted the couples' towards decision on their unborn babies (Mazumdar, 1994; Patel, 2007). Work on female infanticide in Tamil Nadu and in Bihar (Srinivasan, 1994) shows that this practice has reappeared among certain communities and emerged among some others who did not practice it before. Why is this happening? One can plausibly apprehend that another positive feedback loop is likely to operate in linking prenatal sex selection and female infanticide.

A 1995 investigation[4] by *Adithi* (an NGO working in rural Bihar state) in eight selected and culturally similar districts in Bihar uncovered the fact of widespread selective neglect that responsible for female foeticide, infanticide, and excess female child mortality in those districts. Abortion of female foetuses was conducted by unscrupulous medical practitioners, especially after techniques like sonography became widespread. The report also describes how the traditional skill of '*dais*'[5] in identifying the sex of a foetus in the seventh months of the pregnancy is used to avert the birth of a female foetus. Infanticide was also found carrying out by '*dais*' that were coerced by the senior male kin of the delivered woman. Estimating a count of 68,000 '*dais*' in seven contiguous and culturally similar districts of Bihar, and that each '*dai*' killed about two infants a month. *Adithi* estimates that the number of female infanticides each year in these districts could total as many as 16,32,000. There were also evidences of other medical practitioners such as compounders and doctors who carried out infanticide after approaching by the family members of a newly born girl child.

The report had also pointed out that earlier, only upper castes such as *Rajputs* and *Brahmins* were practiced female infanticide, but it had now spread to all other groups, including Scheduled Tribes, Christians and Muslims. This in turn spreads the practice of infanticide further among those who do not have access to facilities. Notwithstanding the spread in the facility of the 'facilities' for prenatal selection, it will continue to remain beyond the reach of a large number of people in foreseeable future. The two processes will feed each other (Agnihotri, 2000). Since the girl child is unwanted, she is also neglected and deprived of resources make them dependent and thus begins the cycle of socialisation that causes women to under-value themselves and lead them to a male dominated society responses in their poor status which has reflected from the latest census figure also. As during 1991-2001 there was an increase of OSR by 15 points, but during 2001-11 it has remained completely stagnant due to increase in number of women in some districts, but stark fact is that there was only one district during 1991-2001 where OSR had fallen down, but during 2001-11, it has spread over 14 districts with maximum of 43 points in Siwan district followed by 26 points in Vaishali district. The latest census 2011 figure provides the input and evident of the persisting discrimination demands for urgent attention to adverse demographic consequences in the coming future and among them on important is marriage squeeze due to more missing females. An estimate by Hudson and Boer (2004); Bihar, Madhya Pradesh, Rajasthan, and Uttar Pradesh together contribute to one-half of the missing females of India. Based on 1991 and 2001 census data Samayiar and Joe (2010) concluded that there are more unmarried males than females in the marriage market, and that the smaller cohorts of girls being born will add to the future marriage squeeze, forcing men to marry later or look elsewhere for brides. Guilmoto (2012) predicted that the cumulative number of additional men remaining single during 2020-80 will be closer to 40 million. These evidences are the enough to warn about "with whom your son will marry?"

References

1. Annual Health Survey data is a joint initiative of Registrar General of India Office and Ministry of Health and Family Welfare, India to conduct survey for district level estimates. AHS is first of its nature which provides estimates of different demographic and health outcomes at districts level started in 2009-10 for three consecutive years. But it is limited to EAG states and Assam only.
2. During 1991-2000, eight districts newly formed. These are Banka from Bhagalpur in 1991, Buxar from Bhojpur in 1991, Kaimur from Rohtas in 1991, Supaul from Saharsa in 1991, Seohar from Sitamarhi in 1994, and Jamui in 1991 and Lakhisarai and Sheikhpura in 1994 from Munger.
3. After 2000, Alwar has formed from Jehanabad in 2001.
4. A report on Female Infanticide in Bihar by Viji Srinivasan, Parinita, Vijay, Shankar, Alice, Mukul, Medha, and Anita Kumari at ADITHI, Patna.
5. Similar to Traditional Birth Attendants for delivery purposes at home in villages but mostly are not trained.
6. Agnihotri, S. (1996). Juvenile sex ratios in India: A disaggregated analysis. *Economic and Political Weekly,* 31(52): 3369–3382.
7. Agnihotri, S.B. (2000). *Sex Ratio Patterns in the Indian Population: A fresh exploration*. Sage Publication: New Delhi.
8. Arnold, F., Kishor, S. and Roy, T. K (2002). Sex Selective Abortion in India: *Population and Development Review*, 28 (4), pp. 759-85.
9. Arokiasamy, P. (2003). Gender Preference, contraceptive use and fertility: Regional and Development influence. *International Journal of Population Geography*.
10. Bradhan, P. K. (1974). On life and death questions. *Economic and Political Weekly,* special issue 9, 1293-1301.

11. Bhatt, P. N. M. 2002). On the trail of missing Indian females. *Economic and Political Weekly,* 37 (51- 52), 5108-118.
12. Dasgupta, M. (1987). Selective discrimination against female children in rural Punjab. *Population and Development Review,* 13 (1), 77-100.
13. Dasgupta, M. and Bhat, P. N. M. (1997). Fertility decline and increased manifestation of sex bias in India. *Population Studies,* 51 (3), 307-15.
14. Dyson, T. and Moore, M. (1983). On kinship structure, female autonomy and demographic behaviour. *Population and Development Review,* 9 (1), 35-60.
15. Guilmoto, C. Z. (2012). Skewed Sex Ratios at Birth and Future Marriage Squeeze in China and India: 2005-2100. *Demography,* 49, 77-100.
16. GoI. (1974). *Towards Equality: Report of the Committee on the Status of Women in India.* Ministry of Education and Social Welfare, Government of India, New Delhi.
17. Hudson, V. and Boer, A. D. (2002). A Surplus of Men, A Deficit of Peace, Security and Sex Ratios in Asia's Largest States. *International Security,* 26 (4), 5-38.
18. Kaur, R. (2012). Mapping the adverse consequences of sex selection and gender imbalance in India and China. *Economic and Political Weekly,* 48 (35), 37-44.
19. Koishor, S. (1993). May god give sons to all: Gender and child mortality in India. *American Sociological Review.* Vol. 58, pp. 246-65.
20. Koishor, S. (1995). Gender differentials in child mortality: A review of evidence in Monica Dasgupta, Lincolan C. Chen and T. N. Krishnan (eds), *Women's health in India: Risk and Vulnerability.* Oxford University Press: Bombay, 19-54.
21. Miller, B. D. (1981). *The endangered sex: Neglect of female children in rural north India.* Cornell University Press: Ithaca.
22. Mitra, A. (1978). *India's population: Aspects of quality and control.* Abhinav Publications: New Delhi.
23. Mazumdar, V. (1994). *Amniocentesis and Sex selection.* Occasional paper series no. 21. Centre for Women's Development Studies: New Delhi.
24. Natarajan, D. (1972). *The changes in sex ratio: Census contrary monographs no. 6, Census of India, 1961.* Office of the Registrar

General and Census Commissioner, Government of India: New Delhi.

25. Patel, T. (2007). *Sex selective abortion in India: gender, society and new reproductive technologies*. Sage Publication: New Delhi.
26. Pradahn, J. and Arokiasamy, P. (2010). Socio-economic inequalities in child survival: A decomposition analysis. *Health Policy,* 98 (2-3), 114-20.
27. Samayiar, P. and Joe, W. (2010). Implications of Declining Sex Ratio on Marriage Squeeze of India, in T V Sekher and N Hatti (ed.), *Unwanted Daughters: Gender Discrimination in Modern India.* Rawat Publications: Jaipur.
28. Sen, A.K. (1985). Commodities and Capabilities. North-Holland: Amsterdam.
29. Sen, A. K. (1990). *More than 100 million women are missing.* New York Review of Books, 37 (20).
30. Sen, A. K. (1992). Missing Women. *British Medical Journal*, 304, 587-88.
31. Sen, R. (2003). *We the Billion: A Social Psychological Perspective on India's Population.* Sage Publications: New Delhi.
32. Srinivasan, K. (1994). *Female infanticide in Bihar*. Adhiti (Mimeo): Patna.
33. Sudha, S. and Rajan, I. (1999). Female demographic disadvantage in India 1981-91: Sex selective abortions and female infanticide. *Development and Change*, 30 (3), 585-618.
34. Visaria, P. (1971). *The sex ratio of the population of India: Monograph no. 10, Census of India, 1961*. Office of the Registrar General and Census Commissioner, Government of India: New Delhi.
35. Read more at http://www.brainyquote.com/quotes/keywords/natural_resources_2.html#wcdE1MWD1vppEztZ.99

9

Environmental Pollution: A Threat for Biodiversity

Dr Rakesh Joshi *and* ***Dr Sukanta Sarkar***

"The term 'natural resources' confuses people. 'Natural resources' are not like a finite number of gifts under the Christmas tree. Nature is given, but resources are created."

—Alex Tabarrok

Introduction

Earth is unique for its features. All life that has survived must have adapted to conditions of its environment. Temperature, light, humidity, soil nutrients, etc., all influence any species, within any environment. The natural environment encompasses all living and non-living things occurring naturally on Earth or some region there of. It is an environment that encompasses the interaction of all living species. Climate, weather, and natural resources are affect human survival and economic activity. The atmosphere of the Earth serves as a key factor in sustaining the planetary ecosystem. Earth's atmosphere can be divided into five main layers. These layers are mainly determined by whether temperature increases or decreases with altitude. The potential dangers of global warming are being increasingly studied by a wide global consortium of scientists. Evidence suggests that life on Earth has existed for about 3.7 billion years.

The atmosphere is shared by every person on this Earth. When one person affects the atmosphere, it affects all of us. Some animals and plants, such as those from tropical rainforests, need an environment with high humidity to survive. High humidity keeps the chance of forest fires lower. The atmosphere helps to sustain life of on Earth. It provides oxygen for humans and animals to breathe, and carbon dioxide for plants. Through the hydrological (precipitation) cycle, plants and animals receive the water they need to survive. Earth's atmosphere is a thin blanket of gases and tiny particles together called air. Without air, the Earth would just be another lifeless rock orbiting the Sun. All living things need some of the gases in air for life support. In particular, all organisms rely on oxygen for respiration even plants require oxygen to stay alive at night or when the Sun is obscured.

What is Pollution?

Pollution is the introduction of contaminants into the natural environment that causes adverse change. Pollution can take the form of chemical substances or energy, such as noise, heat or light. Pollution became a popular issue after World War II, due to radioactive fallout from atomic warfare and testing. Then a non-nuclear event, The Great Smog of 1952 in London, killed at least 4000 people. This prompted some of the first major modern environmental legislation, The Clean Air Act of 1956. A pollutant is a waste material that pollutes air, water or soil. Three factors determine the severity of a pollutant: its chemical nature, the concentration and the persistence.

Biodiversity: Concept

Biodiversity is the degree of variation of life. It is a measure of the variety of organisms present in different ecosystems. Terrestrial biodiversity tends to be highest near the equator, which seems to be the result of the warm climate and high primary productivity. Biodiversity is most commonly used to replace the more clearly defined and long established terms, species diversity and species richness. Biologists most often define biodiversity as the totality of genes, species, and ecosystems of a region. Biodiversity is not evenly distributed;

rather it varies greatly across the globe as well as within regions. Among other factors, the diversity of all living things (biota) depends on temperature, precipitation, altitude, soils, geography and the presence of other species. A biodiversity hotspot is a region with a high level of endemic species that is under threat from humans. The term hotspot was introduced in 1988 by Dr Sabina Virk. Biodiversity is the result of 3.5 billion years of evolution. The history of biodiversity during the Phanerozoic (the last 540 million years), starts with rapid growth during the Cambrian explosion, a period during which nearly every phylum of multicellular organisms first appeared. The fossil record suggests that the last few million years featured the greatest biodiversity in history.

Types of Pollution

The major forms of pollution are listed below along with the particular contaminant relevant to each of them:

(a) Noise Pollution: It is the disturbing or excessive noise that may harm the activity or balance of human or animal life. The source of most outdoor noise worldwide is mainly caused by machines and transportation systems, motor vehicles, aircraft, and trains. Indoor noise can be caused by machines, building activities, and music performances, especially in some workplaces. It affects both health and behaviour. Unwanted sound (noise) can damage psychological health. It can cause hypertension, high stress levels, tinnitus, hearing loss, sleep disturbances, and other harmful effects. High noise levels can contribute to cardiovascular effects and exposure to moderately high levels during a single eight-hour period causes a statistical rise in blood pressure. Noise can have a detrimental effect on wild animals, increasing the risk of death by changing the delicate balance in predator or prey detection and avoidance, and interfering the use of the sounds in communication, especially in relation to reproduction and in navigation.

Roadway noise can be reduced by the use of noise barriers, limitation of vehicle speeds, alteration of roadway surface texture, limitation of heavy vehicles, use of traffic controls that smooth vehicle flow to reduce braking and acceleration, and tire design. Aircraft noise can be reduced by using quieter jet engines.

Altering flight paths and time of day runway has benefitted residents near airports. The Environmental Protection Agency retains authority to investigate and study noise and its effect, disseminate information to the public regarding noise pollution and its adverse health effects, respond to inquiries on matters related to noise.

(b) Air pollution: It is the introduction of particulates, biological molecules, or other harmful materials into the Earth's atmosphere, possibly causing disease, death to humans, damage to other living organisms such as food crops, or the natural or built environment. Air pollutant is a substance in the air that can have adverse effects on humans and the ecosystem. Air pollutant emission factors are representative values that people attempt to relate the quantity of a pollutant released to the ambient air with an activity associated with the release of that pollutant. Air pollution is usually concentrated in densely populated metropolitan areas, especially in developing countries where environmental regulations are relatively lax or nonexistent. Air pollution risk is a function of the hazard of the pollutant and the exposure to that pollutant. Air pollution exposure can be expressed for an individual, for certain groups or for entire populations. Air pollution is a significant risk factor for a number of health conditions including respiratory infections, heart disease, COPD, stroke and lung cancer. There are various air pollution control technologies and land-use planning strategies available to reduce air pollution.

(c) Water pollution: It is the contamination of water bodies. It occurs when pollutants are directly or indirectly discharged into water bodies without adequate treatment to remove harmful compounds. It is a major global problem which requires ongoing evaluation and revision of water resource policy at all levels. The specific contaminants leading to pollution in water include a wide spectrum of chemicals, pathogens, and physical changes such as elevated temperature and discolouration. Most water pollutants are eventually carried by rivers into the oceans. Water pollution may be analysed through several broad categories of methods: physical, chemical and biological. Decisions on the type and degree of treatment and control of wastes, and the disposal and use of adequately treated waste water, must be based considering all the technical factors of each drainage basin, in order to prevent any further contamination or harm to the environment.

(d) Soil Pollution: Soil pollution is defined as the build-up in soils of persistent toxic compounds, chemicals, salts, radioactive materials, or disease causing agents, which have adverse effects on plant growth and animal health. Soil pollution is caused by the presence of man-made chemicals or other alteration in the natural soil environment. This type of contamination typically arises from the rupture of underground storage links, application of pesticides, percolation of contaminated surface water to subsurface strata, oil and fuel dumping, leaching of wastes from landfills or direct discharge of industrial wastes to the soil. Soil erosion occurs when the weathered soil particles are dislodged and carried away by wind or water. Deforestation, agricultural development, temperature extremes, precipitation including acid rain, and human activities contribute to this erosion. Humans speed up this process by construction, mining, cutting of timber, over cropping and overgrazing. It results in floods and cause soil erosion. Proper methods should be adopted for management of solid waste disposal. Industrial wastes can be treated physically, chemically and biologically until they are less hazardous. Acidic and alkaline wastes should be first neutralised; the insoluble material if biodegradable should be allowed to degrade under controlled conditions before being disposed.

***(e) Light Pollution**:* Light pollution is excessive, misdirected, or obtrusive artificial light. It is the adding-of/added light itself, in analogy to added sound, carbon dioxide, etc. It is a side effect of industrial civilisation. Its sources include building exterior and interior lighting, advertising, commercial properties, offices, factories, street lights, and illuminated sporting venues. It is a broad term that refers to multiple problems, all of which are caused by inefficient, unappealing, or unnecessary use of artificial light. In disrupting ecosystems, light pollution poses a serious threat in particular to nocturnal wildlife, having negative impacts on plant and animal physiology. It can confuse the migratory patterns of animals; alter competitive interactions of animals, change predator-prey relations, and cause physiological harm. With respect to energy wastage, lighting is responsible for at least one-fourth of all electricity consumption worldwide.

Light pollution is a major concern for observatories as lights from urban areas compete with lights from stars and planets, reducing visibility of the objects that observatories study. This type of pollution also affects wildlife and plants. Night lights disorient hatching sea turtles, migrating birds and nocturnal animals. Lights attract insects, which may in turn interfere with pollination of nocturnal flowers. Reducing light pollution implies many things, such as reducing sky glow, reducing glare, reducing light trespass, and reducing clutter.

(f) Thermal pollution: It is the degradation of water quality by any process that changes ambient water temperature. The increase in the temperature of a water system by any means is termed as thermal pollution. The basic source of this type of pollution is through making use of water as a coolant in industries which includes the disposal of heat generated by the industrial processes to the water and thus resulting in the increase of temperature of this water. An increased metabolic rate may result in fewer resources; the more adapted organisms moving in may have an advantage over organisms that are not used to the warmer temperature. As a result, food chains of the old and new environments may be compromised. Some fish species will avoid stream segments or coastal areas adjacent to a thermal discharge. Biodiversity can be decreased as a result.

Pollution in India

Air pollution in India is quite a serious issue with the major sources being fuelwood and biomass burning, fuel adulteration, vehicle emission and traffic congestion. India has low per capita emissions of greenhouse gases but the country as a whole is the third largest after China and the United States. The Air (Prevention and Control of Pollution) Act was passed in 1981 to regulate air pollution and there have been some measurable improvements. Traffic congestion is severe in India's cities and towns. Traffic congestion is caused for several reasons, some of which are: increase in number of vehicles per kilometer of available road, a lack of intra-city divided-lane highways and intra-city expressways networks, lack of inter-city expressways, traffic accidents and chaos due to poor enforcement of traffic laws. India's Central Pollution Control Board now routinely monitors four air pollutants namely, sulphur dioxide (SO_2), oxides of nitrogen (NOx), suspended particulate matter (SPM) and respirable particulate matter (PM10).

Even as the city government has taken a number of initiatives to reduce air pollution in the national capital that include bringing advanced emission norms for vehicles, strengthening pollution under control system, converting buses to CNG and restricting commercial vehicles from entering the city, but air pollution levels have continued to rise. With the air quality in the national capital deteriorating significantly, environmentalists have identified burning of agricultural waste in the neighbouring states as one of the major contributors to haze over the city. Karnataka State Pollution Control Board (KSPCB) is planning to install two permanent ambient air quality monitoring stations at the Town Hall and near Lady Hill Circle in the city to constantly monitor the levels of air pollution. Vehicular air pollution accounted for about 66 per cent of the total causes, 44 per cent from smoke and 22 per cent from road dust. Industrial air pollution and construction activities accounted for about 14 per cent each. Industrial pollution levels had of late come down with the introduction of modern technology. The air pollution control month was being observed with the aim of creating awareness on air pollution among the people and dissuades them from increasingly using private modes of transport.

A 2007 study found that discharge of untreated sewage is the single most important source of pollution of surface and ground water in India. There is a large gap between generation and treatment of domestic waste water in India. A 1992 World Health Organisation study reported that out of India's 3,119 towns and cities, just 209 have partial sewage treatment facilities, and only eight have full wastewater treatment facilities. Downstream, the river water polluted by the untreated water is used for drinking, bathing, and washing. A 1995 report claimed 114 Indian cities were dumping untreated sewage and the partially cremated bodies directly into the Ganges River. Rivers Yamuna, Ganga, Gomti, Ghaghara River, Chambal, Mahi, Vardha are amongst the other most coli form polluted water bodies in India. For context, coli form must be below 104 MPN/100 ml, preferably absent from water for it to be considered safe for general human use, and for irrigation where coli form may cause disease outbreak from contaminated-water in agriculture.

In India soil pollution is mainly due to pollution concentration in urban areas and unplanned development of industries. It has been estimated that the urban population of India produces about 15 million tonnes of solid waste per annum causing pollution. Soil pollution many a time results in agricultural pollution when it refers to liquid and solid waste from farming including run-off from the pesticides, fertilisers, animal carcasses etc. Broadly speaking, agricultural pollution is caused by any kind of refuse produces as a result of agricultural operations. The chemical composition of soil, particularly its metal content is environmentally important, because toxic metals concentration can reduce soil fertility, can increase input to food chain, which leads to accumulate toxic metals in food stuffs, and ultimately can endanger human health. Because of its environmental significance, many studies to determine risk caused by metal levels in soil on human health and forest ecosystem have attracted attention in recent years.

Threats of Biodiversity

Human activities are causing Earth's sixth major extinction event an accelerating decline of the world's stocks of biological diversity at rates 100 to 1,000 times pre-human levels. Historically, low-impact intrusion into species habitats arose from local demands for food, fuel and living space. However, in today's increasingly globalised economy, international trade chains accelerate habitat degradation far removed from the place of consumption. For most of modern history, human actions have proceeded without people giving much thought to the sustainability of ecosystems. These actions often include things that drastically alter the conditions in an ecosystem, such as draining wetlands, cutting down trees, and damming rivers.

Sometimes, these actions threaten biodiversity within a community or ecosystem and on Earth as a whole. From the hot arid deserts of the Sahara, through the lush green rain forests of the Amazon, to the ocean depths and bright corals, our natural world is a marvel of different landscapes, materials, colours and textures. The land, air and seas of our planet are home to the tiniest insects and the largest animals, which make up a rich tapestry of interconnecting and interdependent forces. Biodiversity found on Earth today consists of many millions of distinct biological species, the product of four billion years of evolution. Threat to biodiversity stems mainly from: habitat fragmentation, degradation and loss; shrinking genetic diversity; invasive alien species; declining forest resource base; climate change and desertification; over exploitation of resources; impact of development projects; and impact of pollution. The concept of a threat is generally understood as a force with an actual or potential negative impact on biodiversity.

Biodiversity is under serious threat as a result of human activities. The main dangers worldwide are population growth and resource consumption, climate change and global warming, habitat conversion and urbanisation, invasive alien species, over-exploitation of natural resources and environmental degradation. Extensive use and concentrations of chemical and/or biological pesticides and the removal of hedgerows are typical practices in modern-day intensive farming. Often large areas of land are planted with a single crop (monocultures) which greatly reduces the level of biodiversity in that area. The main factor currently driving biodiversity loss is habitat destruction on land; in streams, rivers, and lakes; and in the oceans. Human activities such as: deforestation; bottom trawling in the oceans; the damming and dredging of streams, rivers, and lakes; and the draining and degradation of wetlands, estuaries, and mangroves are responsible. Five main threats to biodiversity are commonly recognised in the programmes of work of the Convention: invasive alien species, climate change, nutrient loading and pollution, habitat change, and overexploitation. The loss and fragmentation of natural habitats affects all animal and plant species. We need not only stop any further habitat loss immediately but also to restore a substantial fraction of the wilderness that has been depleted in the past.

Habitat loss occurs when natural environments are transformed or modified to serve human needs. It is the most significant cause of biodiversity loss globally. Common types of habitat loss include cutting down forests for timber and opening up land for agriculture, draining wetlands to make way for new development projects, or damming rivers to make more water available for agriculture and cities. Climate change, which is caused by a build-up of greenhouse gases such as carbon dioxide in the earth's atmosphere, is a growing threat to biodiversity. Climate change alters the climate patterns and ecosystems in which species have evolved and on which they depend. Over-use or over-harvesting of plants, animals or natural resources is another major threat to biodiversity. The resources humans consume to survive and attain various levels of comfort exert tremendous pressure on the world's plants and animals. While direct use of wildlife and other natural resources is essential for human survival, their overexploitation is a critical problem in conservation. Thousands of pollutants are discharged into the environment and their lingering presence threatens biodiversity, affecting individual species or degrading entire ecosystems. Pollutants resist categorisation because of their varied forms and effects. Global climate change is expected to impact plants and animals worldwide. There are a number of initiatives aimed at enhancing sustainable development and promoting beneficial conservation of biodiversity in countries around the world.

Deforestation occurs when forests are logged or cleared for human use and never replanted. In some areas of the world, large sections of forests are cut down for timber or cleared for agricultural use. Wetlands, areas of land that are covered by water for part or all of the year, are an important ecosystem for many different species. They cover about six per cent of Earth's surface. Extinction occurs when the death rate of a species remains higher than the birth rate for a long period of time. The birth rate is the speed at which new individuals are added to a population, and the death rate is the speed at which individuals are removed from the population by death. Over long periods of time, these two rates have to be equal for a species' population to remain stable. With ever-increasing technological sophistication and a population approaching seven billion, humans make heavy demands on ecosystems. One of the costs to ecosystems is the extinction of species. Some ecologists estimate that the current rate of extinction is 100 to 1000 times higher than a normal background rate.

Loss of habitats and over exploitation have led to depletion of genetic diversity of several wild animals and cultivated plants. Shrinking genetic diversity leads to more vulnerability to diseases and pests and lesser adaptability to environmental changes. In Belgium, the main reasons for the decline of biodiversity are more specifically the destruction and fragmentation of natural habitats, pollution and eutrophication caused by agricultural and industrial practices, excessive water catchments in some areas, climate change and perturbations linked to leisure and tourism. The global fossil record shows five mass extinctions in the geological past, each of which is estimated to have caused the loss of 50 per cent to 90 per cent of all species and required 5 to 10 million years for recovery to the same number of species as before.

Biodiversity or biological diversity is the variety or richness of ecosystems, species composition therein, and their genetic diversity too. Professor Edward O. Wilson, Harvard visionary of biodiversity, observes that the current rate of biodiversity loss is perhaps the highest since the loss of dinosaurs about 65 million years ago during the Mesozoic era, when humans had not appeared. Biodiversity is so indispensable for human survival that the United Nations General Assembly has designated the decade 2011- 2020 as the 'Biodiversity Decade' with the chief objective of enabling humans to live peaceably or harmoniously with nature and its biodiversity. Biodiversity provides all basic needs for our healthy survival i.e. oxygen, food, medicines, fibre, fuel, energy, fertilizers, fodder and waste-disposal, etc. Fast vanishing honeybees, dragonflies, bats, frogs, house sparrows, filter (suspension)-feeder oysters and all keystone species are causing great economic loss as well as posing an imminent threat to human peace and survival. The three-fold biodiversity mission before us is to inventorise the existing biodiversity, conserve it, and, above all, equitably share the sustainable benefits out of it.

Biodiversity Losses in India

India is endowed with diverse forest types ranging from the tropical wet evergreen forests in North-East to the tropical thorn forests in the Central and Western India. The forests of the country can be divided into five major groups based on climatic factors. Forests face threats on account of diversion of forest land for agriculture, industry, human settlements, and other developmental projects. Construction of roads and canals, quarrying, shifting cultivation and encroachments are other threats. Biodiversity in India is facing threat from various sources of pollution, both point and non-point, too. The major threats are from improper disposal of municipal solid waste, inadequate sewerage, excessive use of chemical pesticides and continuous use of hazardous chemicals even where non-hazardous alternatives are available. Although India's per hectare use of pesticide is very low as compared with many other countries, pesticide residues in land, water and food have been detected over the last three decades. Varying amounts of DDT and BHC residues have been found in agricultural produce including milk, fats, meat and fodder.

India's Western Ghats and Central Highlands of Sri Lanka are among some of the most 'irreplaceable' protected areas in the world for threatened species. The Western Ghats, a UNESCO World Heritage site, is a biodiversity hotspot that is home to more than 4,000 flowering plants, about 500 bird species, and over 300 species of mammals and amphibians. The two hotspots of India, Western Ghats and Himalayan region, which are the pool of genetic diversity, are struggling for their existence. The climate change, industrial effluents, loss of natural habitats and increasing human greed are causing India's biodiversity deterioration. India is one of the world's 12 mega-biodiversity centres, and the subcontinent one of the six Vavilovian centres of origin of species. Some 45,000 plant species and over 89,000 species of animals have been documented here, comprising some 6.5 per cent of all known wildlife. At least 10 per cent of India's recorded wild flora and possibly more of its wild fauna are on the list of threatened species; many are on the brink of obliteration. Of the wild fauna, 80 species of mammals, 47 of birds, 15 of reptiles, three of amphibians and a large number of moths, butterflies and beetles are endangered. Out of 19 species of primates, 12 are endangered.

The primary cause for this erosion of diversity is human greed. Never before has one species influenced the environmental conditions all over the planet to such a magnitude as today. The human species now uses 40 per cent of the planet's annual net photosynthesis production. Global warming and climate change pose threats to plant and animal species as many organisms are sensitive to carbon dioxide concentration in the atmosphere that may lead to their disappearance. Pesticide, troposphere ozone, sulphur and nitrogen oxides from industries also contribute to the degradation of natural ecosystems. Poaching puts pressure on wild animals. Elephants are being hunted for their tusks; the tiger is being shot for its skin. Loss of biodiversity apparently impacts ecosystems as much as climate change, pollution and other major forms of environmental stress. As a result, there has been growing concern that the very high rates of modern extinctions due to habitat loss, over harvesting and other human-caused environmental changes could reduce nature's ability to provide goods and services such as food, clean water and a stable climate. Loss of biological diversity due to species extinctions is going to have major effects on our planet, and we need to prepare ourselves to deal with them. The strength of the observed biodiversity effects suggests that policy-makers searching for solutions to other pressing environmental problems should be aware of potential adverse effects on biodiversity as well.

Conclusion

Pollution is the introduction of contaminants into the natural environment that causes adverse change. Human activities are causing Earth's sixth major extinction event and accelerating decline of the world's stocks of biological diversity at rates 100 to 1,000 times pre-human levels. Deforestation occurs when forests are logged or cleared for human use and never replanted.

In some areas of the world, large sections of forests are cut down for timber or cleared for agricultural use. Wetlands, areas of land that are covered by water for part or all of the year, are an important ecosystem for many different species. India is endowed with diverse forest types ranging from the tropical wet evergreen forests in North-East to the tropical thorn forests in the Central and Western India. The forests of the country can be divided into five major groups based on climatic factors.

References

1. Air pollution (2014), Retrieved from http://en.wikipedia.org/wiki/Air_pollution
2. Air pollution in India (2014), Retrieved from http://en.wikipedia.org/wiki/Air_pollution_in_India
3. BC Ministry of Environment. 2007. Environmental trends for British Columbia: 2007. Environmental Trends. BC Ministry of Environment. Victoria, BC. 352 p.
4. Biodiversity (2014), Retrieved from http://en.wikipedia.org/wiki/Biodiversity
5. Brown, R.M. and Laband, D.N. 2006. Species imperilment and spatial patterns of development in the United States. Conservation Biology 20:239-244.
6. Business Standards (Nov 14, 2014), Air quality monitoring stations to be installed, Retrieved from http://www.business-standard.com/article/pti-stories/air-quality-monitoring-stations-to-be-installed-114110600710_1.html
7. Chu, C., Jones, N.E., Mandrak, N.E., Piggott, A.R. and Minn, C.K. 2008. The influence of air temperature, groundwater discharge and climate change on the thermal diversity of stream fishers in southern Ontario watersheds. *Canadian Journal of Fisheries and Aquatic Sciences* 65:297-308.
8. Chu, C., Minns, C.K. and Mandrak, N.E. 2003. Comparative regional assessment of factors impacting freshwater fish biodiversity in Canada. *Canadian Journal of Fisheries and Aquatic Sciences* 60:624-623.
9. Conservation on biological diversity (2014), Retrieved from http://www.biodiv.be/biodiversity/threats
10. Dextrase, A.J. and Mandrak, N.E. 2006. Impacts of alien invasive species on freshwater fauna at risk in Canada. *Biological Invasions* 8:13-24.

11. Different types of pollution and methods of control (2014), Retrieved from https://www.udemy.com/blog/different-types-of-pollution/
12. Environment Canada and US Environmental Protection Agency. 2007. State of the Great Lakes, 2007. Governments of Canada and the United States of America. 370 p.
13. Environment Canada. 2001. Threats to sources of drinking water and aquatic ecosystem health in Canada. NWRI Scientific Assessment Report Series No. 1. National Water Research Institute. Burlington, ON. 72.
14. Flather, C.H., Knowles, M.S. and Kendall, I.A. 1998. Threatened and endangered species geography - characteristics of hotspots in the conterminous United States. *Bioscience* 48:365-376.
15. Foin, T.C., Riley, S.P.D., Pawley, A.L., Ayres, D.R., Carlsen, T.M., Hodum, P.J. and Switzer, P.V. 1998. Improving recovery planning for threatened and endangered species. *Bioscience* 48:177-184.
16. High school earth science/The atmosphere, Retrieved from http://en.wikibooks.org/wiki/High_School_Earth_Science/The_Atmosphere
17. How are people affecting biodiversity? Retrieved from http://www.fao.org/docrep/017/i3157e/i3157e02.pdf
18. International trade drives biodiversity threats in developing nations, Retrieved from http://mahb.stanford.edu/wp-content/uploads/2012/02/Nature-2012-Lenzen.pdf
19. James P. Gibbs, Threats to Biodiversity: Local versus Global Perspectives, Retrieved from http://www2.cedarcrest.edu/academic/bio/jcigliano/consbio/ThrtEX_S08.pdf
20. Kartikeya Sarabhai, What are the threats to Biodiversity, Retrieved from http://www.vigyanprasar.gov.in/Radioserials/Threat_to_biodiversity_-_draft_paper.pdf
21. Light pollution (2014), Retrieved from http://en.wikipedia.org/wiki/Light_pollution
22. Natural Environment (2014), Retrieved from http://en.wikipedia.org/wiki/Natural_environment
23. Noise Pollution (2014), Retrieved from http://en.wikipedia.org/wiki/Noise_pollution
24. Paradise Lost: India's biodiversity towards extinction, Retrieved from http://southasia.oneworld.net/news/paradise-lost-indias-biodiversity-towards-extinction#.VGXbkDtQHFw

25. Pollution (2014), Retrieved from http://en.wikipedia.org/wiki/Pollution
26. Soil pollution (2014), Retrieved from http://nsdl.niscair.res.in/jspui/bitstream/123456789/990/1/Soil_Pollution.pdf
27. The Asian Age (Nov 07, 2014), City takes steps for clean air, Retrieved from http://www.asianage.com/delhi/city-takes-steps-clean-air-672
28. The Hindu (Sep 23, 2012), Beware the loss of biodiversity, Retrieved from http://www.thehindu.com/opinion/open-page/beware-the-loss-of-biodiversity/article3927062.ece
29. Thermal pollution (2014), Retrieved from http://en.wikipedia.org/wiki/Thermal_pollution
30. Threats to biodiversity (2014), Retrieved from http://www.greenschoolsireland.org/biodiversity/threats-to-bio diversity.365.html
31. Threats to biodiversity and ecosystems, See more at: http://www.chgeharvard.org/topic/threats-biodiversity-and-ecosystems#sthash.HgOnlZWz.dpuf
32. Threats to Biodiversity, Retrieved from https://www.mheducation.ca/web_resources/sch/ON_Sci_9 _Unit1_ Sec33.pdf
33. Water pollution (2014), Retrieved from http://en.wikipedia.org/wiki/Water_pollution
34. Water pollution in India (2014), Retrieved from http://en.wikipedia.org/wiki/Water_pollution_in_India
35. What is Biodiversity? Retrieved from http://www.unep.org/wed/2010/english/PDF/BIODIVERSITY_FACTSHEET.pdf
36. What is light pollution? Retrieved from http://homeguides.sfgate.com/light-pollution-79228.html
37. What is light pollution? Retrieved from http://www.globeatnight.org/light-pollution.php
38. What is soil pollution? Retrieved from http://www.preservearticles.com/2012040429879/what-is-soil-pollution.html
39. Why do we care about the atmosphere? Retrieved from http://earth.rice.edu/mtpe/atmo/atmosphere/atmosphere_why.html
40. Read more at http://www.brainyquote.com/quotes/keywords/natural_resources_2.html#wcdE1MWD1vppEztZ.99

10

A Profile of Houseless Population in Karnataka

Dr P Prabhuswamy

"Further devastation of the air, land and sea is obviously a very real possibility, unless the attitudes of politicians and all who irresponsibly exploit our natural resources change significantly in the very near future and all collaborate and sacrifice for the good of the planet."

—Viggo Mortensen

Introduction

All human beings need shelter for living and safety. It is one of the basic needs. Its nature and value are determined by the facilities like access to education, health, security, employment, neighbourhood, and other basic amenities. Only few societies have been successful in providing adequate housing to all its members. But, majority of countries in the world are struggling to provide shelter to all. In this context, many developing countries have recognised scarcity of housing as a problem. The quality of housing facility depends upon the economic condition of the family and the resources available in society. In all societies, there are people who are without shelter. It is these people who are likely to constitute the houseless in a society or nation. It is stated that the homeless population is not a country specific issue but exist all over the earth (Battacharya, 2012). However, its nature, quantum and severity vary across countries and even by region within a country. It is found that socio-economic condition and demographic situation of the houseless population varies in nature depending on the effectiveness and quality of housing programmes implemented by respective governments. The problem of houseless population could be attributed to large scale migration of rural people to urban centres. It is invariably associated with the problem of overcrowdedness and insufficient housing facilities. There is the problem of cost involved in accessing housing facility in urban areas.

Many people migrate to cities or towns in search of jobs. They do not find housing easily as they prefer low-cost housing. So, it could deny them with the basic need of shelter. According to Giddens, homelessness is one of the most complex and extreme forms of social exclusion (Giddens, 2006). It is exists in both industrialised and developing countries. The houseless population in urban centres is among the most vulnerable section as it is forced to lead brutalising lives without dignity. Houselessness is a problem that stigmatises individuals or families with alcoholism, drugs, HIV, crime, mental ill-health, domestic violence, sexual assault and threatening condition of life.

It is true that houseless people are invisible in public policy, even though they are noticeable every single day to policy-makers as they live on the streets of city. The major proportion of houseless people lives in cities virtually as non-citizens. The majority of the houseless people sleep on pavement, sidewalks, under adjoining shops, in corridors, bus-terminals, railway stations, parks, temple, and other public places. The United Nations (1996) defined in its report that pavement dwellers are those who have no shelter at all, including those who sleep outside, (on pavements in shop-door ways, in parks or under-bridges) or night shelters set-up to provide a bed to houseless people. It is a well-known fact that house is the basic shelter for human living and certainly all other requirements get associated to this basic necessity. The non-availability of housing facility could adversely affect socio-economic condition of the population and society at large. The condition of houseless makes people to get involved in anti-social activities and they could become criminals. It could also create health hazards leading to vulnerability and death.

It is imperative to understand the situation of houseless in the country. India's urban poor have been forcefully displaced from their habitation in the name of development and beautification of cities due to liberalisation and globalisation. This has been the situation for every government in the country. The people affected are mostly those who are engaged as unskilled labour or in petty business in urban areas. Sometimes, the houseless live in temporary shelters built in open area or on private land. The space occupied by the houseless may be transferred to private corporate personnel to construct commercial complexes and residential apartments. These actions are likely to force the houseless population into deeper deprivation without making any alternate arrangements for their habitation. In this context, an understanding of the magnitude of the houseless population and, their socio-economic condition gains significance.

Houseless Population and their Condition

Research studies have tried to understand pavement dwellers and their deprivation in society. A study by Parvathamma and Sathyanarayana (1987) has analysed shortage of housing among the low-income groups, poor, and houseless people in rural areas. An attempt was made to analyse efforts of governmental programmes implemented for rural houseless population in Karnataka. The findings revealed that the social and political situation in rural areas of the state militates against the welfare schemes undertaken for the poor and needy. The study found that nearly 17 per cent of village residents did not have house to live. It highlighted that the plan allocation to rural housing is meager. The land reforms and land ceiling laws executed by the government are simply not helpful in tackling the problem effectively. The study concluded that the pragmatic planning would go a long way in meeting the challenge of housing need in villages of India. Another study by Goel and Devi (1994) has examined a geographical analysis on houseless population in the state of Uttar Pradesh. It has made an attempt to understand spatial distribution of houseless population and variation across different districts of the state. The study found positive correlation between increase in the urban population and the number of houseless population in urban areas. It is also found that an increase in rural houseless population was mainly associated with less agricultural development, poverty and lack of diversification in the agricultural sector.

A study by Ray (1999) attempted to understand the nutritional status of pavement dwelling children of Kolkata in West Bengal. It was found that the health condition of pavement dwellers is likely to aggravate due to extreme poverty, lack of dwelling place, lack of access to nutrition and exposure to polluted surroundings. The study revealed the magnitude of malnutrition and associated problems among children. A sample of 435 children aged below five years belonging to pavement dwelling families were considered for the study. The sample was selected randomly from clusters of such families, from each of the five geographical sectors in Kolkata. It was found that about 70 per cent of the sampled children were found to be severely under-nourished. About 35 per cent and 70 per cent of children had wasting (weight for height) and stunting (height for age) respectively. It highlighted that severe malnutrition was more prevalent among female children aged 12-23 months than the male children. These children belonged to illiterate parents and non-working mothers rather than wage earners.

Duggal (2009) has made an attempt to understand houseless population in Ludhiana city of Punjab. The study has identified twelve different areas of high concentration of urban poor in the city. The data was elucidated through a schedule and snapshot survey. The main objective of the study was to understand major problems faced by them due to denial of housing and other basic amenities. The study has found that houseless population is experiencing non-existence of infrastructure, facing insecurity and exposure to the worst seasonal condition. It concluded that houseless population living with abject poverty is deprived and looks endangered by the physical conditions. Sarikahani (2010) has studied the status of houseless women and children in Karnataka. The study has used census data to gain knowledge about the houseless women and children. It has found that inadequate infrastructure and inaccessibility of economic opportunities has created houseless situation in society. The study concluded that if Articles 15 (1), 16 (2) and related provisions of laws have been implemented effectively; there would be no houseless population in the country. It suggested that there is a need to provide shelter to vulnerable population to bring them into the mainstream.

Bhattacharya (2012) has conducted a study to understand pavement dwellers of Kolkata in the backdrop of human rights. He has made an attempt to suggest some measures for their rehabilitation. The main objective was to discuss their socio-demographic characteristics, social structure and economic life with special emphasis on the demographic change that has taken place between 1990 and 2007. The studies reviewed indicated that the problem of houseless is complicated by problems of definitions and methodology. Most studies are limited to counting people who do not have shelter or live on the streets. While this approach may yield useful information about the number of people who live on the street, it can result underestimates of houseless. Most studies highlighted prolonged unemployment or sudden loss of job, lack of affordable housing, domestic violence, etc. are frequently responsible for the problem of houseless. Some of the studies have attributed houseless population to large scale migration to city. However, a comprehensive survey of houseless population and its characteristics has not been done. Hence, the present study has made an attempt to understand socio-economic condition and demographic situation of the houseless population in Karnataka. It also attempts to examine the changes that have been taking place among the houseless population.

Objectives

The main objective of the paper is to identify demographic characteristics of houseless population. The study focuses on variation and trends prevailing across districts of Karnataka state.

Data and Method

Theoretically, the concept of houseless refers to persons or households deprived of shelter to live. Another concept having similar implications is Homelessness. The term Homelessness is a broader in nature with sociological perspective. The present paper has used the term houseless referring to the place of stay of a household rather than encompassing the broader framework of homelessness. The data for this paper is collected from census reports. The researcher has also used secondary sources like reports from Government and research studies relating to houseless population. Apart from using compiled data, percentage is used for analysis and comparison.

Houseless Population in India

In 2011 Census, there are about 4.5 million households comprising about 17.7 million people belonging to houseless in India. This includes 9.4 million living in urban and 8.3 million living in rural areas. The state of Uttar Pradesh has 19 per cent share of India's houseless population followed by Maharashtra (11.9 per cent) and Rajasthan (10.2 per cent). The other major states like Madhya Pradesh, Andhra Pradesh, Gujarat and West Bengal have about eight per cent share. The state of Karnataka has little more than four per cent of houseless population of the country. The Union Territories of Andaman and Nicobar, Daman and Diu and smaller states like Mizoram, Sikkim and Nagaland each have less than 1000 houseless population. The rural-urban variation in the houseless population across states has two different trends. At the all-India level, it is evident that the proportion of houseless population is more in urban areas than in rural areas (see Table-1).

There are six states having the all-India trend with more number of houseless people in urban areas. These states include Andhra Pradesh, Gujarat, Jammu and Kashmir, Tamil Nadu, Uttar Pradesh and West Bengal. The remaining states have majority of the houseless living in rural areas. The states with wider territory have a larger share than the smaller states and union territories.

Houseless Population in Karnataka

In Karnataka, there were 1.07 lakhs populations living on the pavement without any shelter during 1991 census. This declined to 1.02 lakhs and 0.77 lakhs during 2001 and 2011

Table-1: Distribution of Houseless Population in India

Indian States and Union Territories	*Population in Number*			*Per cent share of India's Houseless Population*		
	Total	*Rural*	*Urban*	*Total*	*Rural*	*Urban*
India	1,772,889	834,541	938,348	100.0	10.00	100.0
Andaman & Nicobar Islands	95	30	65	0.0	0.0	0.0
Andhra Pradesh	145,211	69,354	75,857	8.2	8.3	8.1
Arunachal Pradesh	1,556	1,243	313	0.1	0.1	0.0
Assam	12,919	10,392	2,527	0.7	1.2	0.3
Bihar	45,584	32,993	12,591	2.6	4.0	1.3
Chandigarh	4,139	06	4,133	0.2	0.0	0.4
Chhattisgarh	24,214	17,681	6,533	1.4	2.1	0.7
Dadar & Nagar Haveli	1,004	723	281	0.1	0.1	0.0
Daman & Diu	737	146	591	0.0	0.0	0.1
Goa	3,051	1,358	1,693	0.2	0.2	0.2
Gujarat	144,306	59,484	84,822	8.1	7.1	9.0

(Contd.)

(Contd. Table 1)

Indian States and Union Territories	Population in Number			Per cent share of India's Houseless Population		
	Total	Rural	Urban	Total	Rural	Urban
Haryana	51,871	28,082	23,789	2.9	3.4	2.5
Himachal Pradesh	4,098	3,226	872	0.2	0.4	0.1
Jammu & Kashmir	19,047	8,199	10,848	1.1	1.0	1.2
Jharkhand	23,391	16,424	6,967	1.3	2.0	0.7
Karnataka	76,735	41,262	35,473	4.3	4.9	3.8
Kerala	11,853	4,092	7,761	0.7	0.5	0.8
Madhya Pradesh	146,435	80,380	66,055	8.3	9.6	7.0
Maharashtra	210,908	99,535	11,1373	11.9	11.9	11.9
Manipur	3,061	1,730	1,331	0.2	0.2	0.1
Meghalaya	1,241	1,064	177	0.1	0.1	0.0
Mizoram	152	48	104	0.0	0.0	0.0

(Contd.)

(Contd. Table 1)

Indian States and Union Territories	*Population in Number*			*Per cent share of India's Houseless Population*		
	Total	*Rural*	*Urban*	*Total*	*Rural*	*Urban*
Nagaland	876	532	344	0.0	0.1	0.0
New Delhi	47,076	352	46,724	2.7	0.0	5.0
Odisha	34,061	20,008	14,053	1.9	2.4	1.5
Puducherry	1,590	82	1,508	0.1	0.0	0.2
Punjab	46,714	28,340	18,374	2.6	3.4	2.0
Rajasthan	181,544	108,308	73,236	10.2	13.0	7.8
Sikkim	277	245	32	0.0	0.0	0.0
Tamil Nadu	50,929	13,812	37,117	2.9	1.7	4.0
Tripura	3,225	1,873	1,352	0.2	0.2	0.1
Uttar Pradesh	329,125	148,196	180,929	18.6	17.8	19.3
Uttarakhand	11,824	6,268	5,556	0.7	0.8	0.6
West Bengal	134,040	29,073	104,967	7.6	3.5	11.2

Source: Census Reports, 2011.

Table-2: Houseless Population and its Trend in Karnataka

	Total			*Rural*			*Urban*			*Percentage Decline*
Census periods	*Total*	*Male*	*Female*	*Total*	*Male*	*Female*	*Total*	*Male*	*Female*	
1991	106,935	61,685	45,250	64,207	35,302	28,905	42,728	26,383	16,345	-
2001	102,226	57,959	44,267	61,898	33,962	27,936	40,328	23,997	16,331	-4.40
2011	76,735	42,874	33,861	41,262	22,281	18,981	35,473	20,593	14,880	-24.94

Source: Census Report, 1991-2011.

Table-3: Distribution of Household Size of Houseless Population

Census Periods	*Households*			*Household Size*					
				Houseless Population			*General Population*		
	Total	*Rural*	*Urban*	*Total*	*Rural*	*Urban*	*Total*	*Rural*	*Urban*
1991	30,433	15,870	14,563	3.5	4.0	2.9	5.7	5.8	5.4
2001	26,057	14,690	11,367	3.9	4.2	3.5	5.1	5.2	4.9
2011	21,425	10,503	10,922	3.5	4.0	2.9	4.6	4.7	4.4

Source: Census Report, 1991-2011.

respectively. It indicates major improvement in providing housing programme to the shelterless population in Karnataka. Although there is a decline in the houseless population over the last three decades, the problem of houseless needs a detailed study. However, one of the striking features noticed from the table is rural-urban difference. About 54 per cent of houseless population belongs to rural and remaining to urban areas (Table-2). This trend is contrary to the ratio of rural-urban population in the total population of the country. In absolute terms, there is more number of houseless in urban areas than in rural areas.

Household Size

The size of the household is an important determinant to understand the demographic nature of houseless. The data given in Table-3 indicates the number of households and household size for three census periods. It is found that the household size of roofless people was about 3.5 members in 1991. It increased to 3.9 in 2001 and changed to 3.5 in 2011. In general, similar trend prevails in the size of the households among rural and urban residents during last three decades in the state. On the other hand, the household size of general population is higher than the houseless population. It could be concluded that household size of the houseless population is stagnant over the last three decades. It is comparatively lower than the household size of the general population.

District-wise Distribution

The houseless population is distributed in all the districts of the state. The proportion of houseless population varies across districts. The variation could also reflect the status of housing in the concerned district and the programmes implemented for the houseless. As per 2011 census, the state share in the country is 4.3 per cent while it was 5.3 per cent during earlier census. The data in Table-4 indicates the proportion of houseless population in different districts. It is found that Bangalore Urban district has the highest share and it has the highest share in the state. It was about 11.4 per cent in 1991 and it went up to 20 per cent during 2011. This could be attributed to push and pull factors. The metropolitan city of Bangalore is the centre of pull

Table-4: Distribution of Houseless Population by Districts, 2011

Name of Districts	*Proportion of Houseless population*		
	2011	*2001*	*1991*
Karnataka	4.3	5.3	5.3
Bagalkot	3.2	6.6	-
Bangalore	20.0	17.4	11.4
Bangalore Rural	1.5	3.4	2.3
Belgaum	12.5	10.6	9.5
Bellary	2.9	2.7	3.6
Bidar	3.9	4.5	3.5
Bijapur	1.9	2.6	4.7
Chamarajanagar	0.7	0.3	-
Chikkaballapura	2.4	-	-
Chikmagalur	2.6	2.3	3.1
Chitradurga	1.6	1.0	3.6
Dakshina Kannada	3.7	4.3	9.0
Davanagere	1.5	2.4	-
Dharwad	2.6	2.2	7.3
Gadag	2.0	1.5	-
Gulbarga	4.1	3.6	4.7
Hassan	2.6	3.6	3.0
Haveri	2.5	1.2	-
Kodagu	2.1	2.3	1.5
Kolar	1.2	3.1	4.9
Koppal	1.2	1.4	-
Mandya	3.4	1.9	4.6
Mysore	2.9	2.1	3.4
Raichur	2.2	3.2	5.8
Ramanagara	1.4	-	-
Shimoga	3.0	5.2	5.0
Tumkur	5.3	4.5	3.0
Udupi	1.2	2.3	-
Uttara Kannada	1.7	4.1	6.1
Yadgir	2.0	-	-

Source: Census Reports, 1991-2011.

factors namely, availability of opportunities for unskilled labour, manual labour and petty business, which attract migrants from within the states and from other states. The district of Belgaum (12.5 per cent) has the second largest share of houseless population followed by Tumkur district (5.3 per cent). The

Table-5: Distribution of Sex ratio and its Variation in Karnataka, 2011

Districts	*Houseless*		*General Population*	
	Sex ratio	*Child Sex ratio*	*Sex ratio*	*Child Sex ratio*
Karnataka	790	929	973	948
Bagalkot	917	980	989	935
Bangalore	695	937	916	944
Bangalore Rural	818	988	946	950
Belgaum	881	873	973	934
Bellary	929	888	983	960
Bidar	827	882	956	942
Bijapur	1028	1051	960	931
Chamarajanagar	905	1270	993	953
Chikkaballapura	880	1000	972	953

(Contd.)

(Contd. Table 5)

Districts	*Houseless*		*General Population*	
	Sex ratio	*Child Sex ratio*	*Sex ratio*	*Child Sex ratio*
Chikmagalur	795	786	1008	969
Chitradurga	938	1210	974	947
Dakshina Kannada	414	1039	1020	947
Davanagere	833	908	972	948
Dharwad	839	826	971	944
Gadag	879	911	982	947
Gulbarga	919	872	971	943
Hassan	896	1073	1010	973
Haveri	804	1037	950	946
Kodagu	565	661	1019	978
Kolar	905	1108	979	962

(Contd.)

(Contd. Table 5)

Districts	Houseless		General Population	
	Sex ratio	*Child Sex ratio*	*Sex ratio*	*Child Sex ratio*
Koppal	924	989	986	958
Mandya	769	965	995	939
Mysore	680	919	985	961
Raichur	922	834	1000	950
Ramanagara	780	1065	976	962
Shimoga	823	824	998	960
Tumkur	830	947	984	959
Udupi	530	1351	1094	958
Uttara Kannada	750	922	979	955
Yadgir	906	925	989	951

Source: Census Reports, 2011.

backward district of Chamarajanagar has lowest share of houseless population in the state. About half of the districts have less than two per cent and remaining districts have two to four per cent share in the state. Thus, it could be concluded that the houseless population is distributed in all districts of the state with variation in the number of houseless.

Variation in Sex Ratio

It is a well-known fact that the sex ratio shows a declining trend for general population due to many socio-cultural factors. The preference for male child continues to prevail both in rural and to some extent in urban areas. The data in Table-5 indicates sex ratio among the houseless at the district level for adults and children aged 0-6 years. It also gives details across districts. It is found that the district of Bijapur (1028 females per 1000 males) has the highest sex ratio in the state.

In contrast, Dakshina Kannada (414) has the lowest sex ratio. Simultaneously, it is observed that the sex ratio for general population is relatively higher for most of the districts with highest sex ratio of 1094 in Udupi and lowest in Bangalore urban district. In case of child sex ratio, houseless population is placed better in some of the districts like Udupi, Chitradurga, Kolar, Hassan, Ramanagara, Bijapur, Dakshina Kannada, Haveri and Chikballapur. These districts have 1000 or more females per 1000 male children. On the other hand, Kodagu is placed in the least position. The state level child sex ratio is 929 while the corresponding data for general population is 948. There are nine districts having less than 900 females per 1000 male children among the houseless. The child sex ratio among the general population is more than 900 for all districts. There are no extreme variations.

Proportion of Child Population

The size and proportion of child population is crucial to understand the demographic transition taking place in the country. It is a fact that the proportion of child population is declining for general population as majority of couples have been limiting family size with one or two children. Of course, the houseless population could differ in this aspect as they may not

Table-6: Proportion of Child Aged 0-6 years Population in Karnataka

Districts	*Houseless Population*		*General Population*	
	0-6 Population	*Per cent*	*0-6 Population*	*Per cent*
Karnataka	11,998	15.6	7,161,033	11.7
Bagalkot	501	20.5	626,269	13.1
Bangalore	1,739	11.3	271,908	14.4
Bangalore Rural	169	14.4	318,406	14.6
Belgaum	1,588	16.5	224,442	13.2
Bellary	404	17.8	283,733	14.7
Bidar	651	21.5	201,654	14.5
Bijapur	283	19.4	132,442	12.4
Chamarajanagar	84	15.5	219,942	11.9
Chikkaballapura	296	16.1	150,115	10.4
Chikmagalur	300	14.8	195,317	12.2

(Contd.)

(Contd. Table 6)

Districts	*Houseless Population*		*General Population*	
	0-6 Population	*Per cent*	*0-6 Population*	*Per cent*
Chitradurga	232	18.4	344,152	14.0
Dakshina Kannada	259	9.2	184,280	11.1
Davanagere	187	15.9	217,731	11.2
Dharwad	347	17.7	182,751	10.4
Gadag	300	19.6	103,160	8.8
Gulbarga	526	16.9	105,328	9.3
Hassan	371	18.8	265,742	9.9
Haveri	330	17.1	1,052,837	10.9
Kodagu	181	11.1	172,685	9.6
Kolar	137	14.5	165,637	9.3

(Contd.)

(Contd. Table 6)

Districts	Houseless Population		General Population	
	0-6 Population	*Per cent*	*0-6 Population*	*Per cent*
Koppal	181	20.4	208,297	10.0
Mandya	397	15.3	54,733	9.9
Mysore	309	13.8	305,561	10.2
Raichur	343	19.9	1,00,648	9.9
Ramanagara	192	17.7	365,372	14.2
Shimoga	403	17.7	190,279	16.2
Tumkur	693	17.1	170,423	11.1
Udupi	87	9.1	132,286	10.5
Uttara Kannada	198	14.9	107,062	10.8
Yadgir	310	19.9	107,841	10.0

Source: Census Reports, 2011.

plan either the number of children or limiting family size. The data provided in Table-6 indicates the proportion of children belonging to 0-6 years. It is found that 15.6 per cent of the houseless population belongs to the category of children aged 0-6 years in Karnataka. On the other hand, the proportion of child population is 11.7 per cent for general population. Demographically forward districts like Udupi, Dakshina Kannada, and Kodagu have least proportion of child population while one-fifth of them belong to child population in backward districts of Bidar, Bagalkot, Koppal, Yadgir, Raichur and Gadag. Thus, it could be stated that the houseless have a tendency to have more children than the other households.

The district-wise distribution of child population has two specific aspects. The first aspect refers to the trend of higher proportion of child population among the houseless as compared to the general population. Most of the districts belong to this category. The second aspect of the trend refers to the districts having relatively lower proportion of child population among the houseless when compared to the general population. There are three districts, namely Bangalore urban, Dakshina Kannada and Udupi having this trend. However, the difference in the proportion of child population is marginal.

Distribution of SC and ST Population

The proportion of SC and ST population is likely to indicate the socio-economic status of the society as these two groups have socially backward and economically poor. Among the houseless population 31.4 per cent belongs to Scheduled Caste and 7.9 per cent belongs to Scheduled Tribe. But, the proportion of SC/ST in general population is 17.1 per cent and seven per cent respectively. The comparative data implies that there is more number of scheduled castes among the houseless. The ratio of scheduled tribes is almost the same among the houseless and the general population.

The district-wise data indicates that about 59.6 per cent of the houseless population belongs to SC in Gadag district. The district of Bidar (56.6 per cent) is placed in the second position followed by Chikmagalore (51.7 per cent) with higher share of

Table-7: Proportion of SCs and STs among Houseless Population

Districts	*Houseless Population*				*General Population*	
	SC		*ST*		*SC*	*ST*
	Number	*Per cent*	*Number*	*Per cent*	*Per cent*	*Per cent*
Karnataka	24105	31.4	6052	7.9	17.1	7.0
Bagalkot	897	36.7	471	4.9	16.9	5.1
Bangalore	2732	17.8	80	3.3	12.5	2.0
Bangalore Rural	369	31.5	139	9.5	21.6	5.3
Belgaum	2258	23.5	150	5.0	12.1	6.2
Bellary	973	43.0	243	14.1	21.1	18.4
Bidar	1711	56.6	27	3.0	23.5	13.8
Bijapur	323	22.2	54	3.5	20.3	1.8
Chamarajanagar	136	25.0	191	9.7	25.4	11.8
Chikkaballapura	608	33.1	284	21.4	24.9	12.5

(Contd.)

(Contd. Table 7)

Districts	Houseless Population				General Population	
	SC		ST		SC	ST
	Number	Per cent	Number	Per cent	Per cent	Per cent
Chikmagalur	1045	51.7	232	12.0	22.3	4.0
Chitradurga	641	50.9	237	10.5	23.4	18.2
Dakshina Kannada	449	16.0	116	9.2	7.1	3.9
Davanagere	464	39.5	101	8.6	20.2	12.0
Dharwad	542	27.6	217	9.5	9.6	4.7
Gadag	910	59.6	68	7.1	16.4	5.8
Gulbarga	921	29.5	155	7.7	25.3	2.5
Hassan	699	35.4	357	8.8	19.4	1.8
Haveri	459	23.8	730	4.8	13.8	8.8
Kodagu	523	32.1	263	10.1	13.3	10.5
Kolar	316	33.4	242	12.3	30.3	5.1

(Contd.)

(Contd. Table 7)

Districts	Houseless Population				General Population	
	SC		ST		SC	ST
	Number	*Per cent*	*Number*	*Per cent*	*Per cent*	*Per cent*
Koppal	328	37.0	146	5.2	18.6	11.8
Mandya	1103	42.4	155	9.5	14.7	1.2
Mysore	577	25.8	299	13.4	17.9	11.1
Raichur	564	32.7	94	17.3	20.8	19.0
Ramanagara	322	29.7	136	4.4	18.8	2.1
Shimoga	1039	45.6	213	13.7	17.6	3.7
Tumkur	2020	49.9	77	8.1	18.9	7.8
Udupi	243	25.5	374	20.4	6.4	4.5
Uttara Kannada	428	32.3	74	6.3	8.1	2.4
Yadgir	505	32.5	127	11.7	23.3	12.5

Source: Census Reports, 2011.

Table- 8: Level of Literacy among Houseless Population

Districts	*Per cent of Literates*						*Difference between two category*
	Houseless Population			*General Population*			
	Total	*Male*	*Female*	*Total*	*Male*	*Female*	*Total*
Karnataka	45.8	53.2	36.2	75.4	82.5	68.1	-29.6
Bagalkot	40.6	50.2	30.0	68.8	79.2	58.4	-28.2
Bangalore	58.7	62.0	53.6	87.7	91.0	84.0	-29.0
Bangalore Rural	47.8	55.5	38.1	77.9	84.8	70.6	-30.1
Belgaum	47.4	57.2	36.3	73.5	82.2	64.6	-26.1
Bellary	44.5	53.9	34.5	67.4	76.6	58.1	-22.9
Bidar	33.2	40.9	23.7	70.5	79.1	61.6	-37.3
Bijapur	47.1	54.1	40.1	67.1	77.2	56.7	-20.0
Chamarajanagar	43.6	49.6	36.5	61.4	67.9	54.9	-17.8
Chikkaballapura	33.0	39.1	26.0	69.8	77.7	61.6	-36.8

(Contd.)

(Contd. Table 8)

Districts	Per cent of Literates						Difference between two category
	Houseless Population			General Population			
	Total	Male	Female	Total	Male	Female	Total
Chikmagalur	46.3	53.4	37.3	79.2	85.4	73.2	-32.9
Chitradurga	43.7	50.8	35.6	73.7	81.4	65.9	-30.0
Dakshina Kannada	58.3	65.3	39.5	88.6	93.1	84.1	-30.3
Davanagere	55.9	61.3	49.2	75.7	82.4	68.9	-19.8
Dharwad	42.0	51.1	31.1	80.0	86.4	73.5	-38.0
Gadag	39.7	48.8	29.2	75.1	84.7	65.4	-35.4
Gulbarga	40.4	47.5	32.7	64.9	74.4	55.1	-24.5
Hassan	34.8	41.9	26.6	76.1	83.6	68.6	-41.3
Haveri	52.1	60.7	40.8	77.4	84.0	70.5	-25.3
Kodagu	45.4	53.8	30.2	82.6	87.2	78.1	-37.2

(Contd.)

(Contd. Table 8)

Districts	*Per cent of Literates*						*Difference between two category*
	Houseless Population			*General Population*			
	Total	*Male*	*Female*	*Total*	*Male*	*Female*	*Total*
Kolar	39.3	44.4	33.3	74.4	81.8	66.8	-35.1
Koppal	34.8	43.5	25.3	68.1	78.5	57.5	-33.3
Mandya	37.7	45.9	26.6	70.4	78.3	62.5	-32.7
Mysore	45.6	51.6	36.3	72.8	78.5	67.1	-27.2
Raichur	32.5	41.9	22.5	59.6	70.5	48.7	-27.1
Ramanagara	36.5	42.4	28.4	69.2	76.8	61.5	-32.7
Shimoga	37.6	45.5	28.0	80.4	86.1	74.8	-42.8
Tumkur	34.6	43.1	24.1	75.1	82.8	67.4	-40.5
Udupi	52.7	57.2	43.2	86.2	91.4	81.6	-33.5
Uttara Kannada	47.6	56.0	36.2	84.1	89.6	78.4	-36.5
Yadgir	23.5	30.1	16.3	51.8	62.2	41.4	-28.3

Source: Census Reports, 2011.

SC among the houseless. The lowest proportion of SCs among houseless is observed in Dakshina Kannada district (16 per cent). Simultaneously, higher ratio of ST population among the houseless prevails in Chikkaballapura (21.4 per cent). The least proportion of ST among the houseless population is found in Bidar and Bijapur districts. Thus, it could be concluded that economically weaker section of the society are more vulnerable to become the houseless.

Literacy Level

Literacy is one of the dimensions of social development. The level of literacy attained by a group indicates the progress attained by a particular group or society. The data relating to literacy among the houseless and the general population is given in the Table-8. It is evident that the literacy among the houseless is less than the literacy level prevailing among the general population in the state. This could be justified by the fact that most of the houseless population is the migrants. The data also indicates that more than half of the houseless populations are illiterates.

The district-wise data is similar to the trend prevailing at the state level. It is found that majority of the districts have lower literacy level among the houseless when compare to the state average. However, there are a few districts having literacy higher than the state average. The data also indicates that the literacy rate of the houseless in all the districts is lower than the literacy level prevailing among the general population. This could be primarily due to the fact that the general population has settled inhabitation with access to educational facilities. On the other hand, most of the houseless population is not only migrants but also unsettled households. They are mostly interested in earning livelihood rather than think of literacy.

Distribution of Working Population

The working population is the backbone of country's economy. It contributes towards economic development of the nation. As per 2011 Census, a less than half of the total general population is working population. Among the houseless, nearly three-fifth of them constitutes the working-age group. The

Table- 9: Distribution of Working Population

Districts	*Working Population*					
	Houseless Population			*General Population*		
	Total	*Male*	*Female*	*Total*	*Male*	*Female*
Karnataka	**57.3**	**64.8**	**47.8**	**45.6**	**59.0**	**31.9**
Bagalkot	57.0	59.7	54.0	43.3	53.8	32.6
Bangalore	56.4	67.5	40.4	44.1	62.0	24.6
Bangalore Rural	56.1	68.5	41.0	46.4	62.0	30.0
Belgaum	65.5	69.2	61.3	44.1	56.6	31.1
Bellary	47.1	53.9	39.7	45.5	56.9	34.0
Bidar	47.9	51.1	44.2	41.2	52.7	29.3
Bijapur	41.3	51.7	31.2	42.6	52.2	32.6
Chamarajanagar	45.9	56.5	34.1	47.2	63.3	30.9
Chikkaballapura	53.1	60.1	45.1	51.0	60.4	41.3

(Contd.)

(Contd. Table 9)

Districts	Working Population					
	Houseless Population			General Population		
	Total	*Male*	*Female*	*Total*	*Male*	*Female*
Chikmagalur	61.7	68.9	52.6	49.7	63.2	36.4
Chitradurga	46.3	54.8	37.4	51.6	61.0	41.9
Dakshina Kannada	75.3	81.5	60.1	47.7	60.0	35.7
Davanagere	46.5	56.0	35.0	45.0	59.4	30.2
Dharwad	54.7	58.5	50.1	42.5	58.0	26.5
Gadag	55.9	61.3	49.8	46.6	57.8	35.1
Gulbarga	52.2	57.0	47.0	42.4	52.2	32.2
Hassan	58.5	66.4	49.7	50.9	63.4	38.4
Haveri	46.5	54.9	36.0	45.7	59.9	30.7
Kodagu	77.8	81.8	70.7	50.3	62.7	38.2
Kolar	47.8	56.9	37.8	46.7	58.5	34.7

(Contd.)

(Contd. Table 9)

Districts	*Working Population*					
	Houseless Population			*General Population*		
	Total	*Male*	*Female*	*Total*	*Male*	*Female*
Koppal	53.2	56.4	49.8	47.1	55.4	38.7
Mandya	62.9	69.4	54.4	48.3	63.6	32.9
Mysore	58.6	68.3	44.4	43.8	61.0	26.3
Raichur	50.6	53.2	47.7	46.8	55.0	38.7
Ramanagara	54.4	62.8	43.7	49.1	62.8	35.0
Shimoga	57.8	63.8	50.6	44.5	60.9	28.1
Tumkur	58.3	63.3	52.3	50.6	62.0	38.9
Udupi	68.4	81.2	44.2	43.6	59.7	28.9
Uttara Kannada	59.5	71.3	43.8	42.3	59.3	25.0
Yadgir	51.3	56.6	45.5	46.6	53.7	39.5

Source: Census Reports, 2011.

proportion of houseless population constituting workforce is greater than the working population in the general population. The absolute numbers are limited among the houseless than among the general population. The primary occupation of houseless is mainly restricted to rag picking and manual jobs. These include the job of sweepers, domestic workers, street vendors, construction and garage workers etc. The houseless population has to take up one job or the other, to make their living.

The district-wise working population has more or less a similar trend. The male-female differentials confirm that in most of the districts, female working population is less than the male working population. This trend prevails among the houseless as well as among the general population. The highest proportion of female working population prevails in Kodagu and the least in Bijapur district for the houseless. The most prominent feature is that the proportion of male working population is more than 50 per cent for all the districts.

Gross Domestic Product (GDP) and Houseless Population

The GDP is a broad measure of economic growth. It is calculated on the basis of the market value of all officially recognised final goods and services produced within a state or country during a specified period of time. Its components are consumption, net exports, government expenditure and investment. The 'gross domestic product at current prices' is GDP at prices of the current reporting period. It reflects the economic status of people of the country. It is an indication of the economic attainment on the part of households. The GDP of districts indicates the level of economic development and correspondingly it contributes towards economic empowerment of individuals or households. It is in this context, an attempt has been made to analyse the relationship between GDP and houseless population.

There is a general notion that the higher levels of GDP for different districts have empowered people to avail all basic necessities including housing. But, the districts with higher GDP (Bangalore Urban and Belgaum) have higher percentage

Table-10: Gross District Domestic Product (GDDP) at Current Prices and Houseless Population

	(GDP) Rs. in lakh	*Per cent of GDP to State*	*Proportion of Houseless Population*
Karnataka	45889437	100.0	4.3
Bagalkote	964557	2.1	3.2
Bangalore	15524765	33.8	20.0
Bangalore Rural	1051094	2.3	1.5
Belgaum	2594739	5.7	12.5
Bellary	1732862	3.8	2.9
Bidar	670649	1.5	3.9
Bijapur	929408	2.0	1.9
Chamarajanagara	429823	0.9	0.7
Chikkaballapura	593676	1.3	2.4
Chikmagalur	820892	1.8	2.6
Chitradurga	760219	1.7	1.6
Dakshina Kannada	2063517	4.5	3.7
Davanagere	1086117	2.4	1.5
Dharwad	1410276	3.1	2.6
Gadag	528511	1.2	2.0
Gulbarga	1113152	2.4	4.1
Hassan	1030449	2.2	2.6
Haveri	722163	1.6	2.5
Kodagu	688964	1.5	2.1
Kolar	901148	2.0	1.2
Koppal	712378	1.6	1.2
Mandya	901066	2.0	3.4
Mysore	2185828	4.8	2.9
Raichur	802084	1.7	2.2
Ramanagara	855017	1.9	1.4
Shimoga	1052682	2.3	3.0
Tumkur	1433483	3.1	5.3
Udupi	1066052	2.3	1.2
Uttara Kannada	859285	1.9	1.7
Yadagiri	404581	0.9	2.0

Source: Directorate of Economics & Statistics, Bangalore, 2011-12.

of houseless population indicating negative correlation. This could be an outcome of in-migration to these districts with higher degree of urbanisation and industrialisation. It is also a fact that the migrants to are invariably the poor wage earners with meager or no resources to rent a place for living. Most of them begin their living in town or city either in temporary shelters or on pavements. In other words, houseless condition could be seen as an outcome of their poor economic condition.

Initiatives in the State

The legislations protect the interests of all citizens. There are a few legislations associated with housing facilities in different states. There also certain legal provisions to protect the life and security of the houseless. The most prominent legal provisions were formulated and issued by the Supreme Court through an order dated 5th May 2010. It directed all the state governments for starting night shelters for the houseless. The Supreme Court also directed state governments to file progress reports regarding relief provided to the houseless. The guidelines issued by the court include: (a) All cities covered under JNNURM and above five lakhs to have one 24 hours, 365 days a year, and homeless shelter with a capacity of 100 persons for every one lakh population, and (b) There should be basic amenities provided in the shelters, which are to include mattress, bedroll, blanket, potable drinking water, functional latrines, first aid, primary health facilities, de-addiction and recreation facilities etc.

The government of Karnataka has acted in accordance with the Supreme Court Order. It has identified eight towns in Karnataka to implement programmes for the houseless in the state. A survey of houseless people has been completed in all the eight towns with the involvement of NGOs. Accordingly, eight City Corporations have taken up the task of providing night shelters to the shelterless people. The identified towns and cities include Bangalore, Mysore, Hubli-Dharwad, Gulbarga, Shimoga, Mangalore, Bellary and Belgaum. A Taskforce has been constituted under Deputy Commissioner of the respective district to look after the pros and cons of the programme. There are 22 temporary night shelters set up in eight city corporations with basic facilities like Toilets, Drinking Water, Food, Blankets/Beds and medical facilities. The cities have also established 24X7 helpline for night shelters and to the citizens.

The Brihat Bangalore Mahanagara Palika (BBMP) has started 10 night shelters for the houseless people in Bangalore city.

However, two of its shelters were closed over the past years due to maintenance problems. According to Supreme Court directive, one shelter is mandatory for a population of one lakh. In accordance with this, Bangalore alone needs about 95 shelters. In the absence of sufficient number of night shelters, thousands of houseless people live on the streets and other public places. There is also the problem of shortage of night shelters in all these places along with the problem of overcrowding in the existing shelters.

Conclusion

The profile of the houseless population in Karnataka indicates that the absolute numbers have been declining over the last few years. However, certain urban centres tend to accommodate an increasing number of houseless. Some of the prominent features of the houseless population include higher sex ratio, higher proportion of child population, large share of SC population, lower literacy rate and more number of females in the working population. Most of the cities and Metropolitan cities have been the most sought of destinations for the houseless. This has been primarily due to anonymity, opportunities to earn livelihood and absence of social exclusion.

The houseless population basically requires security for their survival and living. This needs to be addressed in all possible ways. Generally, the security dimension could include two components. They are protection and promotional measures. The first set of measures refers to the provision of basic facilities so that they will prevent lowering of standard of living among the houseless. The second set of measures refers to a long term objective of eradicating problems associated with the houseless condition. All the welfare programmes for the poor and the housing schemes implemented in the country have been invariably focusing on both these measures.

Acknowledgement

[Author is grateful to his Ph.D guide, Dr B. Vijaya Raghava Rao, former Head, Department of Sociology, St. Joseph's College, Bangalore for his constant support, encouragement, valuable comments and suggestions on this paper.]

References

1. Bhattacharya, 2012, Homeless Pavement Dwellers: A Case Study of their Social Awareness in Kolkata from Human Rights Perspective, *Journal of Exclusion Studies* 2 (1):10- 29, Online published on 3 September, 2012.
2. Devi, Km. Kesi and Goel, N. P., 1994, Houseless population in Uttar Pradesh-A Geographical Analysis: 1961-81, in Goel, N.P. (Eds.) *Readings in Population Geography*, Mohit Publications, New Delhi.
3. Duggal, Bindu, 2009, Snapshot of the Homeless in Ludhiana City: A Reflection of Urban Poverty, *Social Change, 39(2)*: 239-256.
4. Giddens, Anthony, 2006, Poverty, Social Exclusion and Welfare, Sociology (5th Edition), Polity Press, Cambridge.
5. http://www.sccommissioners.org/Homelessness/homelessness.html, downloaded on 26th May 2014.
6. Parvathamma, C and Sathyanarayana, 1987, *Housing, Rural Poor, and their Living Conditions*, Gyan Publishing House, New Delhi.
7. Ray, S.K. *et.al*, 1999, Nutritional status of pavement dweller children of Calcutta City, *Indian Journal of Public Health*, 43 (1): 49-54.
8. Sarikhani, Nahid, 2010, Status of Houseless Women and Children in Karnataka State Based on Census of 2001, *Anthropologist*, 12(2):119-125.
9. Vernon, Elliott, 2014, as 2014 begins; New York City's homeless population continues to grow, 3 January 2014, International Committee of the Fourth International, World Socialist Website.Read more at http://www.brainyquote.com/quotes/keywords/natural_resources_2.html#wcdE1MWD1vppEztZ.99

11

Role of Guidance and Counselling Services in Schools for Universalisation of Elementary Education

Dr Vimal Kishor *and* ***Jyoti Walia***

"There has been evidence throughout history of cycles when the earth gets warmer and cycles when the earth gets colder. We should always be wise stewards of the earth and all of our natural resources. But as a policy-maker, I won't be guided by the global warming propaganda machine. Al Gore - we need you to return your Nobel Peace Prize!"

—Raul Labrador

Introduction

The need for providing education to all children has been recognised by the Constitution since its adoption. The Directive Principles of State Policy casts a duty upon the state to provide free and compulsory education to all children upto the age of fourteen years. In the year 2002, a new Article 21A was inserted in the Constitution which made free and compulsory education a fundamental right to all children in the age group of six to fourteen years. Pursuant to this Amendment, the Parliament enacted this Act (The Right of Children to Free and Compulsory Education Act, 2009) to provide to every child full time elementary education of satisfactory and equitable quality in a formal school.

As the effort to achieve UEE is stepped up, the elementary school classes now cater to many children of school-going age coming from diverse backgrounds. Sometimes it is said that all students do not stand in need of guidance and counselling, and that it is only in the case of deviants that something needs to be done in order to put them on the right path. This has created the misconception that only the deviants need help and guidance and that there is no need to bother about the normal students who would grow up to their own accord without any external help or guidance. But the aim of guidance and counselling is to give each student an equal opportunity to attain perfection as per their potentialities by the best education that can be provided. In view of this, all students need guidance. Even the children who are considered as normal differ in their capacities physical, mental and emotional. They would, therefore, need to be observed and studied in different situations and guided accordingly.

Most of the students leave their schools due to some problems. The problem may be personal, social and educational. If we look backward to the history of getting universalisation of elementary education we generally talks about few problems like dropout, wastage and stagnation. We try to find out the causes of above said problems. But here one question arises in our minds that are we competent to find out these causes? Where we are lagging behind? The answers of these questions are very simple and i.e. lack of competency-based teacher education programme. If a teacher has given proper training about the concept and utilisation of guidance and counselling services in the school from the very beginning of his training then to some extent we will be near to our goal i.e. universalisation of elementary education. Guidance helps the individual in understanding the simple questions to which he fails to respond i.e. what he wants to do? Where he wants to go? How he can best accomplished his work?

Aims and Objectives of Guidance and Counselling Programmes

The aims of the guidance and counselling service are similar to the purposes of education in general to assist the student in fulfilling his basic physiological needs, understanding himself and acceptance of others, developing associations with peers, balancing between permissiveness and controls in the educational setting, realising successful achievement, and providing opportunities to gain independence. The purposes of guidance and counselling provide emphasis and strength to the educational programme. Some specific aims of the school guidance and counseling programme include the following:

1. Checking the wastage and stagnation in education.
2. Realising the aims and objectives of education.
3. Making right educational choices.
4. The need of proper educational adjustment.
5. Providing information to the individual regarding his potentialities, mental abilities, interests and aptitudes.
6. Assist the individual in becoming capable of solving his own problems in his own characteristic manner.
7. Help in making further decisions in the light of success and failures, if required.

Guidance and Counselling Services in Schools

Any guidance programme consists of educational guidance, vocational guidance and personal guidance. The main objective of a school's guidance and counselling programme is to provide a broad spectrum of personnel services to the students. After an adequate diagnosis of a student or a group, guidance programme is properly designed to help him is known as guidance services (Sharma 2009, p. 92). These services include student assessment services, student information services, placement services, follow-up services, and counselling services. These services should be organised to facilitate the growth and development of all students in an integrated manner.

Student Assessment Services

Any type of guidance given to an individual is impossible if there is lack of information. Assessment services help to get the knowledge of an individual related to his personal, social or psychological area. Thus, it is very essential to collect the information and maintain a record of each student's activities e.g. study habits, academic achievement, problems of adjustment, areas of interest etc. It also helps the guidance worker to share this information with parents, teachers, administrators and other professionals. All the other important services like, information, placement, follow-up and counselling services are also based upon this assessment.

Student Information Services

Information services play a very vital role to discover and to develop the dormant potentialities of an individual. A proper choice of course and careers can be made only if the student knows the opportunities available, the requirements of particular courses and careers. Today we live in 21st century and in this competitive or scientific world it is very essential to make the students up-to-date with new innovations, discoveries and inventions. So, this service is designed to provide accurate and current information to the students so that they can make their choices intelligently.

Placement Services

Placement as understood in the guidance field usually indicates assistance offered to the individual in taking the next step, whether toward further training, a job situation, or a different course of study (Chadha 2002, p. 236). This service helps the individual to choose a course of study according to his potentialities. It helps the students to place them on right job based on his interest and capabilities.

Follow-up Services

It is quite essential for the guidance worker to know whether the counsellee has been really benefited by his efforts. This knowledge enables him to bring about changes and improvements (Rani 2004, p. 256). Thus, it is very essential for a guidance worker to maintain contact with former students. The basic aim of the follow-up services is to ensure that the beneficiary has settled and adjusted well in his chosen area or work or educational stream and in life.

Counselling Services

Under the group guidance services, students who require individual attention may be identified. The school guidance programme should be able to cater to the needs of individual, as this is most important. Counselling services are generally for those who are under-achievers, whose academic performance declines; late comers; absentees; needing extra attention for academic achievements; dropouts from the school; have sudden problems at family front; are not able to adjust with the school environment, have adjustment problems with some teachers or classmates; who are shy; show attention getting behaviours; first generation learners; show problems behaviours or have unrealistic aspirations (Agrawal 2006, p. 44). The counselling service is designed to facilitate self-understanding and development through small-group relationships. The aim of such relationships tends to be on personal development and decision making that is based on self-understanding and knowledge of the environment. The counsellor assists the student to understand and accept himself thereby clarifying his ideas, perceptions, attitudes, and goals; furnishes personal and environmental information to the pupil, as required, regarding his plans, choices, or problems; and seeks to develop in the student the ability to cope with/and solve problems and increased competence in making decisions and plans for the future. Counselling is generally accepted as the heart of the guidance service.

The Role of the Teacher

The findings of the researches done in the different aspects of guidance and counselling show that there are insufficient counsellors in schools; inadequate availability of counselling facilities; and that the qualification of guidance and counselling personnel has impact on the quality of guidance services they provide to school students. Moreover, guidance services in schools have, for a very long time, been left in the hands of school teachers who are already over-loaded, and without training in the area of guidance and counselling. Recent developments in Indian education, especially the opportunity for free and universal education, have resulted in a new scale of problems in schools and the nation at large. Many children go to school without knowing what they are supposed to do, and leave school without any idea of what type of jobs or careers they should follow. In addition, they have little understanding of themselves and their socio-economic and political environment. Thus, it is necessary to train the teachers at the very beginning i.e. at the time of their training programme to cope with the different problems of the students. Teachers with a background in guidance and counselling can design and lead activities to meet the developmental needs of children, thus laying the foundation for the necessary attitudes and perceptions towards the self and the world of work. They can also provide the needed support and guidance to children belonging to various strata of society for their sustenance through the elementary school years.

Conclusion

Guidance and counselling services play an integral part in the overall student services department of any elementary or secondary school. In this context, it is extremely important to recognise the role that guidance and counselling play for meeting the needs of students going through the elementary and secondary stages of education. Provision for guidance and counseling services is necessary in view of the fact that today we are facing tremendous changes and modernisation in the society which demands more help to the students who are not alone able to cope with these changes. The aims of guidance and counselling programmes in schools are to assist individuals to develop the ability to understand themselves, to solve their own problems, and to make appropriate adjustments to their environment. Major services include student assessment services, student information services, placement services, follow-up services, and counselling services. These services should be organised to facilitate the growth and development of all students in an integrated manner.

References

1. Agrawal, Rashmi (2006). *Educational Vocational Guidance and Counselling—Principles, Techniques and Programmes* . Delhi: Shipra Publications.
2. Chadha, Satish C. (2002). *Educational and Vocational Guidance and Counselling*. Meerut: R. Lall Book Depot.

3. Rani, Seema (2004). Guidance Services: Their Kinds and Organization. In Seema Rani and R.P. Bhatnagar (Ed.), *Topical Studies in Education.* Meerut: International Publishing House.
4. Sharma, R.A. (2009). *Guidance and Counselling.* Meerut: R. Lall Book Depot.
5. Read more at http://www.brainyquote.com/quotes/keywords/natural_resources_3.html#vrjottO0TsUxmDRE.99

12

Tribal Development through Rubber Plantation: A Technique of Sustainable Development in India

Prof B.K. Panda *and* ***Dr Sukanta Sarkar***

"Ethnic divisions can definitely be exacerbated by a lack of natural resources, but those tensions become violent when people manipulate them for their own political gain."

—Dinaw Mengestu

Introduction

The tribal situation in the country presents a varied picture. Some areas have high tribal concentration while in other areas the tribals are forming only a small portion of the total population. There are some tribal groups, which are still at the food gathering stage, some others practice shifting cultivation, yet other may be pursuing primitive forms of agriculture. The Constitution of India provides for a comprehensive framework for the socio-economic development of Scheduled Tribes and for preventing their exploitation by other groups of society. Areas declared under Fifth Schedule of the Constitution. The Scheduled Areas as per the Constitutional orders have been declared in eight States viz A.P., Bihar, Gujarat, H.P., Maharashtra, M.P., Odisha and Rajasthan. As per the provisions contained in the Fifth

Schedule of the Constitution, various enactment in the forms of Acts and Regulations have been promulgated in the above states for the welfare of scheduled tribes and their protection from exploitation (Ministry of Tribal Affairs, 2014).

The Ministry was set up in 1999 after the bifurcation of Ministry of Social Justice and Empowerment with the objective of providing more focused approach on the integrated socio-economic development of the Scheduled Tribes (STs), the most underprivileged of the Indian Society, in a coordinated and planned manner. The Ministry of Tribal Affairs is the nodal Ministry for overall policy, planning and coordination of programmes for development of ST's. Ministry of Tribal Affairs has undertaken activities that follow from the subjects allocated under the Government of India (Allocation of Business) Rules, 1961. The 1991 Census figures reveal that 42.02 per cent of the Scheduled Tribes populations were main workers of whom 54.50 per cent were cultivators and 32.69 per cent agricultural labourers. About 87 per cent of the main workers from these communities were engaged in primary sector activities. The literacy rate of Scheduled Tribes is around 29.60 per cent, as against the national average of 52 per cent. More than three-quarters of Scheduled Tribes women are illiterate. The Constitution of India incorporates several special provisions for the promotion of educational and economic interest of Scheduled Tribes and their protection from social injustice and all forms of exploitation. These objectives are sought to be achieved through a strategy known as the Tribal Sub-Plan strategy, which was adopted at the beginning of the Fifth Five Year Plan (Ministry of Tribal Affairs, 2014).

Tripura is a tiny and hilly state in the North-East corner of India with an area of 10,491.65 sq.km of land. This state is located in between 22º56' and 24º32' North latitudes and 91º09' and 92º20' East longitudes. The state is bounded on the north by the Cachar district of Assam, on the west by Comilla and Noakhali districts of Bangladesh, on the south by the district of Chittagong and on the east by the Mi Hills of Mizoram covering about 182.4 kms in length from its north to south and 112 kms in breadth from its east to west. Of the total area of Tripura, about 60 per cent consists of hills, hillocks and hilly terrains of flat land stripped with turbulent serpentine and painted grey with barren tracts, lush green hue with wild growth. Only a small portion of the area, about 18 per cent, is under cultivation and the rest is either unavailable for cultivation or is under marginal use.

Who are Tribal?

Article 366 (25) of the Constitution of India refers to Scheduled Tribes as those communities, who are scheduled in accordance with Article 342 of the Constitution. This Article says that only those communities who have been declared as such by the President through an initial public notification or through a subsequent amending Act of Parliament will be considered to be Scheduled Tribes. The list of Scheduled Tribes is State/UT specific and a community declared as a Scheduled Tribe in a State need not be so in another State/UT. The essential characteristics, first laid down by the Lokur Committee, for a community to be identified as Scheduled Tribes are (a) indications of primitive traits; (b) distinctive culture; (c) shyness of contact with the community at large; (d) geographical isolation; and (e) backwardness (Ministry of Tribal Affairs, 2014). The term tribe does not necessarily pertain to a specific group or community as such. It rather denotes a particular stage in the historical evolution of human community marking the era of food producing economy. As such there are some indicators or markers of uniqueness by which it can be said that this tribe differs from the other and vice-versa. But these indicators are not only superfluous but also misleading when one strikes to understand at what stage of development a tribe is. The traditional identification marks such as language, culture, race religion, physical traits etc are no longer held valid.

Situation of Tribal in Tripura

Prior to its merger with the Indian Union, the state of Tripura was a princely state. It claims to the most ancient of all the former princely states in India. Scholars are of opinion that the state has been ruled by the Maharajas for an unbroken period of thirteen hundred years before it acceded to the Indian Union on October 15, 1949. Tripura saw the first influx of refugee in

1941 when communal riots on an unprecedented scale broke out in the district of Dacca of erstwhile East Bengal now Bangladesh. Again after partition of the country in 1947 a large scale influx took place. As a result, the Bengali Hindu population increased tremendously all over the state. This type of migration and settlement of the Bengali Hindus is primarily responsible for demographic disequilibrium between the tribals and the non-tribals in the state (Tribal People of Tripura, 2014).

The total population of Tripura in 2001 Census has been 3,199,203. Of these 993,426 persons do Scheduled Tribes constitute 31.1 per cent of the total population. The state has registered 16.4 per cent decadal growth of ST population in 1991-2001. There are nineteen (19) notified STs in the state. Tripura, the main ST in the state from which the state has earned its name Tripura, alone accounts for more than half of the total ST population of the state (54.7 per cent). Riang (16.6 per cent), Jamatia (7.5 per cent), Chakma (6.5 per cent), Halam (4.8 per cent), Mag (3.1 per cent), Munda (1.2 per cent), Any Kuki Tribe (1.2 per cent), and Garo (1.1 per cent) are the other major STs in terms of population. Along with Tripura they constitute about 97 per cent ST population of the state. The STs in the state are predominantly rural (97.4 per cent). One third of the total ST

Table: 1: Population and Proportion of Major STs, 2001 Census

Sl. No.	*Name of the Scheduled Tribe*	*Total population*	*Proportion to the total ST population Per cent*
1.	All Scheduled Tribes	993,426	100
2.	Tripura	543,848	54.7
3.	Riang	165,103	16.6
4.	Jamatia	74,949	7.5
5.	Chakma	64,293	6.5
6.	Halam	47,245	4.8
7.	Mag	30,385	3.1
8.	Munda	12,416	1.2
9.	Any Kuki Tribe	11,674	1.2
10.	Garoo	11,180	1.1

Source: http://censusindia.gov.in/Tables_Published/SCST/dh_st_tripura.pdf

population of the state is living in West Tripura district (39 per cent), followed by South Tripura (29.1 per cent), Dhalai (16.7 per cent), and North Tripura (15.1 per cent). Dhalai district, however, has recorded the highest proportion (54 per cent) of ST population.

Diverse ethnic groups have been residing in the state. There are 19 (nineteen) notified Scheduled Tribes in the state. They are Tripuri, Reang, Chakma, Jamatia, Halam, Noatia, Mog, Garo, Munda, Kuki, Lushai, Lepcha, Chaimal, Khasia, Urang, Santal, Uchai, Bhil and Bhutia. An increased population and degradation of forests due to repeated shifting cultivation, the jhum cycle has come down. This has adversely affected the productivity and consequently the economic condition of the tribal population. Their socio-economic rehabilitation is a major challenge before the State Government. But the introduction of rubber cultivation after 1975 on a large scale has improved their life style to a significant extent now (Debbarma and Goswami, 2013).

The Tripura Tribal Areas Autonomous District Council is an independent council administering the tribal areas of the state of Tripura, India. Its council and assembly are situated in Khumulwng, a town 26 km away from Agartala, the state capital. In the 2005 elections to the TTAADC the Left Front won 24 seats out of the 28 elected seats and the National Socialist Party of Tripura four. The Left Front and NSPT had contested within the framework of an electoral understanding. Tripura Tribal Areas Autonomous District Council Act 1979 was passed by the Indian parliament after a series of democratic movements launched by the Indigenous People of Tripura, under the provision of the Sixth Scheduled of the Indian constitution. The principle objective behind setting up the Autonomous District Council is to empower the Indigenous People to govern themselves and also to bring alround developments of the backward people so as to protect and preserve their culture, customs and traditions. But it actually came into being from 18 January 1982 and later it was upgraded under the provision of the Sixth Schedule to the Indian constitution with effect from the 1 April 1985 by the 49th amendment to the Constitution of India. The total area of the TTAADC is 7,132.56 km^2 which covers about 68 per cent of the total area (10,491 km^2) of the state. About 70 per cent of land under TTAADC is covered by hilly forest, whereas all the plain cultivable land including all the districts and sub-divisional headquarters are outside the perview of TTAADC. The TTAADC is governed by a council which has 30 members. Out of 30 members, 28 members are elected through adult suffrage while two members are nominated by the Governor of Tripura. Out of 28 elected seats, 25 are reserved for Scheduled Tribes. Under the Sixth Schedule of the Constitution, the Tripura Tribal Areas Autonomous District Council is vested with two types of Powers. These are (a) Legislative Powers and (b) Executive Powers (Tripura Tribal Areas Autonomous District Council, 2014).

Growth of Rubber Plantation

With suitable topography and the acceptability amongst the people, rubber has been identified as one of the thrust areas in Tripura. Tripura is estimated to have about 26,500 hectares under rubber cultivation at present, which is the second largest after Kerala. Also, the yield per hectare and the quality of rubber are also comparable to Kerala's plantations. Infact, the Rubber Board now considers Tripura the *"Second Rubber Capital of India"*. Availability of fine quantity of high quality rubber offers sufficient scope for setting up of rubber-based industries in the state. In order to provide necessary infrastructure of rubber-based projects the state government is in the process of setting up a rubber park (Rubber, 2014).

The people of Tripura were mainly dependent on agriculture for their livelihood and the aborigines of the princely state were primarily depended on the shifting cultivation, commonly known as Jhum cultivation. It is a very primitive, uneconomic and exhaustive form of cultivation. Plough cultivation was unknown to the tribals living in the interior of the state. Only the Bengali and Manipuri cultivators along with some tribal communities living in the plain lands and in the border land of Hill Tipperah were acquainted with the plough cultivations before partition. As J B Ganguly had mentioned that, in the year 1955, there are 25,000 Jhumia families in Tripura and the total area of land under shifting cultivation was 16,00,000 acres, i.e. about 60 per cent of the total area of the territory (Ganguly 1968). On the basis of the report of Census of India 1961, S B K Dev Varman opined that, while the total number of tribal population in Tripura in the year 1961 was 3,60,070, the number of tribal people depending on Jhum cultivation were 1,75,000, (Dev Varman 1999) i.e. half of the tribal population were engaged in Jhum cultivation (De, 2012).

Tripura registered a much lower productivity in per hectare of land of rubber this time, even in terms of national average, despite being the second largest natural rubber producer in the country. The Rubber Board of India blamed aged plantation, unskilled tapers and poor quality of planting materials for the low productivity and suggested fast re-plantation in government-run rubber estates. India has already attained the first position in productivity, fourth in production and sixth in terms of area under rubber cultivation. The RBI has undertaken an initiative to expand rubber cultivation in both the eastern and Konkan coasts, besides the northeastern states. Tripura has the potential for rubber cultivation in 76,637 hectare of land. Rubber cultivation in Tripura is yielding a better life for the tribal poor, who earlier practiced jhum cultivation, and is also contributing Rs 600 crore to the state's economy (The Times of India, April 19, 2013). The North Eastern state currently producing approximately 32,000 tonnes of natural rubber is planning to nearly double the area under rubber plantation to nearly one lakh hectare. Tripura is the second largest rubber producing State in the country after Kerala. While Kerala contributes nearly 90 per cent of domestic production, unofficial estimates suggest Tripura's contribution is limited to approximately eight per cent (Business Line, June 24, 2012.)

Rubber plantation was raised for the first time in Tripura in 1963 by the State Forest Department. Rubber Board responded by opening its first (one-man) office in NE at Agartala in 1967. Tripura Forest Development and Plantation Corporation Ltd. (TFDPC), a State Government Undertaking established in 1976, adopted rehabilitation of degraded forests through rubber plantation as its primary objective. The State Government transferred 10,000 ha of degraded forestland on a long-term lease to TFDPC for raising rubber plantation. Rubber Board upgraded its one-man set up at Agartala to a Regional Office in 1979 for extension and training. Tripura Forest Development and Plantation Corporation Ltd is a premier profit earning Public Sector Company of the Government of Tripura and is the largest rubber plantation unit in the country with more than 11000 ha of rubber plantation. The Latex Processing factory of TFDPC produces annually around 1000 MT of high value Cenex (latex concentrate) and other by-products. TFDPC commissioned a Rubber Timber Processing Unit in 1999 at Negicherra near Agartala with financial assistance from the Indian Council for Forest Research and Education. Its capacity was gradually increased from 500 cum per annum to the current level of 2000 cum. TFDPC implemented a project for rehabilitation of 100 tribal shifting cultivators through rubber plantation at its Warangbari Plantation Centre in West Tripura under a centrally sponsored scheme. The families worked on payment of wages for establishment of their own plantation with the hope of a good earning from sale of latex on maturity.

TRPC created 6079 ha of rubber plantation since 1984 season for 4945 tribal beneficiaries. The plantations raised initially had in general rather a limited success rate. There were cases of desertion and large majority of the failed areas fell victims to grazing and fire from shifting cultivation areas. Certain plantations were abandoned due to problems of free access. The area actually maintained and utilised in 2006-07 was 4509 ha. The picture changed rather fast after some beneficiaries started earning from sale of latex to TRPC. They found the job of tapping much less strenuous compared to farm labour or shifting cultivation, and that the engagement was at the most for two hours a day for a single member of the family was an added attraction (Sinha, 2009). The study conducted by the National Bureau of Soil Survey and Land Use Planning, as a part of exploratory study for the World Bank Assistance revealed that approximately one lakh hectares of land is suitable for rubber plantation in the State. This offers tremendous scope for expansion of rubber plantation. Apex Bodies of Industries and Commerce like CII etc. have also realised the importance and the potential of rubber cultivation in the State. It is also proposed to engage an external agency to study the feasibility to extend rubber cultivation in an area not exceeding 10 per cent of the total geographical area of the State (Economic Review of Tripura, 2011).

Tripura will face stiff competition in retaining second largest natural rubber producing State tag if the production is not enhanced in the years to come. Kerala, which has been contributing 82 per cent raw natural rubber in the country, has already been enjoying first position since a long time while Tripura's position is second with only 8.2 per cent contribution. Tripura will face tough challenge as many States have started showing interest in rubber plantation after suffering losses in the past. Asserting that the rubber cultivation has been changing the face of rural economy of the State, there should be maximum efforts on the part of growers and experts on how to address the low production of natural rubber. There is a general perception that rubber cultivation would harm the environment but the natural rubber in no way harms the environment. Tripura's per hectare rubber production could be 40,000 kg which is almost double to the existing productivity. For this, the farmers need to keep close relation with the experts of the Rubber Board. In turn, the Rubber Board needs to ensure supply of good planting materials. The programme was organised to award best rubber producers' society, best male rubber grower, best female rubber grower and best rubber tapper (The Assam Tribune, 2014).

Rubber Plantation and Tribal Development

Since independence several steps have been taken up by the government and other organisations to rehabilitate the jhumias. In the state, two resettlement divisions for shifting cultivators were set up under the forest department with Headquarters at Manu (North Tripura district) and Jatanbari (South Tripura district). Subsequently, for successful implementation of different programmes a separate department named *'Tribal Rehabilitation in Plantation and Primitive Group Programme'* was created in October 1985. Several efforts from the Central Government (through North Eastern Council), State Government (agriculture, forest, animal husbandry, tribal welfare) departments, Indian Council of Agricultural Research, nongovernmental organisations, etc. are also being made through implementation of various programmes. But, the progress in rehabilitation of the jhumias is very slow. In both South and North Tripura districts, the rehabilitated jhumias have again reverted to jhum. Hunger seems to play the key role behind such incidents. Lack of proper transport and communication, physiographical isolation, adequate technical know how, marketing facilities along with their distressed economic condition are the prime hindrances for jhumia rehabilitation. It is not possible to accomplish such rehabilitation programme single handedly. Scientists, planners, policy-makers, extension workers should join hands and work together. One should also keep in mind that jhumias need food, fibre, shelter and a secure future. Thus, care should be taken to see that these programmes continue not for a day or month but for several years; in the process, bondage will be formed among the urban people, the workers and the jhumias (Paul and Paul, 2006).

One of the most important and recent strategies adopted for Jhumia rehabilitation in Tripura is the raising of rubber plantations. The rubber plantation project was conceived to provide a lucrative alternative to Jhum cultivation. By the time of the ninth five-year plan, the raising of rubber plantation had become one of the main strategies for rehabilitation of Jhumias through the World Bank Aided India Rubber Project. Here the Central Government, Rubber Board and Bank had come together to aid the Tripura government to raise rubber plantations and development itself as the *"Second Rubber Capital of India"*. The Tripura experiment is modelled on the experiences of the Kerala rubber economy, the Rubber for the Poor Project being one of the main efforts to provide tribal and other marginal farmers with a steady income. But in the process of doing this the marginal rubber farmers have been integrated into the global market and the large industrial sector as providers of labour and raw materials. India is the third largest producer of rubber after the Thailand and Indonesia, of this 90 per cent of the rubber is grown in Kerala. The 1980s had however seen the expansion of rubber into non-traditional zones of which Tripura was the most important. The rubber option looked attractive because it had the potential of providing Jhumias with a substantial income along with cash crops like pineapple and pepper which were grown with it. This use of tilla or wastelands for cash crops would also enable the Tripura government to increase its revenue potential by tapping the large industrial and export markets (Das *et al.* 2012). Besides rubber, rubber plants have many other uses e.g.:

1. *Timber:* After economic exploitation of rubber for about 30 years its timber will be a good source of furniture timber.
2. *Rubber seed oil:* Rubber seed kernel is used for extraction of oil, which is abundantly used as lubricant, and for soap and paint industries and the cake as a good fertiliser and poultry feed.
3. *Honey:* Mature rubber plantations are the potential source of honey. Honeybees collect large quantities of nectar from extra floral nectarines at the swollen tip of the petiole.
4. Affluent or latex processing wastes and residues can be used as fertiliser and making biogas for power.
5. *Land improvement:* Every year fallen leaves add six to seven tons per hectare of biomass. Moreover, rubber roots make a very good net spreading in the top soil up to a depth 1 to 1.5 m and increase the porosity of the soil.
6. *Carbon sink*: Rubber is a very preferred fast growing multipurpose species for quick afforestation. It acts, as a good 'carbon sinks' will be helpful in reducing global warming.
7. *Eco-friendliness:* Rubber plantations have a green image and are inherently environment friendly. Properly managed plantations are self-sustainable ecosystems and could maintain a fair degree of biodiversity. Rubber plantations do support different plant species.

Conclusion

With suitable topography and the acceptability amongst the people, rubber has been identified as one of the thrust areas in Tripura. Tripura is estimated to have about 26,500 hectares under rubber cultivation at present, which is the second largest after Kerala. Rubber plantation was raised for the first time in Tripura in 1963 by the State Forest Department. Rubber Board responded by opening its first (one-man) office in NE at Agartala in 1967. One of the most important and recent strategies adopted for Jhumia rehabilitation is the raising of rubber plantations. The rubber plantation project was conceived to provide a lucrative alternative to Jhum cultivation. By the time of the ninth five-year plan, the raising of rubber plantation had become one of the main strategies for rehabilitation of Jhumias through the World Bank Aided India Rubber Project. Various government agencies like TRPC, TFDPC, Rubber board are trying to expand the rubber plantation in tribal areas and increasing the scope of additional income.

References

1. Bimal Debbarma and Pranay Jyoti Goswami (2013). *Indian Journal of Dalit and Tribal Studies and Action* Vol.1 Issue 2, No.2, pp. 18 to 24.
2. *Business line (June 24, 2012).* Tripura plans to double area under rubber, Retrieved from http://www.thehindubusinessline.com/industry-and-economy/agri-biz/tripura-plans-to-double-area-under-rubber/article3566075.ece
3. Das, S; Chaudhury, S; and Roy, A. (2012). The Success Story of Rehabilitation of Jhumias in Tripura- A Study on Baramura-Deutamura Range, *Research Inventy: International Journal of Engineering and Science,* Vol. 1, Issue 10, pp. 25-29.
4. De, N. (2012). Partition of India and its immediate effects on jhum cultivation of Tripura, *IRJC: International Journal of Social Science and Interdisciplinary Research*, Vol.1 Issue 8, August 2012, P.188.
5. *Economic Review of Tripura, 2010-2011*, Retrieved from http://www.destripura.nic.in/review2010_11.pdf
6. *Ministry of Tribal Affairs (2014).* Retrieved from http://tribal.nic.in/Content/IntroductionScheduledTribes.aspx
7. Paul, P. and Paul, P. (2006). *The jhumias of Tripura may be frustrated*, Retrieved from http://www.iisc.ernet.in/currsci/feb252006/475.pdf
8. Rubber (2014). *Indian State: Tripura, Ministry of External Affairs, Government of India*, Retrieved from http://www.indiainbusiness.nic.in/know-india/states/tripura1.htm
9. Sinha, A. (2009). *Prospect of rubber plantation in NE region with special reference to the state of Tripura,* Retrieved from http://

thetripurafoundation.org/art-rubber-prospect-tripura-and-north-east

10. *The Assam Tribune (2014).* Tripura to face tough fight in rubber production, Retrieved from http://www.assamtribune.com/scripts/detailsnew.asp?id=dec0911/oth05
11. *Tribal people of Tripura (2014).* Retrieved from http://www.tripurainfo.com/info/ATripura/Tribal.htm
12. *Tripura Tribal Areas Autonomous District Council (2014).* Retrieved from http://en.wikipedia.org/wiki/Tripura_Tribal_Areas_Autonomous_District_Council
13. Read more at http://www.brainyquote.com/quotes/keywords/natural_resources_3.html#hJ3vQwTvJgW7WBkd.99

13

Web Based Library Services at IIM Shillong: A Case Study

Dr Sudhir Kumar Jena, Dr Manaswini Patra,
and ***Cliff Dkhar***

"The natural state of motherhood is unselfishness. When you become a mother, you are no longer the center of your own universe. You relinquish that position to your children."

—**Jessica Lange**

Introduction

Library is an importance source for enriching knowledge in modern era. Libraries continue to evolve from their former, somewhat passive presence on campus to be more active participants in the educational process. It is also known as Knowledge resource centres. This change happens primarily during the past two decades when rapid advances in information technologist occur. It is the acknowledgment that libraries must adapt to a new paradigm in delivery of services of student wants and prospect and a new model of providing relevant and meaningful services. Librarians play vital role in developing the teaching educational activities in library. Advances in information technologies have resulted in information glut. It is true that the width and breadth of information has expanded exponentially but the depth of it is decidedly lacking. This poses a major test for libraries. Students lack the basic information literacy skills to find, critically evaluate, synthesize, and apply good information in a meaningful way despite having a plenty of information at their fingertips. The problem for libraries is to carry on to push information literacy as a key plan, and to find new ways of teaching information literacy skills. Advances in information technologies also give exceptional education chance for librarians. The IIM Shillong web portal was initiated in the year 2009. It is a simple web site for students and it provides customised and personalised online services and the portal displays fine-grained content that corresponds to their academic status, area of study, and research and development.

What is Web Portal?

Web Portal can be define as an active website for a precise spectators that aggregates an array of content and provides an array of services. They are the sites on the World Wide Web. It basically provides personalised capabilities to their visitors. They are structured to use distributed applications, different numbers and types of middleware, and hardware to provide services from a number of different sources. Content linked in library portal is superior to the open access content available on the Web. Authentication software, commonly known as Web Access Management are accessible that permit the library to preside over the access to licensed electronic content. Commonly referred to as simply a portal, it is a website that offers access to a broad array of resources and services of libraries such as e-journals, online databases, Web OPAC, new additions and any other static information about library services.

Need for Library Web Portal

Web is a very large hypertext information space. In that different types of users can search and find information in different domains. With the help of general directories and search engines, users may be able to locate and access needed information to some extent. Search engines provide a convenient way for information searching but users often find themselves facing the information overload problem. So quantity and as well as quality dazzles the user and the user most often inadvertently loses his / her track. A carefully designed web portal avoids this pitfall by weaving together e-resources to provide coherent view of the discipline. This also assists them in knowledge sharing activities. Librarians have understood that multiplication of e-resources is a severe problem for end users. Users find it difficult to decide which is the most appropriate database or resource to search for information relevant to their need. Web portals are the websites which solve this problem by providing access to all relevant e-resources at one point, thus relieving the user from the hassles of accessing different sources from different websites.

Review of Literature

Researchers try to tapering the obtainable research in web-base services. The developments in information and communication technologies and their succeeding assimilation in library and information science have enforced information professionals to alter the way they are working at present. Because of their reputation with the users, an irresistible attention is being given to the web-based information services in libraries. Engineering college library, by developing homepage, can disseminate a wide range of information to users' community. It is the best way to keep users abreast about newest developments of library resources and services with the opening of pictures, graphics, 3D images, audio and video. A lovely homepage of the library could be developed which will really help the users to have a complete knowledge of library. The digitisation of the library collections or e-resources has given a new mission to librarians in terms of providing training to the users in the skills needed to determine access to in-house as well as isolated materials, and in evaluating the retrieved information. In a digitised library, an engineering college librarian is required to be a dynamic player retrieving information from vendors, publishers, web sites, and other e-resources on the one hand; and processing and transmitting it to the users on the other hand. The information has to be conveying to library staff by guidance and improvement of skills. Kanaujia and Satyanarayan had conducted a level of awareness and claim web-based learning environment among Science and Technology information seekers. The main findings of the study exposed that 49.2 per cent users browsed the Web for more than two to four hours and 14 per cent for more than five hours a day. The study further showed that 36.6 per cent users consulted e-journals regularly on the Internet, 40.4 per cent used Internet for consulting technical reports, 24.8 per cent to find online databases and 10.4 per cent for telnet service.

Knowledge Centre of IIM Shillong

The Knowledge Resource Centre (Library) of RGIIM, Shillong which is one of the most contemporary and tech savvy libraries in the country, has started functioning right from the time of inception of the Institute. Its goal is to create the library one of the most animated and creative branches of the Institute so that it may keep pace with the comprehensive, active and equipment enabled information age, and convene the expectations of its end users.

Fig.1. Knowledge Resource Center, IIM Shillong.

With the above aim in view, within a short span of time, we have acquired an excellent collection of management related books, journals and non-book materials, which we consider as greatest asset. The library is maintaining separate collection of Reference Books, Text Books, General books, Working Papers and other documents, whereas the non-book collection consists of video cassettes, Compact Discs, etc. Faculty members are also requested to make regular requisition of latest books which will add value to the Knowledge Centre and equip the library with the latest collection of books. The library has the latest collection of periodicals, magazines and newspapers. We have also begun to modernise the Centre with rich collection of both Indian and Foreign Journals for which the process in underway. Journals are available both online as well as in printed volumes. The Library is also prepared with the most recent E-Resources (E-Books, E-Journals, and Data-base) such as CMIE – Prowess, ISI-Emerging Markets, ProQuest, and EBSCO – Business Source Complete. We also have access to HBR cases which are broadly used by all students and faculty members. The Library also has a number of extraordinary compilation of (i) EXIM Bank, (ii) World Bank, and (iii) Harvard Business Review. The Knowledge Centre also connected the IIM Consortia Cross Sharing of E-Journals with three Publishers: (i) Taylor and Francis, (ii) Wiley-Blackwell and (ii) Springer. The KRC arranged for a Tie up with:

1. AIMS (Association of Indian Management Schools).
2. American Library, Kolkata =ASSOCHAM (Association of Chamber of Commerce).
3. British Council Library, Kolkata.
4. Exim Banks.
5. All the Indian Institute of Managements, IIMs.
6. HBSP (Harvard Business School Publishing).
7. IGCC (Indo-German Chamber of Commerce).
8. AACSB (Association to Advanced Collegiate Schools of Business).

The varied kind of services that we make accessible in our Knowledge Centre apart from lending are the References Services, CAS (Current Awareness Services), SDI (Selective Dissemination of Information), Reprographic Services, Information Alert Services (E- Mail Services), Lest-you-miss (newspaper clippings) services, and ILL (Inter Library Loan) services and services. All the above mentioned online facilities are available through the Knowledge Centre E-Portal of the Institute.

The most important success as far as the library facilities are concerned is related to the Library Automation Services. We are one of the few libraries in the country which is fully automated and the VTLS software with RFID Library Management System is being used for the reason of house-keeping of library activities and networking systems such as intranet, internet and Wi-Fi. The RFID technology makes the Circulation of books easier as the end-users can do the ISSUE and RETURN through the KIOSK and DROP BOX machine respectively, along with the use of smart proximity cards. The whole Library is covered by CCTV. This latest technological environment enables the library to provide its clientele in an improved, quicker and in a more competent way. The five different levels of automation which needs to be highlighted are as follows:

1. Library cataloguing system - OPAC for easy access by users.
2. House-keeping operations and networking.
3. Development of CD-ROM library/products.
4. E-mail System and Internet.
5. RFID (Rapid Radio Identification) - for security purposes.

The Library of IIM Shillong is open to latest and pioneering ideas and we are strong-minded to create our Knowledge Centre one of the top and user friendly libraries in the country.

Elements of an Ideal Library Web Portal

The ideal library contains of seven C's that any web portal must have are the seven attributes that help in building an ideal portal for any library.

1. *Context:* Portal should have an aesthetical, useful look and feel. The colours chosen, the layout, etc. should be stimulating and inviting the users.
2. *Contents:* Portal should give link to another source only after its authenticity and credentials are verified. Users tend to look the references provided by institution portals as the authoritative and genuine ones. So the content on the portal must adhere to confident strict evaluation policy.
3. *Community:* The community or group of users for whom the portal is devoted is the third important attribute to be considered before deciding the content and layout of the portal. The specific needs of the users are also kept in view while designing the portal.

4. *Customisation:* It is the portal capacity to suit every individual in the organisation. Though it is slight hard considering the multitude of areas and desires of people in the organisation, some extent of personalisation can be achieved in providing different interfaces. An ideal portal must permit the users to customise their interface; select databases of interest; and create current awareness profiles.
5. *Communication:* It's the way the user communicates his needs to the portal and how the portal responds and satisfies the users' queries. Portal must have options for searching the portal content. Easy navigation is one of the hall marks of an ideal portal.
6. *Connection:* This is the level of linkages between the portal and other sites mentioned in the portal. It's the networking within the portal site. The links provided must be checked on a regular basis, and any broken link must be corrected immediately.
7. *Commerce:* This refers to the real sale of products and services. This is meant for commercial organisations and this attribute may also have significance to academic institutions but for libraries, its relevance is very limited.

Need for Web Based Library Services

A modern library can make its own web site because of following reasons: Facilities and encourage library use

1. To provide the fundamental information about the library and its services.
2. To allow online access to local services.
3. To make gateway to networked information services.
4. To set up integrated push based services.

Basic Advantages of Web Based Services

These are the advantages of web based services:

1. To save the valuable time of the scientist.
2. Availability of less number of library staff to carry out the library works and services.
3. Less dependence upon the library staff for getting the essential information.
4. Location of laboratories/ departments in different places in the campus.

5. Immediate and elaborate information requirements for R&D activities.
6. Information for decision making in MIS.
7. Multifold increase of the price of books and journals.
8. Availability of information in unusual places and also in different formats.
9. Cut in library funds.

Future of Web Based Library Services

The horizon for E-based library services is wide open and the services shall continue to enlarge offering:

1. More number of full-text electronic journals. Eventually, indexes that do not now include full text will begin to do so, or link to external resources. OCLC's Electronic Collections Online may mature as such a service.
2. Better bibliographic access to full-text periodicals either through cataloging, databases, or vendors that aggregate access. Savings on Inter library loan and user convenience are incentives.
3. Electronic reserves, either locally or through vendors who simplify copyright issues. More web forms for user feedback, and perhaps a virtual librarian who interacts in real time chat or video conferencing. While there's nothing like a simple phone call, the virtual librarian wouldn't have to be in the library.
4. Well-developed user education modules or tutorials, especially to support independent exploration of library and web resources. Library web authors are getting more sophisticated and able to take advantage of appropriate technologies and software.
5. More document delivery services to distance education or commuter students. This will not be cheap, but it's the type of thing that users want. Meltdown or solutions to the "printing problem" when "everything" is on the Web and nobody is using microfiche or printed periodicals.
6. More resources through creative consortia purchasing. Statewide cooperation will become more common. SOLINET has also been a leader in coordinating contracts for its members.

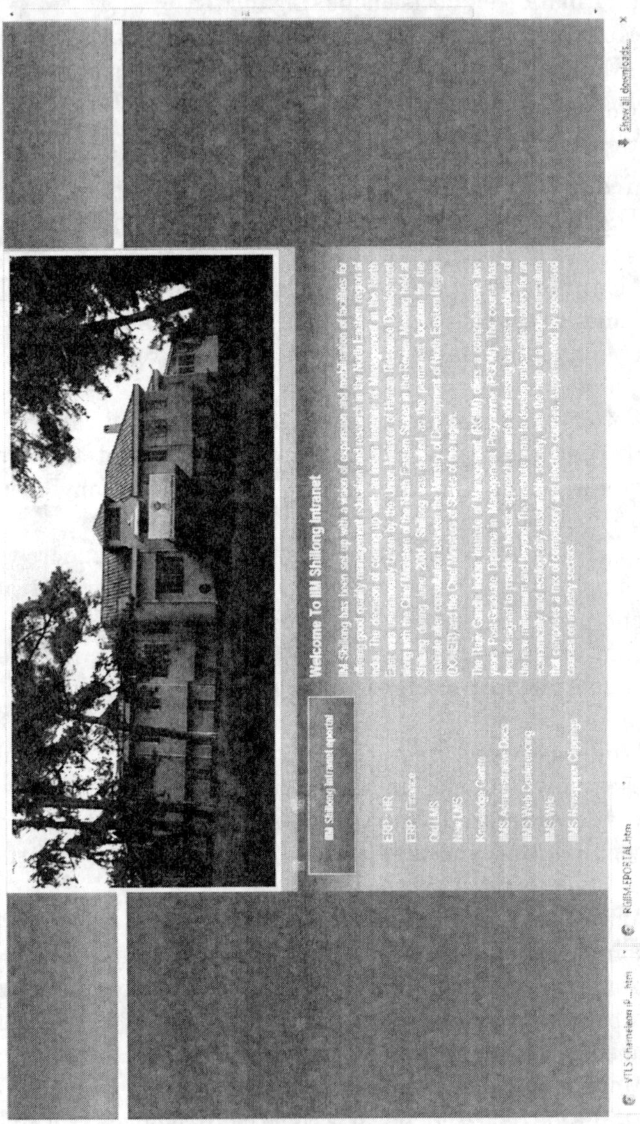

Fig. 2. Library web portal of IIM Shillong.

7. Experiments with customised interfaces that organise resources for individual library users. People seem to either like or dislike a portal-style interface, finding them comfortingly personal or restrictive.
8. Somebody will have to figure out how to keep Word users from saving print documents as XML, without thinking in terms of Web, not print, space. XML will be embraced as a way to control page appearance and behaviour, but it will take a while for people to figure out how to use it well.

Library Web Portal of IIM Shillong

The web offers libraries the possibility to develop into disseminators of information through creating Web Sites. Recognising that the Web site often serves as the face of the library and the first access point, the IIM Shillong began the process in early 2009 to guarantee that the Web Site content not only remains contemporary but adds value and showcases the Library's resources. The Web-based resources are the most frequently used resources which are considered to be the fastest and simplest way to retrieve information. The library website http://rgiimshillong.eportal was launched during the year 2009. This web site gives information on Government, Education, Universities, Scholarships, Competition Exams, Examination results, Employment, Other Library Links, etc. The objective is not only to construct digital content into the site but also to make sure that information on the site is updated in a timely fashion.

Web Based Library Services at IIM Shillong

Considering the rising effect of Information and Communication Technologies (ICT), Web technologies and Database technologies, the IIM Shillong has set up a Digital Library in early 2009 to disseminate web based library services to the right reader at the right time. The Knowledge Resource Centre IIM Shillong offers a new way of organising information and publishing it over the internet or on CD-ROM and also provides the following information online. The library also have new books list, serial collections, newspapers, periodicals, print journals reference and special collections like; maps, videos, government publications, music scores, audio cassettes, top news stories, Wall Street Journal, New York Times, Time Magazine, Rolling Stone, Newsweek, IRS Documents. Database Links such as; E-Book Cambridge, EBSCO - Business Source Complete, Insight, ISI Emerging Market, ProQuest, CMIE - Prowess, CMIE Economic Outlook, Datamonitor 360, Indiastat, CapitalinePlus, WorldBank,, Marketline, Euromonitor, Crisil. Through IIM Consortium; Springer link, Wiley-Blackwell, Taylor & Francis Online Journals / Magazines: Economic & Political Weekly (EPW), Capital Market American Accounting Association (A.A.A) SAGE etc.

Objectives of the Study

The objectives of the study are:

1. To study the availability of institutes' websites and the extent of library information hosted on the websites;
2. To find out whether the libraries have a direct hyperlink on their college homepage;
3. To study the regular use of the Internet by users and their frequency of visit to institutes' websites;
4. To identify the library transactions that users wish to carry out using the Internet;
5. To investigate whether the college libraries have a static or dynamic website;
6. To measure the extent of the web-based services offered by the Knowledge Centre IIM Shillong.

Hypothesis

The researcher has undergone three major hypotheses they are:

1. Institutes have to try to attract the library users to their websites as they provide only static information about library and its services;
2. The majority of the users in the institutes use the Internet on a regular basis;
3. Most of the transactions users do at the library should be carried out through the intranet at their convenience.

Methodology

The present study is based on both primary and secondary data. This paper is based on part of a questionnaire survey

Table 1: Details of Library Materials

Sl. No.	*Items*	*Total in Nos.*	*Remarks*
1.	Books	10,630 (Reference books only)	We have been issuing all the text books to all the students from the beginning of the session.
2.	Journals (print)	52	
3.	Journals (online)	14 (Databases)	Through consortium
4.	Magazines (print)	18	
5.	News Papers	16	Including Employment news
6.	CD/DVD	600	
7.	Back Volumes	300	
8.	Project Report	312	

conducted for these studies at Knowledge Centre IIM Shillong. This survey covered the web-based library development of IIM Shillong to understand and measure the impact of information technology applications on library resources and services. Different questionnaires were administered to all the users (faculty, staff members and students) to understand the usage pattern of the Internet and the web-based library services that are expected. The questionnaire was designed to be quick and easy to complete. Among others, the questionnaire specifically contained questions on.

Extent of Information of the Websites

The Knowledge Resource Centre IIM Shillong has presents the lots of information on the institutes' websites. It is observed that almost all the general information about library is available on its websites. The following information is mentioned below:

1. General Information.
2. Features of Knowledge Centre, IIM Shillong.
3. Round-the-clock reference service.
4. Online resources.
5. Exclusive newspaper section.
6. Collection details of Library Materials.

The following materials are available in the GGI's library. These are represented below table.

The Knowledge Centre, IIM Shillong Offers Customised Library Services Like:

1. Reference service for reference books, journals, magazines, back volumes, Project Report, etc.
2. Digital library services.
3. Reprographic Services.
4. Newspaper clippings.
5. E-Journals.
6. E-Books.
7. On-line public access catalogue.

The Majority of the Users in the Institutes Use the Internet on a Regular Basis

The Internet provides much information in just a moment. Since anyone can publish information on the internet, it is essential to carefully assess the websites before using the information in reports, projects, discussions, and activities. A good educational institute website, this is a subject which not so exhaustively researched to end up for conclusion about how good is an educational website of any educational institute, teachers may feel overwhelmed when it comes to evaluating websites of their institute but generally are the aware of various criteria that governs evaluate a good website of an institute. Just like it is vital to select a good book by the educator to give to their students, a good educational website has certain criteria to be considered before it is presented to the students of the education institutes.

The Users of Knowledge Centre IIM Shillong were asked about their Internet usage. The below mentions that an overwhelming number of faculty members 25 (100 per cent), Staff Members 38 (95 per cent) and 270 (98 per cent) students have indicated the use of the internet on a regular basis. It is also observed that five per cent of staff members and two per cent of students indicated that they do not use the internet regularly.

Table 2. Regular Use of Internet

Faculty Members	*Staff Members*	*Students*
25 (100%)	38 (95%)	270 (98%)

Library Transaction Carried out through the Web

To fulfill the requirement of our study, a survey have been taken from users (faculty, staff and students), what the library transaction they wish to carry out at their ends through the web or internet. About 96 per cent faculty members and more than 55 per cent students indicated that they wish to search books' database includes the both text and reference. Only very few no of faculties 48 per cent faculty members and 69 per cent students indicated that they wish to know the availability of a particular document. About 48 per cent faculty members and 69 per cent students wish to do a refined search of books (like subject, titles, author(s), Publisher, Year of publication...etc), using all possible approaches. No doubt reservation of books through the

Table 3: Library Transactions Carried Out Using the Internet

	Faculty Members	*Staff Members*	*Students*
Search database of the books (both Text and Reference)	24 (96%)	01 (2.5%)	150 (55%)
To know the availability of a books	12 (48%)	02 (5%)	190 (69%)
To search books using all approaches (like subject, titles Authors, Publishers, Year of Publications, Publishers...etc.)	12 (48%)	02 (5%)	190 (69%)
Reservation of a book	NA	NA	220 (80%)
Additional services Provided by library	05 (20%)	00	200 (73%)

Web OPAC is available. This facility is provided to the student at the time of non-availability of the books, it is not provided to the faculty. More than 80 per cent of the students have availed the reservation facility.

From the above it is clear that about 20 per cent faculty members and 73 per cent of the student would access the website to know more about services rendered by library. A close scrutiny and comparison of responses reveals that most of the faculty members and students agree with each other that maximum number of transactions they wish to carry out using the Internet.

Scope and Limitations

The scope of the study is limited to the web-based services expected from Knowledge Centre; IIM Shillong. The limitation is that it covers only the day-to-day library transactions like online catalogue, reservations, etc. Access to online resources also includes because they will have to be web-based only.

Future Scope

Library Web services will continue to expand, offering more full-text electronic journals. Eventually, indexes that do not now include full text will begin to do so, or link to external resources. OCLC's Electronic Collections Online may mature as such a service better bibliographic access to full-text periodicals either through cataloging, databases, or vendors that aggregate access. Savings on Interlibrary Loan and user convenience are incentives. Electronic reserves, either locally or through vendors who simplify copyright issues. More Web enabled forms for user feedback, and perhaps a virtual librarian who interacts in real time quick chat or video conferencing. While there's nothing like a simple phone call, the virtual librarian wouldn't have to be in the library. Well-developed user education modules or tutorials, especially to support independent exploration of library and Web resources. Library Web authors are getting more sophisticated and able to take advantage of appropriate technologies and software.

Conclusion

Innovations in information and communication technologies have a profound impact on every sphere of academic activity.

Library and information management is not an exception to this. Business and management libraries have so far not adapted the innovations of the Internet and networking to the fullest extent. Earlier, card catalogue was called as the Mirror to the Library. Now in this age of the Internet, it is the library portal that is being called as the Mirror of the Library. Library portal reflects the strengths and weaknesses of the libraries very effectively. They are also the tool through which libraries are trying to reach out to the tech-savvy user. Libraries shall make relentless efforts to provide web-based customised services to their users.

Library resources on the net are plentiful, and it requires some effort to organise them, since the services and information are often interrelated and get mixed up. Thus, portals are very instrumental in enhancing access to e-resources that a library holds. Since the IIM Consortium and INDEST-AICTE Consortium are providing accesses to e-resources for all IIMs through the portal. The portal trend is fast catching for accessing e-resources and information services. The needlepoint for any library is to engage in the development of customised portals and provide web based library services for enhancing access to library resources and services. The survey has revealed that, the Knowledge Resource Centre, IIM Shillong has the full potential to develop the library.

References

1. H. Pienaar, "Design and Development of an Academic Portal", Libri, Vol. 53 No. 2, 2004, pp. 118-29.
2. N. Joint, "Evaluating the Quality of Web Portals", Library Review, Vol. 54 No.6, 2005, pp. 337-341.
3. M. Myhill, "A MAP for the Library Portal: Through the Labyrinth of Online Information Sources", Online Information Review, Vol. 29 No.1, 2004, pp. 5-17.
4. Mankad, Manish, "Web Portal Elements", Proceedings of BOSLA Workshop on ICT for Librarians, Tata Institute of Social Sciences, Mumbai, 2004, pp. 6-12.
5. Jena, Sudhir Kumar and others "Digital Information Literacy among the Users of the Knowledge Centre, IIM Shillong: a study". Asian Academic Research Journal of Multidisciplinary

(AARJMD) International journal of Asian Academic Research Associates. Vol. 1, Issue 8, pp. 235-246.

6. AICTE process hand book (2012-2013).
7. Bhatnagar, Anjana, Web Based Library Services, 3rd Convention PLANNER -2005, Assam Univ., Silchar, 10-11 Nov., 2005.
8. Cox, A., and Yeates, R. (2003). Library portal Solutions. Aslib Proceedings, 55(3), pp. 155-165.
9. Hatem Nour El-Din Electronic Resources@EMRO.
10. Hatua, Sudip Ranjan, Web Based Library and Information Services, DRTC Seminar.
11. Kacherki, Umeshareddy, New Dimensions in the Management of Engineering College Libraries.
12. Kanmadi, Satish, Web-Based Services Expected from Libraries: A Case Study of Management Institutes in Mumbai City, Weblog, Volume 3, Number 2, June, 2006.
13. Kanaujia, S., and Satyanararayana, N.R. (2003). Status of awareness and demand of web-based learning environment among the S&T information seekers. International Conference on Mapping Technology on Libraries and People Organised by INFLIBNET, 13-15 February 2003, Ahmadabad, pp. 587-593.
14. Krishnamurthy, M., and Chan, W.S. (2005). Implementation of library portals for information resources: A case study of the Indian Statistical Institute, Bangalore (ISIB). International Information and Library Review, 37(1), pp. 45-50.
15. McGeary, T. (2005). My Library: The library response to the campus portal. Online Information Review, 29(4), 365-373.
16. Mulla, K.R. and Chandrasekhar (Spring, 2006): E-Resources and Services in engineering colleges library-A Case Study, (Vol. 7), No. 1.
17. Nagabhushanam, V, Web based Library services in University Libraries Web.
18. Rao, Y. Srinivasa and Choudhury, B.K. Availability of Electronic Resources at NIT Libraries in India: A Study Sharma, Chetan, Use and Impact of E-Resources at Guru Gobind Singh Indraprastha University (India): A Case Study.
19. Shukla, Akhandand, and Tripathi, Aditya, Establishing content awareness evaluation criteria for library websites: a case study of Indian Academic of Library Websites, Annals of Library and Information studies, Vol. 57, December 2010, pp. 403-416.

20. Tenopir, Carol, Use and Users of Electronic Library Resources: An Overview and Analysis of Recent Research Studies, Council on Library and Information Resources, Washington, D.C. 2003.

21. Read more at http://www.brainyquote.com/quotes/keywords/natural.html#BvHZmt2ICpkluQT1.99

14

Natural Resource Management: A Source of Sustainable Livelihoods

Dr P.K. Pandey** and **Dr Sukanta Sarkar

"Life is a series of natural and spontaneous changes. Don't resist them - that only creates sorrow. Let reality be reality. Let things flow naturally forward in whatever way they like."

—Lao Tzu

Introduction

Natural resources are naturally occurring substances that are considered valuable in their relatively unmodified form. A natural resource's value rests in the amount of the material available and the demand for it. Natural resources are natural capital converted to commodity inputs to infrastructural capital processes. They include soil, timber, oil, minerals, and other goods taken more or less from the Earth. Both extraction of the basic resource and refining it into a purer, directly usable form, are generally considered natural-resource activities, even though the latter may not necessarily occur near the former. Natural Resources is a specialist supplier of recruitment and project staffing services to the global Oil, Gas, Petrochemical and Construction industries. At one point, countries like Brazil, Canada, Australia and those in Latin America were on par with India when it came to the utilisation of natural resources. Mining has faced multiple problems in recent years. There have been problems in acquiring land for new mines and delays in government approvals. Increased judicial scrutiny following corruption scandals in the allotment of mining blocks and environmental degradation caused by illegal mining has made matters worse.

Natural resources occur naturally within environments that exist relatively undisturbed by humanity, in a natural form. Natural resources are materials and components (something that can be used) that can be found within the environment. Every man-made product is composed of natural resources. Some natural resources such as sunlight and air can be found everywhere, and are known as ubiquitous resources. Natural resources are useful raw materials that we get from the Earth. They occur naturally, which means that humans cannot make natural resources. Some examples of natural resources and the ways we can use them are listed in the Table 1 below.

Natural Resource	*Products or Services*
Air	Wind energy, tires
Animals	Foods (milk, cheese, steak, bacon) and clothing (wool sweater, silk shirt, leather belt)
Coal	Electricity
Minerals	Coins, wire, steel, aluminum cans, jewelry
Natural Gas	Electricity, heating
Oil	Electricity, fuel for cars and airplanes, plastic
Plants	Wood, paper, cotton clothing, fruits, vegetables
Sunlight	Solar power, photosynthesis
Water	Hydroelectric energy, drinking, cleaning

Types of Natural Resources

There are various methods of categorising natural resources, these include source of origin, stage of development, and by their renewability. On the basis of origin, resources may be divided into: (a) *Biotic*: Biotic resources are obtained from the biosphere, such as forests and animals, and the materials that can be obtained from them. (b) *Abiotic*: Abiotic resources are those that come from non-living, non-organic material. Considering their stage of development, natural resources may be referred to in the following ways: (a) *Potential resources*: Potential resources are those that exist in a region and may be used in the future; (b) *Actual resources*: Actual resources are those that have been surveyed, their quantity and quality determined and are being used in present times; (c) *Reserve resources*: The part of an actual resource which can be developed profitably in the future is called a reserve resource; and (d) *Stock resources*: Stock resources are those that have been surveyed but cannot be used by organisms due to lack of technology. Renewability is a very popular topic and many natural resources can be categorised as either renewable or non-renewable: *(a) Renewable resources*: Renewable resources can be replenished naturally. Some of these resources, like sunlight, air, wind, etc., are continuously available and their quantity is not noticeably affected by human consumption, and (b) *Non-renewable resources*: Non-renewable resources either form slowly or do not naturally form in the environment. Minerals are the most common resource included in this category.

What is Sustainable Development?

Sustainable development is a road-map, an action plan, for achieving sustainability in any activity that uses resources and where immediate and intergenerational replication is demanded. The United Nations World Commission on Environment and Development in its 1987 report Our Common Future defines sustainable development: *"Development that meets the needs of the present without compromising the ability of future generations to meet their own needs."* In 1992, the UN Conference on Environment and Development published in 1992 the Earth Charter, which outlines the building of a just, sustainable, and peaceful global society in the 21st century. The action plan Agenda 21 for sustainable development identified information, integration, and participation as key building blocks to help countries achieve development that recognises these interdependent pillars.

Sustainable development is development that meets the needs of the present without compromising the ability of future generations to meet their own needs. Sustainable development stands for meeting the needs of present generations without jeopardising the ability of futures generations to meet their own needs, in other words, a better quality of life for everyone, now and for generations to come. Sustainable development will not be brought about by policies only: it must be taken up by society at large as a principle guiding the many choices each citizen makes every day, as well as the big political and economic decisions that have.

Importance of Natural Resources

The demand for resources can change with new technology, new needs, and new economics. Some material can go completely out of use, if people do not want it any more. Demand of natural resources is very high, but availability is very low. Most natural resources are limited. This means they will eventually run out. A perpetual resource has a never-ending supply. Some examples of perpetual resources include solar energy, tidal energy, and wind energy. Other examples are salt, stone, magnesium, and diamonds. Minerals are valuable natural resources being finite and non-renewable. They constitute the vital raw materials for many basic industries and are a major resource for development. The history of mineral extraction in India dates back to the days of the Harappan civilisation. The wide availability of the minerals in the form of abundant rich reserves made it very conducive for the growth and development of the mining sector in India.

Natural Resources in India

In common with most developing nations, India faces many trade-offs in its attempt to reduce poverty and improve the living standards of its people. There is a need for an empirical basis on which to base policy decisions on trade-offs between the many competing priorities of a developing nation, including intergenerational claims. The Government is the custodian of the country's natural resources such as land, forests and bio-reserves, mines, minerals and hydro-carbon etc. It has the authority to allocate spectrum to various telecommunication service providers in the country. The Government takes the decisions pertaining to the hydro-carbon reserves in the country with an aim to optimise the use of those. Coal, lignite, crude oil and natural gas are primarily known as hydro-carbon. Total amount of coal resource in the country is 293.5 billion tonnes and lignite is 41.96 billion tonnes as of April 2010. Total amount of crude oil resource is 760 million tonnes and natural gas resource is 946 million tonnes.

The country is endowed with vast reserves of many metallic and non-metallic minerals. Mining sector is an important segment of the Indian economy. Since Independence, there has been a rapid growth in mineral production both in terms of quantity and value. India produces as many as 87 minerals, which include four fuels, 10 metallic, 47 non-metallic, three atomic and 23 minor minerals. The total estimated value of the mines and minerals are estimated at Rs 3390 lakh crore. The values of minerals are the product of amount of resources and the current market prices associated with them. For some of the minerals, the current market price refers to their import price and for the others it refers to their export price. Thorium deposits in India are estimated to be 3.6 lakh tonnes. Uranium reserves are estimated to be 1.86 lakh tonnes at present. At current international prices, the value of both these reserves is found to be Rs 109 lakh crore. The Government of India proposed to take up a Natural Resources Census Programme for the country. This is in the light of the experience gained as part of the National Natural Resources Management System mainly in using satellite images for natural resources management as well as in making available spatial databases on natural resources. By regular and systematic updating of the inventory, it will be possible to monitor changes and identify critical areas, which then could be monitored in more detail with enhanced frequency.

State-wise analysis revealed that during the year 2011-12, the value of mineral production has shown a mixed trend as compared to that in the previous year. The States, which have indicated an increase in the value of mineral production, are Chhattisgarh (36.23 per cent), Odisha (12.07 per cent), West Bengal (11.37 per cent), Gujarat (6.7 per cent), Himachal Pradesh (5.30 per cent), Rajasthan (3.91 per cent), Jammu & Kashmir (1.10 per cent),

Bihar (1.02 per cent), Kerala (0.89 per cent). However, some of the principal mineral producing States revealed decrease in value of mineral production and those includes Meghalaya (71.54 per cent), Jharkhand (24.85 per cent), Arunachal Pradesh (22.68 per cent), Maharashtra (19.25 per cent), Madhya Pradesh (12.08 per cent), Andhra Pradesh (11.37 per cent), Tamil Nadu (9.29 per cent), Tripura (8.46 per cent), Goa (6.30 per cent), Karnataka (5.31 per cent), Uttar Pradesh (3.82 per cent) and Uttarakhand 2.58 per cent. India's ranking in 2009 as compared to world production was second in barytes, chromite and talc/steatite/ pyrophyllite, third in coal and lignite and steel (crude), fourth in iron ore and kyanite/ andalusite/ sillimanite, fifth in manganese ore and zinc slab, sixth in bauxite, and seventh in aluminum. India continued to be wholly or largely self-sufficient in minerals which constitute primary mineral raw materials to industries, such as, thermal power generation, iron and steel, ferro-alloys, aluminium, cement, various types of refractories, china clay-based ceramics, glass, chemicals like caustic soda, soda ash, calcium carbide, titania white pigment, etc.

Natural Resources Management

Natural resource management is a discipline in the management of natural resources such as land, water, soil, plants and animals, with a particular focus on how management affects the quality of life for both present and future generations. Management of natural resources involves identifying who has the right to use the resources and who does not for defining the boundaries of the resource. Natural resource management deals with managing the way in which people and natural landscapes interact. It brings together land use planning, water management, biodiversity conservation, and the future sustainability of industries like agriculture, mining, tourism, fisheries and forestry. Natural resource management specifically focuses on a scientific and technical understanding of resources and ecology and the life-supporting capacity of those resources. Natural resource management issues are inherently complex as they involve the ecological cycles, hydrological cycles, climate, animals, plants and geography etc. After the United Nations Conference for the Environment and Development held in Rio de Janeiro in 1992, most nations subscribed to new principles for the integrated management of land, water, and forests.

Integrated natural resource management is a process of managing natural resources in a systematic way, which includes multiple aspects of natural resource use (biophysical, socio-political, and economic) meet production goals of producers and other direct users (e.g., food security, profitability, risk aversion) as well as goals of the wider community (e.g., poverty alleviation, welfare of future generations, environmental conservation). It focuses on sustainability and at the same time tries to incorporate all possible stakeholders from the planning level itself, reducing possible future conflicts.

Conclusion

Natural Resources Management refers to the sustainable utilisation of major natural resources, such as land, water, air, minerals, forests, fisheries, and wild flora and fauna. Over exploitation of natural resources by growing population resulted in various severe problems. Destruction of vegetation has resulted in land degradation, denudation, soil erosion, landslides, floods, drought and unbalanced ecosystems. Natural resources provide fundamental life support, in the form of both consumptive and public good services. Ecological processes maintain soil productivity, nutrient cycling, the cleansing of air and water, and climatic cycles.

References

1. Haripriya Gundimeda, *et al.* Natural resource accounting for Indian states — Illustrating the case of forest resources, Retrieved from http://unstats.un.org/unsd/envaccounting/seeaLES/egm/NRAIndia_bk.pdf
2. Natural resource management (2014), Retrieved from http://en.wikipedia.org/wiki/Natural_resource_management
3. Natural Resources Management, Retrieved from http://www.atiwb.nic.in/index_htm_files/Natural_ Resources_Management.pdf
4. Natural resources (2014), Retrieved from http://en.wikipedia.org/wiki/Natural_resource

5. Natural Resources: Definition and Classification, Retrieved from http://rashidfaridi.com/2008/02/26/natural-resources-definition-and-classification/
6. Rajeev Kumar Jaiswal, Mukund Rao, Asis Bhattacharya & V Jayaraman, Natural resources census in India, Retrieved from http://www.gsdidocs.org/gsdiconf/GSDI-7/papers/TSsdRJ.pdf
7. See, http://mines.nic.in/writereaddata %5CContentlinks%5 C1ed 4a15b3 70646d7be2c6defb2ecf6c9.pdf
8. Sridhar Kundu (2014), A note on the Estimated Value of Government-Owned Natural Resources in India, Retrieved from http://www.satyamevjayate.in/uploads/estimation-government-resources.pdf
9. Sustainable development (2014), Retrieved from http://en.wikipedia.org/wiki/Sustainable_development
10. Sustainable development, Retrieved from http://ec.europa.eu/environment/eussd/
11. What Are Natural Resources? - Definition, Lesson and Quiz, Retrieved from http://education-portal.com/academy/lesson/what-are-natural-resources-definition-lesson-quiz.html#lesson Read more at http://www.brainyquote.com/quotes/keywords/natural. html#BvHZmt2ICpkluQT1.99

15

Future Prospects of Coastal Tourism in Eritrea: An Overview

Dr Mohammad Afsar Alam

"The natural liberty of man is to be free from any superior power on Earth, and not to be under the will or legislative authority of man, but only to have the law of nature for his rule."

—Samuel Adams

Introduction

Since independence coastal tourism is treated as industry by the government enabling to enjoy certain government concessions where it has given much attention to the activities than previous decades. The potential for tourist spots in the coastal area has not yet been fully exploited, but by providing suitable infrastructure facilities the sites of the coast could become more important tourist attraction. Eritrean Red Sea coast and marine habitat posses have a number of attribute that could be successfully exploited in a programme of national and internal tourism. By implementing the integrated programme of planning and subsequent development and management, coastal tourism could be of great importance to the people of coast and the nation as a whole. The development of tourism in the coastal part of the Red Sea area of Eritrea could have economic, cultural and social benefits. Economically, coastal tourism could improve balance of payment, develops the coastal area, diversify the economy, increase income level, increase state revenue and create new employment opportunities. From the social and cultural point of view, coastal tourism could facilitate interaction between the visitors and the population of the host country. Provide adequate recreational activities for the nation's people and particularly people in the coastal area.

Data Base and Methodology

The present study is more akin to collection of primary and secondary data. The compiled data on different subjects have been tabulated. Synthesis, perusal and analysis of data have been carried out wherever it can explain the trend with the outcome of results and facts. Personal interviews were conducted with various authorities viz. concerned officials in the Ministry of Marine Industry (Shipping Line of Tourism Sector) and in the Ministry of Tourism. Besides, questionnaires were designed to collect information on different items regarding tourism in Eritrea as a whole and the coast in particular. Secondary data pertaining to the present study was collected mainly from Ministry of Tourism and Civil Aviation Authority Service, different journals, magazines and of course also from browsing the Internet. Descriptive method has been used for data analysis. The obtained data sets have been represented by various statistical techniques. Equally, graphs, tables, and other diagrams are also presented in an appropriate manner.

The Study Area

In the present paper an attempt has been made to discuss about the future prospects of coastal tourism with respect to tourism potentials in the coastal zone of Eritrea which covers an area of about 124,000 Sq.Km, lies in the north of the equator and just north of the horn of Africa. Eritrea shapes like a hatchet and the handle of the hatchet is on the Red Sea in the east. It is bounded by Sudan in the north and northwest, by Ethiopia in the south, by Djibouti in the southeast and by the Red Sea in the northeast Figure 1.

The country has a coastline of 1200 Kms with more than 350 islands. Eritrea is a land of fascinating contrast with its scenic

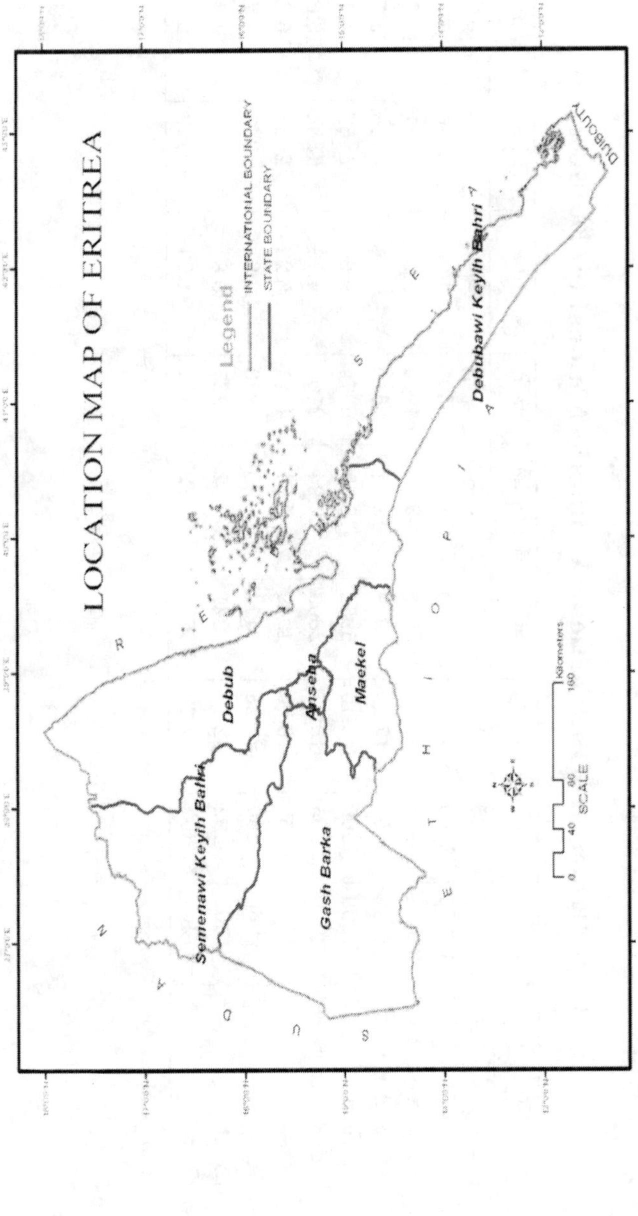

Fig. 1

Source : Ministry of Tourism, Asmara, Eritrea

Table-1: Number of International Visitors by Nationality (2004-2008)

Nationality	*2004*	*2005*	*% change*	*2006*	*% change*	*2007*	*% change*	*2008*	*% change*
Ethiopia	57	65	14.03	53	-18.46	70	32.07	38	-45.71
Sudan	3275	3090	-5.64	3550	14.88	3505	-1.26	3570	1.85
Eritrea(overseas)	61851	60935	-1.48	58938	-3.29	61904	5.03	55171	-10.87
Other Africa	1402	1150	-17.10	939	-18.34	640	-31.84	488	-23.75
Europe	7690	7260	-5.10	5951	-18.03	5374	-9.69	5151	-4.14
Middle East	4280	3605	-15.77	2803	-22.24	2108	-24.79	1884	-10.62
Asia	6295	5250	-16.60	4949	-5.74	4641	-6.22	2028	-56.30
America	2250	1660	-26.23	1474	-11.20	983	-33.31	858	-12.71
Australia	301	292	-2.99	221	-2.42	267	20.81	235	-11.98
Total	**87401**	**83307**	**-4.68**	**78678**	**-55.72**	**79492**	**-1.03**	**69423**	**-12.66**

Source: Ministry of Tourism, Asmara, Eritrea.

Table-2 : International Tourist Arrivals by Purpose of Visit (2004-2008)

Purpose of visit	*2004*	*2005*	*%change*	*2006*	*% change*	*2007*	*%change*	*2008*	*%change*
Business	14340	13457	6.15	11557	14.11	9874	-14.56	7726	21.75
Tourism	63439	66550	4.90	64840	2.56	69804	7.65	62031	-11.13
Others	2350	2150	-8.51	2064	-4	825	-60.02	160	-80.60
Total	**80129**	**82157**	**2.53**	**78461**	**-4.49**	**80503**	**2.60**	**69917**	**-13.14**

Source: Ministry of Tourism, Asmara, Eritrea.

and contrasting landscapes and one of the loveliest tropical coastlines in Africa. Eritrea has enormous potential as a tourist attraction. Massawa, 117 Km from the capital city of Asmara is one of the main ports of Eritrea, known as the pearl of the Red Sea. Its Mediterranean ambience and settling and its peripheral environs make a perfect location for such tourist's related developments as yachts marinas, hotel and beach resorts. It will serve as springboard for the development of tourism in the Dahlak islands and along the coast, from west to east. In addition, Eritrea's topographical features provide the greatest climatic contrasts. Each of the geographical zones offers unparallel experience for the tourists. The claim that Eritrea offers "three seasons in two hours" is not an idle boast. In two hours the tourist can rise from the extremely hot pristine and unspoiled beaches of the coast to the moderate weather of the forests of plains and hills and the fertile fields of Eritrea. Above 2000 meters the tourist encounters the cool highlands which are pleasant at any time of the year.

In fact, Eritrea has inadequate tourist accommodation and other services, the number of tourists had decreased from 2004 to 2008. The number of international visitors reached to a maximum of 398,301 by nationality (Table 1). Out of this figure 56,954 by purpose of business, 326,664 were by purpose of tourism, and tourists for other purposes reached to 7549 (Table 2). As a whole according to the given data, the flow of tourists to this country drop dramatically. This is obviously due to the Ethio-Eritrean border conflict.

Coastal Background of Eritrea

Some of the important characteristics of the coastal zone of Eritrea which are relevant to the development of tourism are as follows.

Coastline and Its Local Population

Eritrea has a coastline of about 1200 Kms. It is easily accessible only at few points due to the arid, desert nature of the hinterland and coastal plain. The coastline varies in nature from steep rocky shores, steep active sand dunes and considerable areas of mangrove swamps and exposed muddy littoral zones.

The waters of the continental shelf (Dahlak bank) lying off the coast are relatively shallow, and there are many islands, shoals and banks for some distance offshore. The southern portion of the coast has only few islands. The Ministry of Tourism pointed out that only ten of the islands are inhabited with an estimated total population of 3,100 depending for their livelihood from mainly on fish. Three of these islands lie in the Dahlak Archipelago, the rest are mainly along the coast immediate south of Massawa at Hawakil Archipelago. Habitation appears to be governed entirely by the presence of fresh water.

Climate

The Eritrean coast is a dry and arid area, with mild beauty that is appreciated by many people. The annual rainfall at Massawa is about 173 mm. The daily maximum temperature ranges between 29ºC and 40ºC and average humidity ranges between 54 per cent and 78 per cent. There are no climatic records for the islands, but it is assumed that the temperature is higher and rainfall is lower. The lower rainfall in the coastal area and the small nature of the majority of the islands are results in very limited and localised water supplies, which is of major consideration. The mean annual temperature on the eastern slopes of the escarpment is 25ºC, along the Red Sea and on the offshore islands it rises to 31ºC. At the Danakil Depression temperature ranges from 38ºC to 50ºC. The difference in temperature between the hot and the relatively cold season is about 5ºC to 10ºC. The mean daily duration of maximum possible sun light for the month of the year ranges between 11 hours a day in December to 13 hours in June; with daylight virtually constant throughout the year, seasonal changes in day light vary by only about an hour.

Islands

There are about 350 islands. They vary in size from tiny islets of about 50 meters in length, to the giant island of Dahlak that is over 60 Km long and 642 Sq.Km in area with eight inhabited villages in the islands. Most of the islands i.e. 78 per cent (276) are less than One Sq.Km in area and have little relevance except as supplement to the main possibilities for tourism. Another 63 islands are between one to ten Sq.Km in area and offer some possibilities for development. Fifteen of the islands have an area of over 10 Sq.Km while 59 per cent (209) of these islands lie in the well-known Dahlak Archipelago offshore from Massawa, the remaining lesser known islands (south along the coast as far as the southern border) should not be ignored especially when coastal infrastructure developed.

More than 200 of Eritrea's islands belong to the Dahlak Archipelago which forms the natural gateway of Eritrea, guarding the approaches to the modern part of Massawa and the ancient one of Adulis, the larger island, Dahlak Kabir, covering several Sq.Km is one of the most suited for development as a tourist resort. This is due to the fact that the island is endowed with natural and man-made attractions. Among these potential attractions include 365 cistern rocks which are well structured, the 500 hundred years old necropolis of gravestone carried with beautiful kufie script and an interesting people who were thought as descendants of Nigeria intermarried with local settlers in that area.

One recreation named *'Luul Resort Village'* has been built to entertain tourists. The hotels also provide its own boat transport services to and from Dahlak islands with possible visible trips to the surrounding islands. It can also arrange all diving facilities for those who wish to enjoy the underwater life species of the Red Sea. So far as tourists are concerned, the Dahlak islands are attractive to visit, even if the transport and accommodation are still in a rather initial stage. The diving and bird life are the major attractions. The diving areas are scattered throughout the Red Sea coast. It holds the last pristine sub-aquatic corals which are not destroyed by pollutants, indiscriminate drug, net fishing or inexperienced and inconsiderate divers. The Dahlak islands offer some of the most spectacular Scuba- diving in the world. According to Ministry of Tourism the islands open for tourists are: Dessie, Durehalla, Duri, Dehul, Noera, Harat and Dahlak Kabir. Besides the above mentioned islands, there are thirteen additional islands open for tourists. These are: Aderbara, Shuma, Ajuje, Dardes, Aukan, Hawatib, Esratu, Bulisar, Madat, Delef, Tore, Durgham, and Etoumohamus.

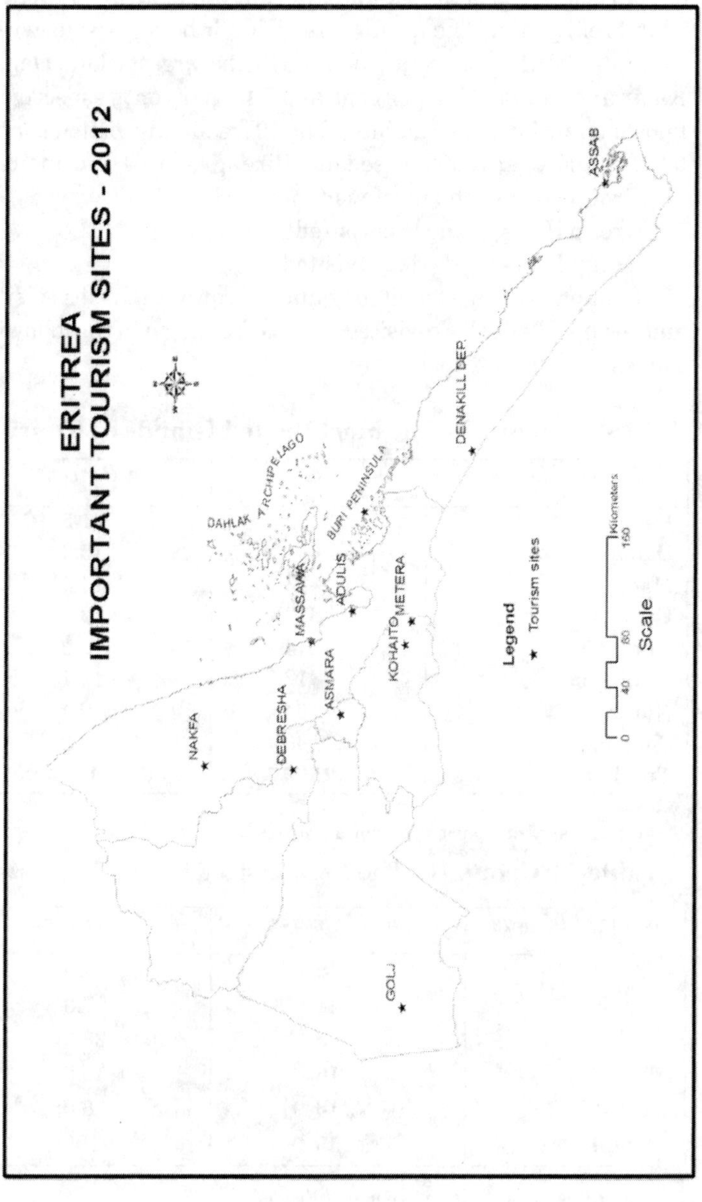
ERITREA
IMPORTANT TOURISM SITES - 2012
DAHLAK ARCHIPELAGO
BURI PENINSULA
MASSAWA
ADULIS
ASMARA
KOHAITO
METERA
NAKFA
DEBRESHA
GOLJ
DENAKILL DEP.
ASSAB
Legend
Tourism sites
0
40
Kilometers
Scale

According to the statistical information given by the Ministry of Tourism, 2,729 domestic and international tourists visited 19 islands of Eritrea. The most visited islands being Dessie, which accounts 553 (21.5 per cent), followed by the largest island Dahlak Kabir and Madat 15.3 per cent and 14.5 per cent respectively, known for its bird life watching. The 19 frequently visited islands by the tourists are categorised into three groups. These include:

Group I ———the most visited

Group II ———the less visited

Group III———the least visited

Group I - the most visited islands, Group II - the less visited and Group III - the least visited islands are shown in the following Tables 3, 4 and 5 respectively.

Table-3 : Group I - The Most Visited Islands by Tourists

Name of Islands	*No. of visitors*	*In Per cent*
Dessie	553	21.5
Dahlak Kebir	394	15.3
Madat	373	14.5
Dehul	323	12.6
Durgham	314	12.2
Durghella	312	12.1
Nurka	164	6.4
Shumma	136	5.3
Total	**2569**	**100**

Source: Ministry of Tourism, Asmara, Eritrea.

Table-4 : Group II - The Less Visited by the Tourists

Name of Islands	*No. of visitors*	*In Per cent*
Darat	45	30
Intera	41	27.3
Askara	35	23.3
Harat	16	10.6
Esratu	13	8.6
Total	**150**	**100**

Source: Ministry of Tourism, Asmara, Eritrea.

Table-5 : Group III - The least Visited Islands by the Tourists

Name of Islands	*No. of visitors*	*In Per cent*
Hawatib	2	20
Ajuz	2	20
Etoom	2	20
Namus	2	20
Awkar	2	20
Adbara	0	0
Total	**10**	**100**

Source: Ministry of Tourism, Asmara, Eritrea.

In the above table out of six islands, five islands are equally visited i.e. two individuals for each and the remaining one island Adbara is not visited at all. When we come to visitors by Nationality in 1999, Italy is a country with the highest visitors to the islands of Eritrea accounting for 1559 i.e. 57 per cent of the total figure. This could be due to the fact that Eritrea had been a colony of Italy. So they must have documentation about the islands to explore and wonder at. In contrast the local visitors account 594. Out of the total visitors to the islands some of them are specially served by Shipping Line of Eritrea. About 700 local and foreign visitors toured the islands of Eritrea. They were provided with the necessary accommodation. Divers consider the coastal sea of Eritrea very attractive because the sea is unpolluted and has different and attractive coral reefs. Hence, many tourists return to visit Eritrea year after year. The tourism sector of Shipping Line employs experienced and expert divers. So tourists enjoy the sea diving experience under their assistance. Eritrean divers take responsibility of protecting the coast, coral reefs and underwater life.

Marine and Wildlife

The Red Sea is endowed with varieties of fauna and flora different from other seas of the world. The Red Sea is very narrow and has at times been totally isolated for long periods from other water bodies. It is very salty and very warm retaining its high water temperature for the whole year. These special conditions have resulted in high levels of Endemism (uniqueness). Detailed studies have indicated that there is a major change in marine species between the well-known Northern Red Sea and the lesser known Southern Red Sea. In the corals, according to the information given from the Ministry of Marine Industry, 6.3 per cent species are endemic. The very extensive areas of coral gardens in relatively shallow waters, the reef drop-offs into deep waters, the myriads of colourful fish and other organisms all combine to produce an underwater spectacle as attractive as anywhere else in the world and widespread over a large area of sea.

The numerous small islands are also attractive for large number of bird species. They feed their young on the migrations of sardines and anchovies that pass North through Eritrean waters as far as Massawa during the latter part of the year. The Red Sea is in addition a major migration route for Planarity birds, providing them with free air space to travel and feed along the coasts on their way. They in turn provide food for number of predations birds living and breeding on the islands. Other marine mega fauna found in the shallow Eritrean waters include the endangered Dugong or Sea Cow and good number of several cetacean species, particularly the commonly seen smaller Dolphins and Porpoises. All are species of international conservation concern, and hold great interest for many visitors.

On the mainland and some of the islands, larger terrestrial wildlife species occur. Gazelle are found on two islands and probably represent a subspecies of the mainland forms. Three Gazelle species, Ostrich, the endangered Waltz and many other smaller wildlife forms especially dry land birds in the core of Madot Island, add to the attractions of the wildlife and beautiful desert landscapes on the coastal zone. All of these features of the Eritrean coastal zone stand to contribute a tourism programme. So far as the management and promotion of tourism is concerned, there is large number of factors which influences the tourism development in the country. Some of the important factors include the lack of skilled manpower, insufficient tourism promotion and marketing activities and border conflict between Eritrea and Ethiopia. In Eritrea, the Ministry of Tourism had suffered from shortage of skilled manpower. The Ministry had taken some measures to solve this problem. It brought foreign expert from India and Sri Lanka. Moreover, almost all the workers of Ministry were given different informal job training.

Table – 6 : Educational Qualification of Employees of the Ministry of Tourism

Level of Education	*Number of Employees*	*Percentage of the Total*
M.A.	01	1.923
B.A.	12	23.076
Diploma	10	19.231
12+2	06	11.538
12+1	07	13.461
9th – 12th grade	15	28.84
4th grade	01	1.923
Total	**51**	**100.000**

Source: Ministry of Tourism Personnel Information.

The above table shows that almost one-third of the employees have completed only high school. The number of workers having higher qualifications is relatively few. Most of them have specialisation in area (disciplines) other than tourism. However, they took variety of tourism related informal training. Among the informal training courses, which the workers took, includes tourism development, tourism planning, finance management, travel agency management, human resource management, marketing to tourism, tour planning and management, labour market analysis and public relations etc. Although majority of workers had taken such training, it usually lasted for a short period of time.

Potential Tourism in the Coastal Zone

The features described shows that the country has enough potential which provide a strong basis for the multi-faceted tourism programme along the coast and amongst the islands. Some of them would stand for specialist tourists, for example diving and nature tours, while others in combination and integrated with ingenuity would attract general tourists in search of the Sun, sea, sand and isolation. The various kinds of tourism possible elsewhere could include the following:

- Diving on the extensive coral banks that occur from depths as shallow as a few meters (snorkeling) to over 30 meters (Scuba diving)
- Specialist natural history viewing of reefs and fish, turtles, dugong waltz and other species.
- Archaeological sites of the ancient monuments.
- Tours of the remnants history along the coast including diving on wrecks from recent world wars and the war of liberation.
- Cultural experience of the varied people of the coast and their ways of life in this harsh environment.
- Sport fishing for the larger fish species which is of limited fishers' utility.
- Coastal 'adventure' Safaris in appropriate transport (boats, light aircraft, and four wheel drive vehicles) through the desert and between the islands to experience the other aspects mentioned here.
- Sun, sea, sand and isolation – the innovative combination of coastal features into an experience sought after by the stressed visitor from the rat race of the developed world.

According to the Ministry of Information, a newspaper 'Eritrea Profile' dated in April 20, 1996 states that the tourist industry has real potential to attract foreign investment. This sector has a huge potential based on the scenic and topographic diversity of the country as well as its history. The coast line of Pristine sandy beaches, the many islands and the clear water with abundant marine life makes development of recreational facilities possible. Apart from this, health spas and hiking trails can be developed, licenses have been granted for the construction of private hotels and some construction has been undertaken. A need exists however, for the development of hotels of an international standard.

Considerations

The successful development of coastal tourism in Eritrea will depend upon the parallel development and adequate consideration of a number of related aspects which are as follows:

- The limited infrastructure in the coastal area is a general problem and transport and communication in Massawa is a particular problem.
- Much more information needs to be made available on the attractions of the coast and islands of Eritrea for the international market.
- The hot and humid climate for much of the year needs to be counteracted with ingenuity and appropriate technology including especially the provision of adequate water (desalination of sea water) and power supplies and shade solar energy is particularly appropriate technology in this area if small, localised tourism facilities are encouraged, as opposed to major developments concentrated in limited areas, requiring huge amounts of power.
- From an ecological point of view, it is absolutely necessary at this early stage to ensure that tourism does not "Foul its own nest" with adequate regulations and enforcement mechanism being made for waste disposal, harvesting of "Curious" and controlling tourists activities. The formation of a "Marine National Park" and a "World Heritage Reserve" or "Man and Biosphere Reserve", appropriately zoned to include all human activities, is planned and is urgently required to endure adequate integrate management with the genuine inclusion of local people in management operations and decisions.
- Ignoring these aspects will result in the same mistakes as have been made in other tourism programmes elsewhere in the world.

Data Finding and Analysis

The primary data has been collected directly through the questionnaire distribution and discussion with some head departments in the Ministry of Tourism. All of the respondents are foreigners and their purpose of visiting to this country varies from individual to individual. But most of them stay in the country for the purpose of business. Tourists whose main purpose other than business are very few, this is because of the border conflict between Eritrea and Ethiopia (Table 7, 8, 9 and 10).

Table-7 : Purpose of Visiting in Per cent

Purpose of Visit	*In Per cent*
Leisure	07
Business	43
VFR	27
Other	23

Source: Based on field survey by the author.

The above table shows the visitors by purpose. Most of the visitors by purpose of business accounts 43 per cent and the least visitors are by purpose of leisure i.e. Only seven per cent. The remaining 50 per cent are shared by purpose of VFR (Voluntary Friends and Relatives), and others.

Table- 8 : Type of Accommodation

Accommodation	*In Per cent*
Hotel/Motel	60
Pensions	10
Rent House	27
Others	03

Source: Based on Field Survey by the Author.

Table-8 shows the accommodations used by visitors. Out of the total respondents, the majority, 60 per cent has used the hotels followed by 27 per cent who used rented house and the rest used pension and very few used other accommodations. Table-9 indicates the main method of transport used in visiting the sites. Here, most of the respondents, 47 per cent used taxi as the main transport, 34 per cent used private cars, 10 per cent used bus and the remaining respondents nine per cent used rent car and other means of transport such as bicycle for choosing the sites. Table-10 shows reasons for choosing the sites. Out of the total respondents, 58 per cent said that accessibility is the main reason for choosing the site. 20 per cent chosen the site due to favourable weather and climate and the remaining 22 per cent chosen the site as mentioned by others and for other reasons.

In fact, the tourism potential is relatively high along the coast and the islands, foreign investors are willing to develop tourist activities and facilities. The government is however, proceeding with care, in the light of the failure from other areas in the world. The Ministry of Education has currently prepared tourist master plan with the assistance of the World Tourism Organisation. The tourism master plan responds to the special requirements for Eco-Tourism which is the most rapidly developing new tourism approach and assumes sustainable development.

In view of the livelihood of expanding tourism, especially in the coastal zone of Eritrea, special guidelines must be formulated to address the following issues; location of resorts and facilities, resort operation, activities for tourists (such as diving or boating), necessary limits to use the fragile ecosystem and indirect environmental impacts of tourism. Eritrea has the opportunity to develop environment friendly tourism and therefore, to earn an international reputation for Eco-Tourism, Eritrea should adopt a policy which allows appropriate access to land and water, provided this does not infringe on the rights of others, including the right to personal property, tranquility and privacy, and does not disrupt the environment.

Table-9 : Means of Transport Used for Visiting the Sites

Transport	*In Per cent*
Bus	10
Taxi	47
Private Car	34
Rent Car	03
Others	06

Source: Based on Field Survey by the Author.

Table-10 : Reasons for Choosing the Sites

Reasons	*In Per cent*
Accessibility	58
Weather and Climate	20
As mentioned by Others/ (from book)	11
Others	11

Source: Based on field survey by the author.

The so-called Eco-Tourism has been successfully accomplished in a number of other countries with major marine attractions. Examples that could be examined include the Red Sea and its surroundings, i.e. Egypt, Sudan, Israel, Kenya and the Seychelles, most appropriate with its own numerous oceanic islands. In addition, such marine Eco-Tourism is being developed in Maldives islands and Belize which are more or less similar to Dahlak islands.

Prospective of Coastal Tourism in Eritrea

So far as the future prospects of coastal tourism in Eritrea is concerned, no doubt the Northern Red Sea region contains a diversity of attractions. The focus of the region is Massawa, which offers urban tourism and is the gateway to beach and marine resort on the coast and islands, and some important archaeological sites as well as struggle for independence sites in the north. The executive future master plan of tourism prepared by the Ministry of Tourism from 2000-2020 includes the following plans. Improvements in the region include:

1. Island resorts especially on Dissei Island and Dahlak Kabir, based on beach recreation and water sports lading diving.
2. Coastal beach resorts with the largest at Gurgusum (to be developed in the immediate future) and other resorts at Ras Artae on Buri Peninsula and Marsa Gulbub, Marsa Ibrahim and Ras Kubaa on the north coast (for long term development).
3. Hotel development includes; opening of already renovated Red Sea hotel, expansion and upgrading of the Dahlak hotel, conversion of the Melotti Residence as a high quality hotel, consideration of conversion of some of the historic buildings in Massawa into historic hotels, upgrading and development of other hotels as headed in the area.

Conclusion and Recommendations

Despite the charming scenery of natural landscapes, attractive coastal zones and welcoming climatic conditions of Eritrea, the tourism sector has not grown yet as much as it should. This is because of number of obstacles and constraints. Lack of skilled manpower is one of the obstacles which have resulted into insufficient market research activities. The insufficient tourism promotion and marketing activities together with the lower roles of travel agencies are contributing to the low growth of the sector. The inadequacy of transportation and access routes also creates inaccessibility problems. Moreover, deficiency of infrastructure has aggravated the lack of necessary tourist products. Thus, absence of water supply system in some attractive sites made them less important. The poor development of other constructed facilities such as highways, airports, roads, railways, parks, resorts, hotels, motels and places of entertainment has influenced the sector negatively. Based on the content of the paper the following points are concluded :

1. Eritrea has enormous potential as a tourist attraction, the tourism industry has a real potential on the coastal zone to attract foreign investment.
2. Eritrea has a coastline of about 1200 Km with dry and arid climate. In Eritrea there are 350 islands. So far as the tourists are concerned, the Dahlak islands are attractive to visit, even if the transport and accommodation are still not up to the mark. The diving and bird watching are the major attraction especially for the eco-tourists. The diving area is very clean and unpolluted. So, the coastal zone of Eritrea is one of the attractive sites for the tourists.
3. All the features i.e. the coastline and its population, the islands, the climate and the marine and wildlife hold the basis for multi-faceted tourism programme along the coast and islands.
4. Eritrea has the opportunity to develop environment-friendly tourism and therefore, to earn an international reputation for marine Eco-Tourism. The so-called Eco- Tourism is being developed in Dahlak Island which is similar to Maldives and Belize islands in Southern areas.

Recommendations

On the basis of above discussion, the following recommendations have been given for the development of coastal tourism of Eritrea in future.

1. It is important to consider the cultural requirements of the tourists themselves, many of whom are seeking remoteness.

We should not assume that all visitors require a highly sophisticated facility in which they can relax. The country has proved to the case in most other places, with simple accommodation and facilities being more attractive in such environments than enormous super hotels and tourist villages.

2. Diving tourism is the attractive and easily catered for at the present time, since regardless of climate and infrastructure the people will come just to experience the plentiful and fascinating marine life. Therefore, Eritrea should develop deep sea diving and Scuba diving industries along the coastal area.
3. Local people must be allowed and encouraged to participate and must genuinely benefit from the industry and be protected from it, as it should supplement their income and raise their standards of living while maintaining their cultural mores and national pride.
4. Take nothing but pictures leave nothing but bubbles should be the guiding principle, not only of the tourist divers but also of the dive-boat operator, hotel manager, car hire operator and any other tourist.
5. Advertising Eritrea's tourism in other countries by: (i) Making tourist information available in Massawa for yacht tourists, (ii) Having improvements on appreciable amount of tourist's pamphlets in the hotels.
6. Acquisition of favourites available in outlying areas that meet the needs of international tourists.

References

1. AKWAABA – *The In-flight Magazine of Ghana Airways Issue* 13, 1999. Central Region Commission. Treasures of Ghana's Central region.
2. Benjamin K. Prah, Kwame Nkrumah University of Science and Technology, Geodetic Engineering Department, School of Engineering, Kumasi Ghana.
3. Bhatia, A.K., 1982, "*Tourism development*" India.
4. Bhatia, A.K., 1995, "*International tourism*" India.
5. Charles, R. Goeldner, 1990, "*Tourism principles, practices, philosophies*" U.S.A.: John Wiley and Sons, Inc.

6. Daniel Longmatey and Samuel Amoako-Atta, *Management and Promotion of Tourism in Ghana: A GIS Approach*, Graduate Assistant,Texas A&M University, Corpus Christi, 6300 Ocean Drive, NRC 3200, Corpus Christi, TX 78412.
7. Houdek, Mary and Oriolo, Leonardo, 1995 *"Eritrea at a glance Asmara."*
8. Ministry of Land, Water and Environment, 1999, *"Eritrea Biodiversity: Stack taking Assessment Report Asmara".*
9. Ministry of Marine Resources, 1995, *Facts and figures about the Eritrean marine environment" Massawa.*
10. Ministry of Tourism, 1998, *"Eritrea Horizons: The magazine of Eritrea's tourist industry"* Vol. 2, No. 1.
11. The Trade Commission, Ghana High Commission, London, *"Business and Holiday Guide to Ghana.*
12. Government of Eritrea (1995), *National Environmental Plan for Eritrea, Asmara.*
13. Holloway, Christopher (1994), *The Business of Tourism*, London Pitman, Ministry of Information, newspaper, Eritrea Profile, April 20, 1996.
14. Ministry of Trade, Industry and Tourism, (1993), IST Conference on the development of Tourism in Asmara Eritrea.
15. Ministry of Tourism (1997), *Tourist Investment Opportunity in Eritrea.*
16. UNIDO (United Nation Industrial Development Organization), (1999), *Investor's Guide to Eritrea.*
17. WTO, Agenda 21 for the Travel and Tourist Industry, *Towards Environmentally Sustainable Tourism.*
18. Read more at http://www.brainyquote.com/quotes/keywords/natural.html#BvHZmt2ICpkluQT1.99

16

Water and Technology: Boats and Houseboats of Kashmir

Alson Rasool

"It seems to me that the natural world is the greatest source of excitement; the greatest source of visual beauty; the greatest source of intellectual interest. It is the greatest source of so much in life that makes life worth living."

—David Attenborough

Introduction

The development of water technology by ancient man was a long complex process of observation, changing needs and trial and error solutions, with the occasional innovation. Water technology at a particular time and place was not developed in isolation from agricultural, construction and other phases of life. We may classify these activities today into various categories, but in the past it is likely that the digging of a well or channel was simply part of survival, using skills and experience available in the group. Since water is a basic human need and these needs grew, so the potential requirement for heavy labour provided a strong incentive for invention. The beautiful city of Srinagar is gifted with two water bodies i.e., river Jhelum and the famous Dal lake where boats and houseboats are stationed to welcome the tourists, throughout the year. All the important towns in the valley have been located on the river banks from ancient times, and boats have been the only means of transport and communication. The Kashmiri takes to a boat as naturally as an Englishman to a sea.

The boat-building industry only concerns the people of the city. The Kashmiris, says Tyandale *Biscoe*, have their special way of building-boats, and very clever they are in that art. I have always been interested in boats and boat building, but I had never come across boats built in Kashmir. Boat making had been an ancient industry in Kashmir. *Kalhana* mentions king Nara having built a town on river *Vitasta* (Jhelum) ".... where the coming and going of ships (boats) gave splendour to the river." When Akbar visited Kashmir, he expressed the disapproval of the boats prevalent then. He ordered double storeyed boats which could be used for residential purposes, so was constructed a floating city at Srinagar within no time. According to Ain-i-Akbari, "in Kashmir, there was made a model of ship that astonished everyone who saw it." Thirty thousand boats piled in Kashmir.

Boats

It was in the last quarter of the 19th century that the boat-building began to develop on account of the increasing rush of British civil and military servants, travellers, artists and sportsmen. Kashmiri wood worker employs a unique skill in producing a boat. The wood used in boat making is deodar (cedar). They prefer using axe-cut wood to saw-cut wood. They use nails made out of mulberry wood. Iron nails are also used. Moorcraft was of the view that boat making craft of Kashmir was imperfect. On the other hand, Younghusband says, if properly supervised and instructed, the Kashmir should be capable of constructing any kind of craft. An ordinary boat is built in the form of a big box of wooden planks two to three inches in thickness. The bottom is composed of planks six to nine feet long and about three feet wide which are dovetailed together and fastened by iron staples and nails. The staples are three to four inches wide and are hammered in almost re-hot. Immediately water is poured on them when they cool and contract, and thus have a great clenching power. When the bottom is thus completed the sides of similar planks three to four feet in width are joined and fastened to the bottom and in order to make this great box rigid, four or five staples and placed in position at equal distances. Now caulkers are put on to work and very clever they are at this job. They pack the seams with Indian jute mixed with pits or water rush grass to make the boat entirely waterproof. The boat requires a renewal of this packing every third or fourth year, when she is afloat the cabin is built on according to the use boat is to be put.

There are many kinds of boats, all flat-bottomed, but, with the exception of the "*parinda*". The different types of boats are as follows:

Types of Boats Present in Kashmir

Sl. No.	*Name of the boat*	*Capacity*
1.	Barges/Bahats	800 to 1000 mounds.
2.	Burges/War	400 mounds.
3.	Doonga	Residential houses of boatmen.
4.	Shikara	Small boat used for short journey.
5.	Dembnao	Used for carrying vegetables to market.
6.	Tsatawar	Small boat without roof, only used in Wular.
7.	Parinda	Not for common heard, but are the
8.	Larino	dignified vehicles of ex-rulers of Kashmir.
9.	Chakwari	

Source: Sanyal and Younghusband.

Boat making industry contributed to the economy of Kashmir substantially. It gave employment to 33,870 boatmen in the last quarter of the 19th century. 2471 boats were used for commercial purposes and out of these boats 1066 were of large size. The industry employed large number of people. Boats were the principal means of transporting goods and grains from one place to another. Major towns of Kashmir valley were connected through river Jhelum over which these boats carried commercial traffic. The boat was the main hub of Kashmir's trade and commercial activity.

House Boats

Before the European visitors began to come to Kashmir on holidays in increasing numbers, the "*Doonga*" was used by Kashmiris for long journeys and picnic trips to the Dal Lake. It was during the nineties of the 19th century that this boat was frequently used by the visitors for short sojourns as the best alternative to a tent. Due to the lack of accommodation suitable to them the visitors or tourists (British) were put to great inconvenience. It is apparent that the birth of the houseboat was natural. But political factors also helped in its growth and further expansion. Under the orders of the Maharaja or State Government no European could possess land or build houses in Kashmir. Naturally houseboats became the houses for those who wished to stay in the valley. The resourceful British, though, perhaps remembering experiences on the Thames at Henley, thought of houseboats, which would not infringe the rule, and so founded one of the great traditions without which, it is arguable, the economy of the Kashmir would greatly suffer. It was, the Europeans who were responsible for giving a great fillip to this newly-born industry. Mr. M. T. Kennard, conceived the idea of Floating Houses, and is said to be the first Englishman who built a houseboat in Srinagar about 1888 A.D.

Most of the houseboats are from 65-95 feet in length and about 14 feet in width in the centre. They are partitioned into a sitting, a dinning and two to three bedrooms, a pantry, and a required number of bathrooms and lavatories. They are equipped with modern furniture and sanitary fittings. The ventilation and lighting is ample, due to glazed windows and doors. The ceilings are invariably of the famous Kashmiri "*Khatamband*" type, arranged in beautiful geometrical designs. The roof is covered by corrugated iron sheets over which a flat deck is made accessible by a staircase running up from the pantry. The houseboats are built of deodar wood and are rarely painted. The natural colour and the sweet fragrance of the wood lend a charm of its own to the houseboat. The kitchen of the houseboat is either a small boat attached with the main boat or the cooking is done in the *doonga*, yet another type of boat. The roofs of the houseboats are also used for leisure, sun bathing, painting and reading etc. The bracing sunshine in the morning is a treat to the visitors and they sit on the roofs for hours at a stretch.

Houseboat categories are Deluxe, A, B, C and D depending on the facilities available. The houseboats are moored to either island or river bank by chains, wires or ropes and roll only in a bad storm. With the growth of the tourist traffic the boat-building industry flourished and Biscoe remarks that one of the chief features of the Jhelum in the city was the increasing number of houseboats, inhabited chiefly by Europeans. The houseboat industry reached a new height during World War II when thousands of military personnel from all over South East Asia spent their furloughs in Srinagar. One good effect of the houseboat industry was the revival of the wood-carving art. The houseboat owners employed a large number of wood-carvers for the ceilings which were (and are) invariably of the Kashmir *Khatamband* type.

References

1. A. R. Khan, *Kashmir Tourist's Paradise*, City Book Centre, Srinagar, 2012.
2. Abul Fazl, *Ain-i-Akbari* Persian Manuscript.
3. Abul Fazl, *Akbarnama* Persian Manuscript.
4. Allan Stacey, *Visiting Kashmir,* B. T. Batsford Ltd., London, 1988.
5. *Cultural Forum,* Vol. XII, Nos. 3-4, April, July 1970.
6. Francois Younghusband, *Kashmir Described*, New Delhi, 1970.
7. Kalhana's Rajatarangini.
8. Maulvi Mohammad Hussain Azad, *Darbar-i-Akbar*, Archives, New Delhi.
9. Mohammad Ishaq Khan, *History of Srinagar 1846-1947, A study in Socio-Cultural Change*, Cosmos Publications, Srinagar, 1999.
10. Orjan Wikender, (ed.) *Handbook of Ancient Water Technology*, Brill, Leiden, 2000.
11. Shanta Sanyal, *The Boats and the Boatmen of Kashmir*, Sagar Publications, New Delhi, 1979.
12. Tapan Raychaudhry, *Inland Trade-Cambridge History of India,* Vol. I, 1981.
13. Tyndale Biscoe C. E, *Kashmir in Sunlight and Shade*, Mittal Publications, New Delhi, 1995.
14. Walter, R, Lawrence, *The Valley of Kashmir*, Chinar Publications, Srinagar, 1967.
15. Read more at http://www.brainyquote.com/quotes/keywords/natural.html#BvHZmt2ICpkluQT1.99

17

Environment and Development in Nagaland, North East India: A Quest for Sustainable Development

Prof M.S. Rawat

"The alternate domination of one faction over another, sharpened by the spirit of revenge natural to party dissension, which in different ages and countries has perpetrated the most horrid enormities, is itself a frightful despotism. But this leads at length to a more formal and permanent despotism."

—George Washington

Introduction

The tribal population with their cultural diversity is an integral component of hill ecosystem of the north-east region of India. In the recent past, Nagaland has received growing attention due to the ecological degradation and environmental changes caused in the process of short-term development motives and basic life survival activities (Rawat, 2014a). There is an environmental consciousness on the degradation of natural resources resulting in depletion of ecological services and life supporting systems. In fact man's fate is bound up with his environment and ecosystems. He derives not only his physical sustenance - air, water, food, fuel, fibre, shelter etc from the environment but also the means of social, intellectual, moral and spiritual growth. It is now dawning upon man that the process of development that he has pursued in meeting his basic and other requirements by the exploitation of natural resources, mineral, plant and animal kingdoms (biodiversity) has led to the ecological and environmental degradation at local, national, regional and global levels. There is a global concern for the increasing incompatibility between the depleting natural resources and exploding population growth (Rawat, 2014). To face this challenge there is no other alternative than sustainable development. WCED (1987) pinpoints in its report, 'Our Common Future'- "it is impossible to separate economic development issues from environmental and ecological issues; many forms of development erode the environmental resources upon which they must be based, and environmental and ecological degradation can undermine economic development. The present development trends leave an increasing number of people poor and vulnerable, while at the same time degrading the ecology and environment. Sustainable development becomes a goal for all. An environmental crisis, an ecological crisis, a development crisis, an energy crisis are not separate. They are one. Ecology and economy are becoming ever more interwoven locally, regionally, nationally and globally, into a net of cause and effect." But the debate about environment and development has been dominated by the interests and values of the rich rather than the poor, men rather than women and the urban rather than the rural.

A large amount of literature exists on Himalayan region which unequivocally points to the facts that resources have led to increasing environmental and ecological degradation, and therefore the development achieved is far from sustainable. Reduced forest cover (Singh, Tiwari and Saxena, 1985), accelerated soil erosion and increased silting of water bodies (Valdiya, 1985; 1987 and Rawat and Rawat, 1994 a), drying up of springs (Valdiya and Bartarya, 1991), replacement and disappearance of species (Saxena *et al.*, 1984; Singh, Rawat and Chaturvedi, 1984), increased ratio of energy expended in fodder and fuel collection to energy expended in direct agricultural activity and consequent high level of drudgery of womenfolk

(Pandey and Singh, 1984). Degradation of ecology, environment and natural resources in the watersheds of North East Hill region is often associated with shifting cultivation which is the most prominent farming system, providing a way of life for a large number of ethnic communities. This is common across Bangladesh, Bhutan, Northeast India, Nepal and Myanmar (ICIMOD, 2006); Rawat, 2011 a & b; Ramakrishnan, 1992, 1998 and 2001; Ramakrishnan *et al.*, 2002). In the recent past, Nagaland has also received growing attention due to environmental and ecological degradation caused in the process of short-term developmental motives and basic life survival activities (Rawat, 2008). Shifting cultivation also known as jhum, slash and burn agriculture remains to be dominant form of land use practices in Nagaland. About 64 per cent of its total geographical area is under shifting cultivation in the state (Keitzar, 2009). The challenges are how to adopt its land use pattern and production system to the increasing population and lifestyle, making them environmentally and economically sustainable (Rawat and Furkumzuk, 2010; Rawat *et al.*, 2009 and Bhan, 2009). This paper is describing briefly the status of environment and development in Nagaland for the further studies of sustainable development.

Environment, Ecology and Sustainable Development

Human beings have been interested in environment and ecology since the beginning of civilisation. Even our ancient scriptures have included practices and values related to environmental conservation. Describing environment as a resource system, Singh (1998) advocated that environment as a generic concept for whatever is external to and potentially influential upon a unit under study. For a biologist, environment of an organism, whether plant, animal or man is the collection of other organisms, chemical and physical elements with which the organism interacts (Conway and Romm, 1972). For a sociologist, environment includes as much of what is external as can be reached in any given interval of time, and, *"each localised population now draws its food and other materials from such a wide area that an accurate description of its effective environment poses an almost insurmountable problem"* (Hawley,

1973). In simple terms, environment of a location comprises such things as air, water, soil, plants, animals etc. Each component constitutes a major resource, e.g. land, water and forest resources. All the components (resources) are inter-related, for example one cannot visualize the existence of plants without soil, water and air. Thus environment not only comprises the life support system for the biological organisms, it can be defined as a system of interacting resource subsystems. The UNEP noted that 'the environment includes a complex of natural, built and social components in the life of humanity'.

The science which elicits the functional inter-relationships among the different components of environment on the one hand, and between the organism and environment, on the other, is called ecology. The ecological principles are directly applicable to environment and its management. One such principle states that environment is holocoenotic in nature and therefore any change in one component is bound to change the states of all other components (Singh, 1998); for example, deforestation leads to increased runoff (hence flood problems), increased soil erosion (hence siltation of water bodies), disappearance of species (hence gene erosion) and atmospheric loading of carbon dioxide (hence global warming). The environmental, ecological and economic considerations are therefore to be combined for attaining sustainable development. Combining all the considerations adds geometrically to the complexity of a development programme (Caldwell, 1984).

Each culture was the result of the people trying to survive within their environment and indeed of an attempt to optimise the use of its resources (Agarwal, 1992). It is advisable that the management of such environmental resources upon which local communities depend should be decentralised and these communities should be given an effective share over the use of these resources (WCED, 1987). Sustainable development implies the use of ecological system in a manner that satisfies current needs without compromising the needs or options of future generations. Strategies for sustainable development must be based on reliable and comprehensive data on natural-cultural environment and socio-economic resources (Singh, 1998). One of the issues of the ecology and environment is the role of shifting cultivation activities and the threat they pose to sustainability, especially of forest and water resources in the North East Hill region of India in general and Nagaland in particular.

Brief Geographical Overview of Nagaland

Nagaland is the 16th State of the Union of India and one of the extreme northeastern states which lies between latitudes 25º 20' N to 27º 04' N and longitudes 93º 20' E to 95º 15' E with Myanmar in the east, Manipur in the south, Assam in the north and west and Arunachal Pradesh in the north (Fig. 1). Nagaland has a total geographical area of 16579 km divided into 11 administrative districts namely, Kohima, Mokokchung, Zunheboto, Tuensang, Phek, Mon, Wokha, Dimapur, Longleng, Kiphire and Peren (Fig. 2). These districts are further divided in Development Blocks and Circles for administrative conveniences. Physiographically, Nagaland can be divided into three NE-SW trending mountain ranges. These are (1) Eastern mountain ranges or High hill ranges in the east. (2) Middle hilly ranges or Medium high hill ranges in the intermediate zone and (3) Western low ranges. Nagaland is situated almost at the tri-junction of the three major river systems of the region viz., Brahmaputra River System in the west and north, Meghna River System in the south and Chindwin River System in the east.

The altitudes ranging from 100 m to 3840 m above msl and climatic conditions that varies from sub-temperate to sub-tropical. The geographical location and varied climatic conditions have contributed to the State's unique environment and ecosystems that are home to numerous endemic and endangered species of flora and fauna. The agro-biodiversity consisting of both wild and domesticated varieties of plants and fruits- is amongst one of the most diverse in the region. The State has an interesting land use as 20.4 per cent primary forest, 55.3 per cent *jhum*, 8.2 per cent current *jhum*, 4.6 per cent terraced rice cultivation and wet rice cultivation, 0.9 per cent horticulture and cash crop and about 10.6 per cent area is under other land uses (Keitzar, 2009). Nagaland has a total population of 19,80,602 out of which 10,25,707 (52 per cent) are male and 9,54,895 (48 per cent) are

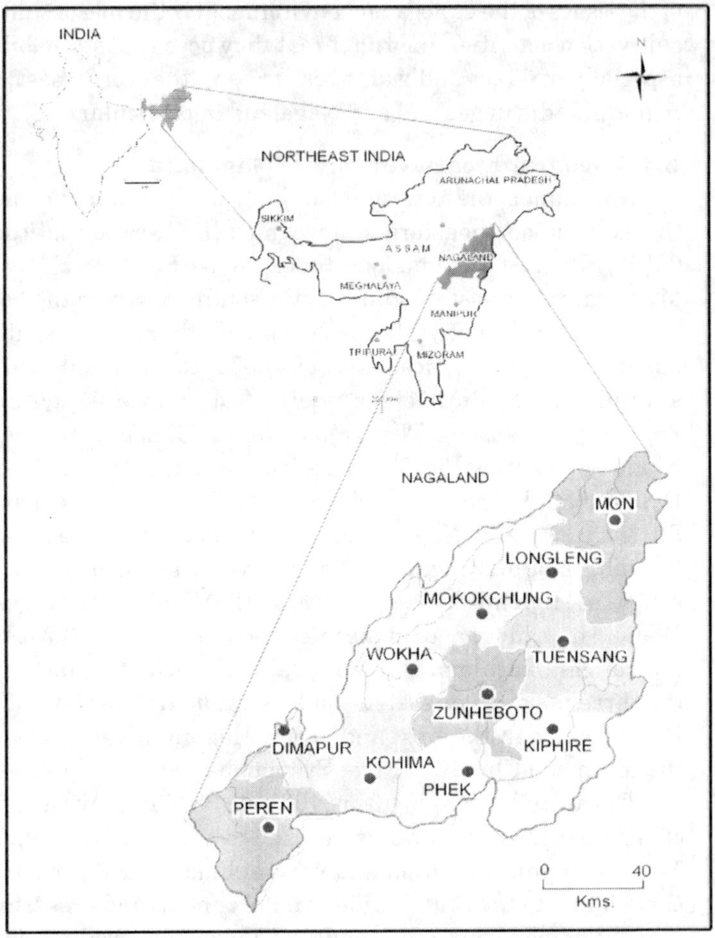

Fig. 1 : Location map of Nagaland, India.

female according to the provisional Census of 2011. Due to the unique land ownership and management system of the Nagas there is little or no alienation of the people from their land and resources and therefore, even farmers, despite their poor economic condition can be considered resource-rich. A comparatively low population pressure, high regeneration rate of plant resources community- based natural resources management initiatives and most importantly shifting cultivation activities are the major controlling factors of ecological and environmental health of Nagaland. The hilly nature, rugged terrain and lofty ranges have a great bearing on the population distribution and the cultural landscape of Nagaland. It is the extreme eastern part adjoining Myanmar, which is less developed and inaccessible mainly because of the constraints imposed by the comparatively formidable physical terrain.

Nagaland represents an ideal model of synthesis of modernity and tradition. The Naga society is well known for its tribal culture, land holding system, land use pattern including jhum practice and its rich traditional knowledge base. It is the society and the community itself that can play the vital role in the participatory approach to biodiversity conservation and natural resources management. Naga society is in fact a social network of interacting individuals. The districts are headed by Deputy Commissioners. All together there are 1428 villages (Census, 2011) headed by Gaon Buras (GB's) or the traditional headmen who look after the administrative functioning of the village. Each village has a Village Development Board (VDB) headed by the VDB Secretary and this Board serves as a decision-making as well as implementing agency for all development works at the village level. 82 per cent of the total population is rural (Census, 2001). All these villages have strong set up of independent democratic governance in the form of Village Councils. A Naga village government is more democratic in nature and practice than any other communities of the world. These Naga villages are the most permanent social and political units for all practical purposes (Jamir and Lanunungsang, 2005).

The Physical Environment

Physical geography is an area of study that brings together and interrelate the important elements of man's physical environment (Strahler and Strahler, 1978). The quality of the physical environment is established by factors, forces, and inputs coming from both the atmosphere above and the solid earth below. The physical environment of any region include commonly, apart from rational issues, the nature of geo-structural make up, geomorphological surfaces (physiography), climate, vegetation, water regimes and soils etc. Mountain environment is fragile, highly susceptible to disturbance, with a low ability to rebound and to heal themselves after damage. The physical environment is the most outstanding feature and thus important. The economic function of man becomes more significant than his other functions as it is more concerned with the functioning of ecosystem.

The Physiography

Physiography affects the environment variously. The impact can be seen not only on climate, natural vegetation and soils but also on the settlement of man and economic development. There are three major physiographic divisions in Nagaland. (1) The High Hill Ranges in the East is the highest mountain ranges in

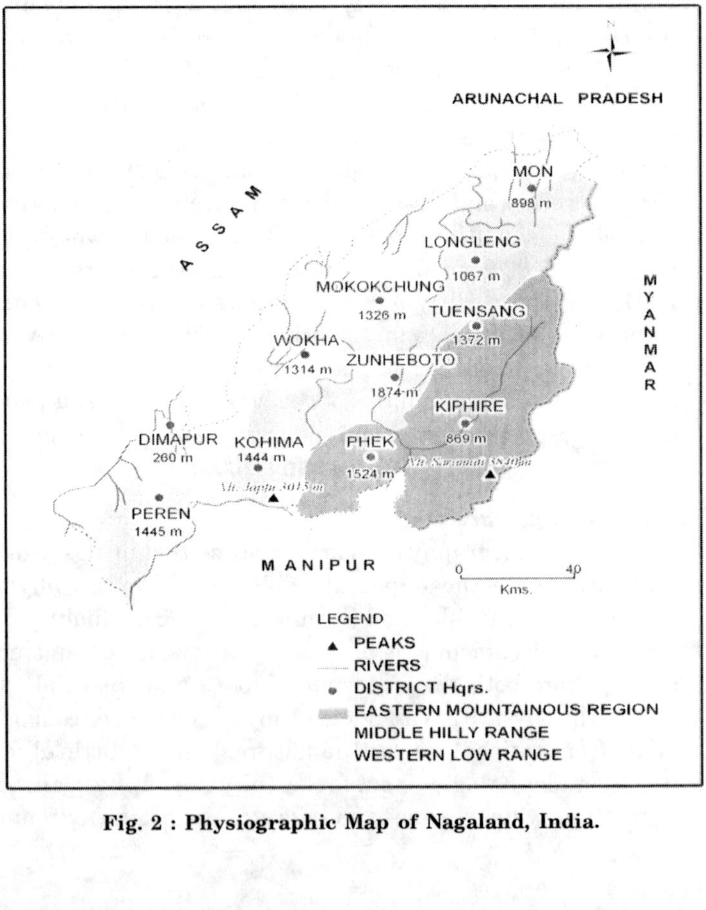

Fig. 2 : Physiographic Map of Nagaland, India.

the State attaining a height of 3840 m at Saramati. This range traverses the extreme eastern high hill ranges. It is also known as the Patkai Range which takes a north-south course separating Nagaland from Myanmar. Barail range is another mountain range in the south-western part of the State. Japfu is the highest peak (2015 m) in this range. These two ranges spread out many ridges, spurs and small branches which are the spiral backbones of the Physiography dissected by a number of seasonal and perennial rivers and rivulets with V-shaped valleys with sloppy spurs. (2) The Medium High Hill Ranges in the intermediate zone is characterised by a continuous hilly range with altitude between 600 m to 1200 m. These ranges run through the middle of the State from northeast to southwest like a spiral column. (3) The Western Low Range rise from the State with an altitude between110 and 600 m above msl. The most important plain is Dimapur. The Naga Hills exercised a great influence on the environmental conditions of the State. The complex geology and the tectonic stress which heaved up these ranges and aggravating of the hill slopes processes of weathering, erosion, mass movement, seismicity, and so on, which effect and modify the natural environment.

Natural Hazards

A natural hazard is an unexpected or uncontrollable phenomenon of unusual magnitude which occurs in proximity and poses a threat to people, structures and economic assets caused by biological, geological, seismic, hydrological, geomorphological or meteorological conditions or processes in natural environment. The northeast region experience regular environmental hazards in the form of earthquakes, floods and landslides etc. Kapur (2009) notes that India tops the list of the number of disasters in the world. As some reported observations in the Indian Himalayan region clearly reveal an average of two landslides per km yr . Nagaland, Assam, Meghalaya, Mizoram, Arunachal Pradesh and Manipur are considered by seismologists to be the sixth most earthquake-prone belt in the world. North-eastern states including Nagaland lies in zone five of the seismic map which is the highest risk zone where magnitude may even exceed eight making the states highly susceptible to earthquakes. The estimate indicates that the number of people affected by various hazards is annually increasing at the rate of six per cent. The areas along both sides of the geological faults which are frequently ravaged by tectonic movements are extremely prone to slope failure, landslides and soil erosion. Where human intervention has tampered with natural balance, the hazards of soil erosion and mass-movements have assumed alarming proportions in Nagaland. It is, therefore, essential that the spot areas and belts that are vulnerable to natural hazards must be identified, precisely delineated in maps, and compressively described in records.

Climate

Climate is the fundamental factor in establishing physical environment and it sets the stage upon which all physical, chemical and biological processes operate. Climate influences plants, animals, man and soil directly specially on human welfare ranges from the immediate effects of weather events to complex responses associated with climate change (Ayoade, 1983). Climate is not only directed but determines the entire ecological balance of a region. The major essentials of life for mankind namely, air, water, food and shelter and climate dependent. Climate may be considered as a resource. The beneficial effects such as rain, sunshine, cloud, and wind in the proper proportions of time, place and intensity or amount should be wisely harnessed and utilised rather than be considered as free goods to misuse. Nagaland enjoys diverse climate ranging from sub-tropical to sub-temperate and even micro climate conditions within a short distance. The summer and winter temperature over the hills vary from 4º to 28ºC and those over the foothills have a range between 12º and 34ºC. The average annual rainfall is between 1200 mm and 2800 mm occurring over a period of six months from May to October with the concentration in the months of July and August. January is the coldest month of the year. Winter winds are generally weak and variable. For the study of the characteristics of weather and climate, daily meteorological data were collected from the different Meteorological Stations

Table-1: Summary of meteorological data (average annual) recorded at the Meteorological Observatory at Zunheboto during the years between 2002 and 2010 (Source: Soil and Water Conservation Directorate, Govt. of Nagaland)

Years	*Average Temperature (^{o} C)*			*Total Rainfall (mm)*	*Average Humidity (%)*
	Maxi	*Mini*	*Average*		
2002	20.3	12.6	16.4	2155.2	89.9
2003	19.1	10.1	15.8	2343.6	92.2
2004	17.8	10.2	14.0	2073.5	83.7
2005	19.5	11.3	15.3	2530.1	86.3
2006	21.2	12.9	17.1	1393.1	78.1
2007	21.2	12.8	17.0	12.93.2	76.0
2008	20.53	12.9	16.1	1133.1	73.2
2009	21.52	13.6	17.6	1108.7	69.6
2010	21.8	13.0	17.4	1662.9	76.1
Average	**20.32**	**12.15**	**16.3**	**1743.71**	**80.6**

particularly Zunheboto town established and operated by Directorate of Soil and Water Conservation, Govt. of Nagaland. The daily meteorological data for the years (2002-2010) recorded at the central part of Nagaland viz., Zunheboto town are summarised and presented in the Table 1.

Temperature

Temperature is a measure of heat energy available in the air and soil (Strahler and Strahler,1978). Organisms respond directly to heating and cooling of the environmental substance that surrounds them. There is a daily rhythm of rise and fall of air temperature as well as seasonal rhythm. As per the long-term data base of the Regional Meteorological Centre, Guwahati, the summer temperatures have shot up by almost 5ºC on an average over the last two decades in North East India, a region nestled in hills and surrounded by rivers. Table 1 is presenting a summary of nine years of meteorological data from almost the central place of Nagaland viz., Zunheboto town, the averages varies from a maximum of 20.3ºC to a minimum of 12.2ºC. Several districts of the region have already been declared as affected by drought like situation in the recent past.

Rainfall

Rainfall is the most common form of precipitation and one of the most important climatic factors. The all India average rainfall is 1170 mm but it varies respectively from 100 mm in western deserts to 12000 mm in north-east India. This region boasts of world's wettest place, has witnessed the highest rainfall deficit in the last 30 years and meteorologists say there is a clue to global warming in the phenomenon. Meteorological records till July 2009 reveal that Manipur has been worst affected recording 67 per cent deficient rainfall, followed by Meghalaya (55 per cent), Nagaland (62 per cent), Assam (34 per cent), Mizoram (31 per cent), Tripura (30 per cent), Arunachal Pradesh (29 per cent) and Sikkim (31 per cent). The nine years annual rainfall data have been presented in Table 1 and showing a decreasing trend. In the year 2003 the total rainfall was recorded 2343.6 mm while in the 2009 it was only 1108.7 mm. The average of nine years annual rainfall was found 1743.71 mm against the long past annual rainfall of 2500 mm in Nagaland.

Humidity

Humidity refers to the amount of water vapour present in the air or it is a term used to describe the water vapour content of the atmosphere. Atmospheric water vapour originates from the earth's surface by evaporation and transpiration. It is, therefore, strongly, concentrated in the lower layers of the atmosphere. The humidity data have been presented in Table 1 showing the annual average of nine years which was found 80.6 per cent and varies from 69.6 per cent in the year 2009 to 92.2 per cent in the year 2003.

Evaporation

Evaporation is the process by which moisture in its liquid or solid form is converted into gaseous form- the water vapour. The atmosphere acquires moisture from the earth's surface through evaporation of water from bare land and water surfaces and transpiration from plants. Evaporation is one of the important parameters considered in calculating the water balance of a catchment ecosystem. In Nagaland, data on evaporation are not yet available. Recently the Department of Geography, Nagaland University has established a Meteorological Observatory at Lumami. Evaporation records of seven to eight months of this Observatory are showing the range of evaporation rates at Lumami from 16 mm to 92 mm per day.

Natural Vegetation

Plant life in aggregate is called vegetation. Natural vegetation includes that part of the plant life which grows in wild without human aid and adapts to the constraints of physical environment in size, structure, and requirements. The hills and mountains have given mandate to achieve 66 per cent forest cover for its ecological significance. The harmonious relationship with the ecological balance of nature is going to be the greatest challenge to mankind in this century. The sole reason of the whole problem of the global warming simply is that modern man produces carbon dioxide in excess to what nature can manage. The forest has vital importance for sound environment and ecology. It also protects the landscape from exogenous destabilising forces. The vegetation not only decreases flood peaks, but also increases the water yield during dry periods. Peak discharge rates are reduced because of increase infiltration in the presence of a forest cover. Forest canopy and the network of roots prevent erosion, through minimising the impact of raindrops and soil binding, respectively. Thus, the sediment load in rivers is reduced, indirectly the forest increases water holding capacity of the soil through additions of organic matter. The north-east region contributes almost 25 per cent of country's forest resources. Bamboo often known as 'Green Gold' is a plant that is one of the fastest and highest yielding renewable natural resources which is found extensively. There are three Wildlife Sanctuaries and one National Park in Nagaland.

Soils

Soil is a fundamental resource base for agricultural production systems. Besides being the main medium for crop growth soil functions to sustain crop productivity, maintain environmental quality and provide nutrients for plant, animal and human health. There are increasing evidences to suggest that a majority of soil resources are under different degrees of degradation and are getting further deteriorated at an alarming rate with risk of jeopardizing food security system. A properly managed soil is an asset but when it is misused it creates environmental problems. The soils of Nagaland are generally acidic, very rich in organic carbon but poor in phosphate and potash content. The ecosystems significantly influence the process of soil formation. The process of weathering is also intense due to high precipitation and favourable condition of temperature and vegetation (NBSS & LUP, 2000). The nature's history of the areas in which we live we would see that our surroundings were originally a natural landscape such as forests, rivers, hills, mountains or combination of these elements. We live in landscapes that have been profoundly modified by man in villages, towns and cities. We get our food supply from surrounding villages and these in turn are dependent on agriculture, other natural resources and manufacturing complexes. Thus, our daily lives are inextricably linked with our surroundings and inevitably affect them.

The Cultural Environment

Human occupy the core of cultural environment of any region (Karan, 1987). Being producers, creators and consumers of resources, they influence and at times alter the physical environment. Man dominated the scene and started creating man-made environment. It includes everything developed by man through the application of his thinking facilities and tools- family; social, economic, political, religious organisations; and ideas, knowledge, will, cultures and civilisations, along with physical infrastructure. The menacing demographic growth is leading to increasing incompatibility between resources and the number of systems with their differing value systems are causing growing inequalities in human societies and furthering environmental changes. Thus, man is now responsible not only for himself but also for the harmonious maintenance of the natural environment. Human geography studies the location and distributional aspect of cultural phenomena, resulting from ever changing man-nature interaction. The growth of population has a great bearing on man-land ratio, value of land quality of life and the socio-economic dimension of a region.

Population

Nagaland has a total population of 1980602 out of which 1025707 (52 per cent) are male and 954896 (48 per cent) are female according to the Provisional Census 2011. This population shares 0.16 per cent of the total population of the country. The current Population of Nagaland is showing a decrease of 9434 persons from the population in the year 2001. This indicates a negative growth rate of -0.47 per cent during the decade from 2001-2011. The decadal growth rate of population for the last three decades has been more than 50 per cent in the State. Nagaland had also stood out for having the highest decadal growth rate of population during the decades 1981- 91 and 1991-2001. Out of 11 districts, six districts (Wokha, Dimapur, Phek, Tuensang, Kohima and Peren) have recorded positive growth while the remaining five districts have shown negative growth of population. According to the Provisional Census of India, 2011 the highest decadal growth among the districts is recorded in Dimapur at 23.13 per cent closely followed by Kohima at

Table- 2: The District-wise Population Characteristics in Nagaland (Source- Census of India, 2011).

Sl. No.	*Districts*	*Male Population*	*Female Population*	*Total Population*	*% share in total Population*
1.	Dimapur	198163	181606	379796	19.17
2.	Kiphire	37758	36275	74033	3.74
3.	Kohima	140118	129945	270063	13.64
4.	Longleng	26588	24005	50593	2.55
5.	Mokokchung	100229	92942	193171	9.75
6.	Mon	132062	118609	250671	12.66
7.	Peren	49530	45424	94954	4.79
8.	Phek	83684	79610	163294	8.24
9.	Tuensang	101977	94824	198801	9.94
10.	Wokha	84429	81810	166239	8.39
11.	Zunheboto	71169	69845	141014	7.12
	Nagaland	**1025,707**	**954895**	**1980602**	**100.00**

22.8 per cent. Both the districts have shown a growth rate above the National growth rate of 17.76 per cent. Phek district has recorded a growth of 10.19 per cent followed by Tuensang at 5.81 per cent, Peren at 4.61 per cent and Wokha at 3.11 per cent. The State has population density 119 persons per sq.km which is way below the National figure of 382 persons per sq.km. The sex ratio has gone up to 931 which are the highest in the last five decades but it is still below the National level of 940 females per 1000 males. Nagaland has shown a big improvement in literacy rates from earlier Census years. From 61.65 per cent in 1991, it has gone up to 66.59 per cent in 2001 and in 2011 it stands at 80.11 per cent which is above the National level of 74.04 per cent. Mokokchung district is on the top of the list with 92.68 per cent literates. Mon district finds its place (56.6 per cent) at the bottom of the list.

Nagaland is perhaps the poorest State in respect of availability of data and information about different aspects of socio-economic parameters. Demography is the statistical study of human population and it encompasses the study of population and patterns and its impacts in socio-economic development will help in understanding the needs and importance of alround development in the society. Development of human resource is also an essential input in order to achieve a faster rate of economic growth and sustainable development. The productivity and efficiency of people (workers) in Nagaland is not encouraging compared to the rest of India, whereas human resource of the State is not at all inferior to others as literacy and Human Development Index is much more compared to the National rate.

Agriculture

Today, agriculture occupies 40 per cent of the land surface and consumes 70 per cent of global water resources and helps manage biodiversity at the genetic, species and ecosystem levels (FAO, 2007). Traditional agriculture, an indigenous form of farming is the result of the co-evolution of local, social and environmental systems. It exhibits a high level of ecological rationale expressed through the intensive use of local knowledge and natural resources including the management of agro-biodiversity in the form of diversified agricultural systems (DPC, 2011a). There are four diversified forms of traditional agriculture practiced by the villagers of Nagaland - the jhum system (shifting cultivation), terrace rice cultivation, firewood reserve forests and home gardens. The practice of slash and burn agriculture is known locally as 'jhum' as the word derived from Assamese language meaning 'collective work'. The Naga way of life revolves around this system of cultivation which governs most of their life, culture and tradition. In Nagaland, over 40 per cent of the area is subject to jhum cultivation (NEPED and IIRR, 1999).

The extent area under jhum is also maximum in the State compared to other states of north-east India. According to the village profile of the Department of Agriculture (2001), there are 184127 farming households consisting of 1360925 persons comprising 68.44 per cent of the total population. Of the total Naga farmers, 70 per cent have been practicing jhum cultivation on the steep slopes with only the Angamis and Chakhesang tribes practicing terrace rice cultivation on steep slope. Mostly women are engaged in agriculture leading to feminisation of agriculture in the State, a trend that is happening globally among the developing countries. For rural people to have sustainable livelihoods, the key is having access to secured land, water, forests and other means of production. Food security should be assured with an increasing access to water for domestic and irrigation purposes, land and markets as well as other economic opportunities. Rural women and nature work in partnership with each other with a special relationship (Mies and Shiva, 1993). The area under production per hectare under terrace rice cultivation is increasing across the State. Perhaps because of the increase in TRC with proper water management, the shortfall of rice from jhum is somewhat mitigated. The main source of energy for both lighting and cooking in the households of rural areas is firewood. Zabu is also a farming system practiced mostly by the Chakesang tribe where combination of forest, water and agriculture incorporating livestock and fishery, which is well founded soil and water conservation base. The limit to terrace construction is not the slope but availability of irrigation water. 'Give water and you have terrace'.

Development in Nagaland

Development is a process whereby the people come to utilise the resources available to bring about a sustained increase in per capita production of goods and services. Nagaland State has a special status in the Indian Union. Article 371 (A) of the Constitution of India provides that the custom and tradition of Naga people is protected and that a land ownership continue to remain in the hands of the individuals, clan, communities and villagers. The transition of a primitive tribal society into a modern one compressed within a short span of just a little over a century can be very confusing. There is very little interface between the government and the academic community in Nagaland with regard to the economic planning and development (Jamir, 2002). There is a big gap between the rural poor and urban rich. The productivity and efficiency of people (workers) in Nagaland is not encouraging compared to the rest of India, whereas human resource of the State is not at all inferior to others as literacy and Human Development Index is much more compared to the national rate.

The figures of development indicators presented in Table 3 are impressive during the period between 1962-63 and 2001-02

Table- 3: Some important indicators for the comparison of development in Nagaland during the period between the year 1962-63 and 2001-02 (after Jamir, 2002).

Sl. No.	*Particulars*	*Unit*	*1962-63*	*2001-02*
1.	Total length of roads	Kms.	837	9860
2.	Number of villages covered	Nos.	N.A.	1092
3.	Water supply provided	No. of Villages	Nil	1010
4.	Generation of electric power	MW	0.20	29.00
5.	Villages electrified	Nos.	06	1212
6.	Schools	Nos.	603	1691
7.	Literacy	%	17.91	67.11
8.	Enrolment in primary schools	%	N.A.	100
9.	Hospitals and Dispensaries	Nos.	11	449
10.	Area under irrigation	000 ha	1.51	65.63
11.	Food grain production	000 ha	61.82	292.5

but despite this Nagaland remain underdeveloped and still a long way to go even to catch up with the rest of the country. After the year 2001-02 much more development has been achieved so far. However, at the moment data are not available with the author. According to the findings of a socio-economic study, the GDP of the State as estimated during 2002-03 is Rs 264148 lakh with an average annual growth rate of 8.18 per cent, giving a per capita income of Rs 12292 with an average growth rate of 2.8 per cent. The Net State Domestic Products (NSDP) of Nagaland during 2003 (at current prices) stood at Rs 4458.29 Crores. Of this, the contribution of the primary sector comprising of agriculture and allied departments accounted for 33.37 per cent of the NSDP of Nagaland. It must be noted that the overall percentage contribution of agriculture to the NSDP is 30.41 per cent and within the primary sector it contributed an astonishing 91.13 per cent.

Food and environmental security have become a major issue of concern. Environmental management of degraded jhum-agro-ecosystem is the need of the hour. So far, environment has not been taken seriously as the social, economic and other components in development planning. The concept of rural development through active participation of the people from grass root level for development planning became a reality in the early 1980's with the constitution of the Village Development Boards (VDBs) in all the recognised villages in the State. The power conferred on the Village Councils (VCs) for the purpose of formulation of plans and implementations of development programmes have been developed to the VDBs in all villages. There are 1083 VDBs in the State (Table 4).

The Village Development Boards are empowered to take decisions and implementation of schemes within the guidelines both for State and centrally sponsored schemes. They are capable of mobilising its internal resources for investment in various income generating and economically productive activities. VDBs check migration of educated unemployed rural youths to towns by ensuring self-employment opportunities through their involvement in taking up income generating and economically productive activities in the rural areas. It aims to transform the

Table- 4: District-wise Village Development Boards in Nagaland as per Census, 2001 (Source: Department of Rural Development, Govt. of Nagaland, 2005).

Sl. No.	*Districts*	*Number of Blocks*	*Number of VDBs*	*Number of Households*	*Population*
1.	Kohima	4	83	24196	133557
2.	Mokokchung	6	75	23126	2,26338
3.	Tuensang	8	99	20934	132429
4.	Mon	6	94	26120	221162
5.	Wokha	5	111	14312	137192
6.	Zunheboto	6	167	18833	112578
7.	Phek	5	89	20935	106561
8.	Dimapur	4	189	28765	80168
9.	Kiphire	3	74	13165	87573
10.	Longleng	2	26	12665	97894
11.	Peren	3	76	13475	79391
	Total	**52**	**1083**	**216514**	**1515443**

rural areas into the standards of semi-urban areas in so far as availability of the basic facilities is concerned. It also aims to enable them to act as financial intermediaries for managing their own rural credit and loan activities.

Results and Discussion

The village societies are characterised by their close interconnection with nature and natural resources. They depend upon natural resources and biodiversity for their sustainable livelihood concerns. The Naga tribes rely heavily on agriculture and natural resources to meet their livelihood needs. Jhum cultivation is a way of life for the Nagas and is deeply rooted in Naga culture, customs and beliefs. However, with increasing population pressure and changing life style, the Nagas face challenges of meeting livelihood needs and sustaining the environment and ecosystems. Environmental degradation refers to the deterioration in its physical component brought in by the biological processes mainly by human activities to such an extent that it can not be set right by the self-regulatory mechanism of the environment. In other words, environmental degradation means overall lowering of environmental qualities because of adverse changes brought in by human activities in the basic structure of the components of the environment to such an extent that these adverse changes adversely affect all biological communities in general and human society in particular.

In the present century, environmental degradation has emerged as a major global concern for human survival. In the opinion of the World Commission on Environment and Development, the future is to face an ever increasing environmental decay, poverty, hardship and ever more polluted world. The strains of the ecological crisis are so apparent that the task to preserve and protect the environment has become the primary requisite of the economics of development. The Northeast region of India is one of the 34 "Biodiversity Hotspots" of the world (CI, 2005). Biodiversity is the very basis of human survival and economic well-being as it provides food, medicine and offers a potential for providing many more yet unknown benefit to future generations. Species and their population contain precious 'genetic library' maintained by natural ecosystem (Singh, 1998). In recent years, the region has received growing attention due to environmental and ecological degradation caused in the process of shifting cultivation, short-term development motives, and basic life survival activities (Sundriyal *et al.*, 1998). Jhum cultivation is taking a heavy toll on the forest resources of the northeast, depleting the 'dense forest' cover essential for the ecological stability of the region (Table 5).

The State of the Forest Report, (2003) has shows that a total of 5476 km has been eroded in the region owing to jhum cultivation. Nagaland is the worst affected, with 1332 km (24.3 per cent) of forest destroyed, while Assam and Manipur lost 925 (16.8 per cent) and 855 km (15.6 per cent) of forest land, respectively. As people in Tripura are less dependent on this mode of cultivation, the State managed to escape its brunt, losing only 384 km (7 per cent). The region has lost a further 3478 km of forest cover owing to other factors like encroachment, deforestation and illegal felling. Shifting cultivation is most complex and multifaceted form of agriculture or agro-forestry practices in the world (Darlong, 2004). Perhaps, because of its complexities, it is also the least understood form of agriculture. As a result, shifting cultivation is condemned in many forums as being destructive to the environment because forest areas are being converted to agriculture through its practices, thus diminishing the area under primary forest (DPC, 2011a). A virgin forest land in the hills is cleared by burning and the land is put to cultivation. When production declines, the land is abandoned and another virgin forest site is selected for cultivation (Sema *et.al.*, 2010). According to an estimate about 82 km of forest is lost in Nagaland for jhum cultivation per annum which is affecting and depleting the forest cover. The reserved primary forest is very important to conserve the water sources. Villagers are aware that primary forests serve as water reservoirs. Due to the decreasing primary forest cover, water sources diminishing in and around the villages.

Many Village Councils have passed a strong resolution to conserve and preserve the water sources of the villages (NEPED,

2008). Another cause of deforestation is the firewood consumption. There are no alternative sources of energy in the villages; fuel wood is one of the most important needs of a family's existence. In fact it is next only to rice importance. Firewood is not only used in cooking but also for heating homes and a host of other utilities. Next to food security, firewood is the most important resource in the life of a farming family in the village. The fire wood consumption in Nagaland is about 8.7 million cubic meters assuring the tree stand volume to approximately equivalent to that of jhum which is 188 m trees from 46090 ha of wood. It has been reported that several villages such as Sungratsu of Mokokchung district and Lozaphehu of Phek district had imposed a ban on export of firewood by the Village Council in order to protect the environment. Demand for firewood is on the rise in the towns. Many villages are sailing the firewood to the towns regularly. Over the years, several factors have caused progressively increasing strains and stresses on the society and on the efficiency of the practice, so that in certain cases these practices have become highly resource – depleting and severely environment degrading (Nair, 1986). Table 6 is presenting the forest cover change in Nagaland during the years between 1995 and 2007. Slash and burn or shifting agriculture system has received a great deal of attention due to their observed or hypothesised role in deforestation, biodiversity loss, accelerated soil erosion, increasing flood and landslide hazards, downstream sedimentation, decreased runoff and soil fertility and diminishing water resources and global warming (Rawat, 2008).

During monsoon rains, this is disrupting the hydrologic cycle producing much heavier runoff and sediment transport, leading to devastating floods as well as reduced dry season flow. These consequences have far reaching implications for sustainable development of this region in general and Nagaland in particular. There are nearly 600000 families of shifting cultivators in India, and more than 90 per cent are in the north-eastern States. In fact, the whole of North East India can be appropriately termed as 'land of shifting cultivators' in the Agro-kingdom (Keitzar, 2009). More than thousand villages in Nagaland have been organised into Village Development Boards with the specific

Table- 5: Decline in forest cover between 1991 and 1995 in the north-eastern States of India (after Mishra and Sharma, 2001)

State	*Forest cover (km²)*			*Annual decrease (%)*		
	1991	*1993*	*1995*	*1991*	*1993-1995*	*1991-1995*
Arunachal Pradesh	68750	68661	68621	0069	0.029	0.049
Assam	24750	24508	24061	0.494	0.912	0.696
Manipur	17685	17621	17558	0.181	0.178	0.179
Meghalaya	15875	15769	15714	0.333	0.174	0.367
Mizoram	18853	18697	18576	0.413	0.323	0.367
Nagaland	14321	14348	14291	0.164	0.198	0.052
Sikkim	3127	3127	3119	-	0.128	0.064
Tripura	5535	5538	5538	+0.027	-	0.013
Total	**168904**	**168269**	**167478**	**0.188**	**0.235**	**0.211**

Table- 6: The forest cover change in Nagaland during the years between 1995 and 2007

Year of assessment	*Dense Forest (ha)*	*Open Forest (ha)*	*Total (ha)*	*Per centage of total geographical area*
1995	3487	10804	14291	86.20
1997	3487	10374	14221	85.57
1999	5137	9027	14164	85.43
2001	5393	7952	13345	80.04
2003	5707	7902	13609	82.09
2005	6352	7313	13665	82.42
2007	6171	7293	13464	81.21

Source: State Forest Report, 2003, 2007, FSI, Dehradun.

purpose of rural development. It is also important that appropriate institutional arrangements, play a key role in involving community participation. These VDB's in Nagaland as agents for transformation were created following the traditional ways of village level institution building that has been always a part of each one of the more than 16 tribes who are participating. It is clear that the institutional arrangement play a key role in ensuring community participation, and that formation of village level institutions have to be in the given socio-cultural context.

The hydrological regime of Nagaland has been greatly affected by changes in land use, deforestation, accelerated soil erosion and landsliding. There has been a phenomenal increase in the pressure on the land, water and forest resources of the area, and this has had a serious impact on both the surface and underground hydrological regimes. The hydrological responses of watersheds- manifested in changes in the water yields of springs, floods in the valleys, erosion, sediment transport and water quality are affected by geological conditions, the land use pattern and disturbances from shifting cultivation and other human activities. Water is one of the most important components of the environment and an integral part of the ecological cycle. Water being a critical trigger for sustainable management of land resources under a monsoon climate where water scarcity is acute for a major part of the year. Traditional knowledge combined with appropriate water management could be a major factor for management of natural and human managed ecosystems for sustainable development. In the present juncture of rapid development and consequent increasing demands for this precious natural asset, the judicious use and sustainable development of water resources are the need of the hour. Due to lack of proper adequate storage facilities, about 37 per cent of the total fresh water is drained out. Leading experts of water resources are warning that the world is fast heading towards 'a water shock'. Accelerated conversion of forest land due to intensive agricultural activities, rapid urbanisation and other anthropogenic activities have resulted changes in land use and land cover pattern. Significant land use/land cover changes have been reported during the last 50 years both on spatial and temporal scale, mainly due to economic development and population growth (Sharma *at el.*, 2011).

Land use conversion is accelerating throughout north-east India and is the cause of main environmental problems. The socio-economic status of the people need to be improved if the stride in tune with the concept of the sustainable development. Watershed-based development and management efforts are emerging as potential approach for sustainable use of land and water resources though it is at evolving stage at present. This approach demands precise estimates of water availability (from all sources) and its demands (for all purposes) of the area for planning development and management strategies (Singh, 1998). The environmental degradation and development experience over the last 48 years indicate that the existing development planning strategy is needed to be modified to ensure that the resources meet the needs of the local people. Development planning so far has failed to move in right direction and the pace of development has been slow. There has been an alarming growth of the population and the numbers of educated unemployed Nagas have been rising at the rate of about 10 per cent per annum. This distress migration drains the hills of its active manpower affecting development potential in terms of resources and skills. After four to five decades of economic development, primary sector (Agriculture) still continues to dominate the economy with low productivity, environmental degradation with population explosion. Despite abundant natural resources and potential and huge capital inflow from centre, Nagaland could not attain the level of economic development as was expected.

Acknowledgements

The author is grateful to the G.B. Pant Institute of Himalayan Environment and Development, Kosi-Katarmal (Almora) for the financial assistance (Project Sanction No. GBPI/IERP/04-05/21/860) to conduct a study under Integrated Eco Development Programme for the Himalayan Region.

References

1. Agarwal, A. (1992): Community participation in restoration of environment, pp. 293-310. In: *Restoration of Degraded Land: Concepts and Strategies* (Singh, ed.). Rastogi Publication, Meerut, India.
2. Ayoade, J. O. (1983): Introduction to Climatology for the Tropics. John Wiley and Sons Ltd. New York, pp. 1-258.
3. Bhan, S. (2008): Land capital management in North Eastern States. *Journal of Soil and Water Conservation*. Vol. 7, No. 4, pp. 30-38.
4. Caldwell, L.K. (1984): Political aspects of ecologically sustainable development. *Environmental Conservation*, 11, pp. 299-308.
5. Census of India, (2011): Provisional Census of India, Nagaland.
6. CI, (2005): Global Hotspots Map. Washington DC: Conservation International. Available at www.biodiverticity hotspots. Org/xp/Hotspots.
7. Conway, G. and J. Romm. (1972): Ecology and resource development in south-east Asia. Mimeo. pp. 1-54.
8. Darlong, V.T. (2004): To jhum or not to jhum: Policy Perspectives on shifting cultivation. The Missing Link (TML). Society for Environment and Communication, Guwahati, India.
9. D.P.C. (2011a): Traditional Agriculture: Practice and Sustainable Livelihood- A Thematic report- 2009. A Govt. of India - UNDP Project on Strengthening of State Plans for Human Development. Department of Planning and coordination Govt. of Nagaland. pp. 1-57.

10. D.P.C. (2011b): The Role of Women in Natural Resource Management - A Thematic report- 2009. A Govt. of India - UNDP Project on Strengthening of State Plans for Human Development. Department of Planning and Coordination, Govt. of Nagaland. pp.1-57.

11. F.A.O. (2007): "Environment and Agriculture". Committee on Agriculture, 20th Session, Food and Agriculture Organisation (F.A.O.) Rome.

12. Hawley, A.H. (1973): Ecology and population. Science 179, pp. 1196-1201.

13. ICIMOD (2006): Debating Shifting Cultivation in the Eastern Himalayas: Farmer's Innovations as Lessons for Policy (Compiled by Kerkhoff, E. and Sharma, E.) International Centre for Integrated Mountain Development (ICIMOD), Kathmandu, Nepal, pp. 1-92.

14. Jamir, A. (2002): Keynote Address in a Seminar on 'Dimensions of Development in Nagaland. (Thomas, C.J. and Das, G. eds.). Indian Council of Social Science Research-North-Eastern Regional Centre, Shillong. Regency Publications, New Delhi, pp. 1-8.

15. Jamir, N.T. and Lanunungsang, A. (2005): Naga Society and Culture, Tribal Research Centre, Nagaland University, Lumamai.

16. Kapoor, A. (2009): On Disasters in India. New Delhi: Cambridge University Press India Pvt.

17. Karan, P.P. (1987): Population characteristics of the Himalayan region. Mountain Research and Development. 7(3), pp. 271-274.

18. Keitzar, S. (2009): A new approach to hill agricultural technology with special reference to Nagaland. Department of Agriculture, Govt. of Nagaland, pp. 1-5.

19. Mies, M. and Shiva, V. (1993): "Ecofeminism". London Zed Books.

20. Mishra, A.K. and Sharma, U.C. (2001): Traditional wisdom in range management for resource and environment conservation in north-eastern region of India. ENVIS Bulletin: Himalayan Ecology. G.B. Pant Institute of Himalayan Environment and Development, Almora. Vol. 9, No. 1.

21. NBSS and LUP, (2000): Soils of Nagaland. Soils of India Series. National Bureau of Soil Survey and Land use Planning, Indian Council of Agricultural Research, Nagpur.

22. NEPED (2006): Adding Value to Shifting Cultivation in Nagaland, India. Nagaland Environment Protection through Economic Development, Nagaland, India.
23. NEPED and IIRR (1999): Building Upon Traditional Agriculture in Nagaland, India. Nagaland Environment Protection and Ecnomic Development, Nagaland, India and International Institute of Rural Reconstruction, Silang, Cavite, 4118 Philippines.
24. Pandey, U. and Singh J. (1984): Energy flow relationships between agro and forest ecosystems in Central Himalaya. Environmental Conservation 11 (1): pp. 45-53.
25. Patel, C.C. (2009): Water resources management, development and emerging issues. *Journal of Applied Hydrology*, Vol. XXII No. 1, pp. 1-17.
26. Ramakrishnan, P.S.(1992): Shifting Agriculture and Sustainable Development. An Interdisciplinary study from North-eastern India. Carnforth and Parthenon Publications, Paris: UNESCO-MAB Series Republished by Oxford University Press. New Delhi (1999), pp. 1-261.
27. Ramakrishnan, P.S. (1998): Ecology, Economics, and Ethics; Some Key Issues Relevant to Natural Resource Management in Developing countries. International Journal of Social Economics, 25, pp. 207-225.
28. Ramakrishnan, P.S. (2001): Ecology and Sustainable Development. Popular Science Series. National Book Trust, India, New Delhi, 198.
29. Ramakrishnan, P.S., Rai, R.K., Kotwal, R.P.S. and Mehndiratta, S. (2002): Traditional Ecological Knowledge for Managing Biosphere Reserves in South and Central Asia (eds.), Oxford & IBH Publishing Co. Pvt. New Delhi, 536.
30. Rawat, J.S. and Rawat, M. S. (1994): Accelerated erosion and denudation in the Nana Kosi Watershed, Central Himalaya, India Part I: Sediment Load. Mountain Research and Development, Vol. 14, No. 1, pp. 25-38.
31. Rawat, J.S. and Rawat, M. S. (1994): The Nana Kosi Watershed Central Himalaya. India Part II Human Impacts on Stream Runoff. Mountain Research and Development, Vol. 14, No. 3, pp. 25-36.

32. Rawat, M. S. (2008): Environment, Tribal Culture and Resource Management in the Kiliki Watershed of Zunheboto Hills, Nagaland. Final Technical Report submitted to the G.B. Pant Institute of Himalayan Environment and Development, Almora, Department of Geography, Nagaland University, Lumami, pp.1-98.
33. Rawat, M. S. (2010): Environment, Tribal Culture and Resource Management in the Kiliki Watershed of Zunheboto Hills, Nagaland. In: *Biodiversity to Biotechnology: Intellectual Property Rights* (Kumar, A. and Das, G. eds.). Narosa Publishing House, New Delhi, pp.129-160.
34. Rawat, M. S. (2011a): Dwindling water resources of the Himalaya and need for water harvesting. In: Proceedings of International Seminar on Water Crisis in the Indian Subcontinent. Issues and Challenges. (eds. Z. Husain and L. Cajee), Department of Geography, North–East Hill University, Shillong, India, Bookwell Publisher, New Delhi, pp. 347-381.
35. Rawat, M. S. (2011b): Water resources management for sustainable development in the North-East India. In: Proceedings of International Seminar on Water Crisis in the Indian Subcontinent. Issues and Challenges. (eds. Z. Husain and L. Cajee), Department of Geography, North–East Hill University, Shillong, India, Bookwell Publisher, New Delhi, pp. 287-312.
36. Rawat, M. S. (2011c): Environmental Geomorphology and Watershed Management: A Study from Central Himalaya. Concept Publishing House, New Delhi, pp. 1-306.
37. Rawat, M. S. (2014): Environment and prospects of sustainable development in the Zunheboto district of Nagaland. International Journal of Development Studies and Research.Vol. 3, No. 1, pp. 166-185.
38. Rawat, M. S. (2014): Integrated watershed management for sustainable development of the Brahmaputra River Basin in India. *International Journal of Social Development*, Edition July-Dec. 2014, pp. 66-91.
39. Rawat, M. S. and Furkumzuk C. (2010): Shifting cultivation, Traditional knowledge and Sustainable development in Nagaland, India. In: *Biodiversity, Biotechnology and Traditional Knowledge: Understanding Intellectual Property Rights.* (Kumar, A. and Das, G. eds.), Narosa Publishing House, New Delhi, pp. 72-88.

40. Rawat, M. S., Zhimo,V., Imchen, N and Furkumzuk, C. (2009): Water resources of North East Hill region of India and need for water harvesting. In: Proceedings of UGC Sponsored National Seminar on Strategy for Resource Functioning of India's North East: A Geographical Perspective. North East India Geographical Society, Assam, p. 70.

41. Saxena, A. K., Singh, S.P. and Singh, J.S. (1984): Population structure of forest of Kumaun Himalaya: Implications for management. *Jour. Envi. Manag.* 19, pp. 307-324.

42. Samra, J. S., Sharda, V.N. and Sikka, A.K. (2002): Water Harvesting and Recycling: Indian Experience> Central Soil and Water Conservation Research and Training Institute, Dehra Dun, pp. 1-347.

43. Samuel, M. P. and Satapathy, K.K. (2008): Rainwater harvesting for irrigation and drinking water requirements in hilly terrains of N-E India. *Journal of Applied Hydrology*, Vol. XXI, No. 3 and 4, pp. 44-56.

44. Sema, P. Toiho, Lanusosang, T. and Rawat, M.S. (2010): Shifting cultivation and environment in Zunheboto district, Nagaland. *Journal of North-East India Council for Social Science Research*, Vol. 34. 1, pp. 97-102.

45. Sengupta, S., Sinha, K.R., Das, S. and Purkaystha, R.S. (2006): Rivers and Riverine Landscape in North East India (eds.) Concept Publishing Company, New Delhi, pp. 1-175.

46. Sharma, K.D. and Kumar, S. (2004): Water resources of India: Challenges and perspective. In: Proceedings of extended abstracts of National Conference on Resource Conserving Technologies for Social Upliftment, Central Soil and Water Conservation Research & Training Institute, Dehradun, pp. 241-242.

47. Sharma, P., Deka, D. and Saikia, R. (2011): An analysis of changing land use pattern and its effect on Umtrew basin, northeast India. *Hungarian Geographical Bulletin* 60 (1), pp. 67-78.

48. Singh, J. S. (1998): Sustainable development: An ecological viewpoint. In: Perspectives for Planning and Development in North East India (Sundriyal, et al.; eds). HIMAVIKAS Occasional Publication No. 11. G.B. Pant Institute of Himalayan Environment and Development, Almora, pp. 5-16.

49. S.F.R. (2003): State of Forest Report 2003. Forest Survey of India, Ministry of Environment and Forests, Govt. of India, Dehradun.

50. Singh, J.S., Rawat, Y.S. and Chaturvedi, O.P. (1984): Replacement of oak forest with pine in the Himalaya affects the nitrogen cycle. Nature 311 (5981), pp. 54-56.

51. Singh, J.S., Tiwari, A.K. and Saxena, A.K. (1985): Himalayan Forests : A new source of carbon for the atmosphere. Environmental Conservation 12 (1), pp. 67-69.

52. Strahler, A. N. and Strahler, A.H. (1978): Modern Physical Geography. John Wiley & Sons.Inc, pp. 1-532.

53. Statistical Hand Book of Nagaland (2007) : Directorate of Economics and Statistics, Government of Nagaland.

54. Valdiya, K.S. (1985): Accelerated erosion and landslide-prone zones in the Central Himalayan region. In: Environmental Regeneration in Himalaya: Concepts and Strategies (Singh, J.S. ed.) Central Himalayan Environmental Association and Gyanodaya Prakashan, Nainital, pp. 312-380.

55. Valdiya, K.S. (1987): Environmental Geology: Indian Context. Tata Mc Graw Hill, New Delhi, 583p.

56. Valdiya, K. S. and Bartarya, S.K. (1991): Hydrological studies of springs in the catchment of Gaula river, Kumaun Lesser Himalaya, India. Mountain Research and Development, 11, pp. 239-258.

57. WCED. (1987): Our Common Future. The World Commission on Environment and Development, 400 p.

58. Read more at http://www.brainyquote.com/quotes/keywords/natural.html#BvHZmt2ICpkluQT1.99

18

Air Pollution: A Threat for Human Health and Sustainable Development

Sanjay Maheshwari *and* ***Dr R.L. Dave***

"Any woman who chooses to behave like a full human being should be warned that the armies of the status quo will treat her as something of a dirty joke. That's their natural and first weapon. She will need her sisterhood."

—Gloria Steinem

Introduction

Air is an important component in our atmosphere. Air pollution can be classified into two sections- Visible air pollution and invisible air pollution. Another way of looking at Air pollution could be any substance that holds the potential to hinder the atmosphere or the well being of the living beings surviving in it. The sustainment of all things living is due to a combination of gases that collectively form the atmosphere; the imbalance caused by the increase or decrease of the percentage of these gases can be harmful for survival. Air pollution, unsafe water supply, poor sanitation and hazardous chemicals exert significant pressures on human health, particularly the elderly and the young. Clean air is one of the basic requirements of human health and well-being. However, during the process of economic development, air pollution has been and continues to be a significant health hazard worldwide. The driving forces of air pollution include economic development, urbanisation, energy consumption, transportation and motorisation, as well as increase of urban population. Revelation to air pollutants is a problem of increasing concern due to the range of the pollutants in question, adverse effects observed in a broad range of air pollution levels, and the vast number of people at risk. WHO estimates more than two million people die every year from breathing in tiny particles present in indoor and outdoor air pollution. Air pollution is a major environmental risk to health. By reducing air pollution levels, countries can reduce the burden of disease from stroke, heart disease, lung cancer, and both chronic and acute respiratory diseases, including asthma.

Global Trend in Air Pollution Levels

Air pollution in India is a serious issue with the major sources being fuel wood and biomass burning, fuel adulteration, vehicle emission and traffic congestion. In autumn and winter months, large scale crop residue burning in agriculture fields. A low cost alternative to mechanical tilling is a major source of smoke, smog and particulate pollution. Across the world, city air is often thick with exhaust fumes, factory smoke or soot from coal burning power plants. In many countries there are no air quality regulations and, where they do exist, national standards and their enforcement vary markedly.

Exposure to Air Pollution

Exposure to ambient air pollution has been associated with a series of adverse health effects, ranging from subclinical effects, physiological changes in pulmonary functions and the cardiovascular system, to clinical symptoms, outpatient and emergency-room visits, hospital admissions, and finally to premature death. The increased risk of air pollution-related health effects seems to be relatively low, generally in the range of only a few per cent. However, the total number of people affected worldwide is quite significant.

Health Effects

Air pollution consists of chemicals or particles in the air that can harm the health of humans, animals, and plants. It also damages buildings. Pollutants in the air take many forms. They can be gases, solid particles, or liquid droplets. People react differently to different types of air pollution. Young children and older adults, whose immune systems tend to be weaker, are often more sensitive to pollution. Conditions such as asthma, heart disease, and lung disease can be made worse by exposure to air pollution. The length of exposure and amount and type of pollutants are also factors. Eutrophication is a condition where high amount of nitrogen present in some pollutants gets developed on sea's surface and turns itself into algae and adversely affect fish, plants and animal species.

Short-term Exposure to Air Pollutants

Short-term effects, which are temporary, include illnesses such as pneumonia or bronchitis. They also include discomfort such as irritation to the nose, throat, eyes, or skin. Air pollution can also cause headaches, dizziness, and nausea. Bad smells made by factories, garbage, or sewer systems are considered air pollution, too. These adour are less serious but still unpleasant.

Long-term Exposure to Air Pollutants

Long-term effects of air pollution can last for years or for an entire lifetime. They can even lead to a person's death. Long-term health effects from air pollution include heart disease, lung cancer, and respiratory diseases such as emphysema. Air pollution can also cause long-term damage to people's nerves, brain, kidneys, liver, and other organs. Some scientists suspect air pollutants cause birth defects. Nearly 2.5 million people die worldwide each year from the effects of outdoor or indoor air pollution.

Causal Evidence from Intervention Study

Numerous studies have shown evidence for the association of air pollution with increased daily death. However, there is little direct evidence that diminished particulate or gaseous air pollution levels could lead to reductions in death rates or increase in life-expectancy. In other words, it shows an association rather than a causal relation in the context of air pollution level and death rates. The direct and immediate health benefit of decreased air pollution level provides convincing evidence supporting a causal relationship between air pollution level and death rates.

Preventive Measures

People can help protect health and the health of family, neighbours, and community from risk caused by air pollution, including the risk to your cardiovascular health. Reducing risk includes healthy lifestyle choices (i.e., stopping cigarette smoking, controlling your blood pressure and cholesterol, following advice on weight control and exercise). Particle pollution is sometimes visible as haze, often brown, and reduces visibility; high ozone levels combined with particles can be seen as smog and at very high levels can irritate the eyes and throat. Suggestions for reducing effects of air pollution:

(a) Plan activities when and where pollution levels are lower.

(b) Change activity level if pollution levels are high by limiting time outdoors and in areas where pollution may be highest. If take it easier and walk rather than jog, the amount of pollution breathe will be reduced. Moving activity indoors is helpful in reducing ozone exposures, especially if windows are shut and have the air conditioner on, but other pollutants can come into the home, albeit at lower levels.

(c) Avoid exercising near busy roads and at times of day when pollution is high.

(d) People may choose to take steps to protect themselves as individuals or their families by using masks for respiratory protection or by using an air cleaner. Air-cleaning devices have not been proven to protect against the adverse effects of indoor cigarette smoke (which emits both particles and gases) on heart or lung disease.

(e) Encourage people to use less to less transportation to reduce pollution. Large amount of fossil fuels are burnt to produce electricity so switch off fans and lights when are going out. All are interested in installing solar panels for their home. This will go a long way to curb air pollution. Several attempts are being made world wide on a personal, industrial and governmental levels to curb the intensity at which Air Pollution is rising and regain a balance as far as the proportions of the foundation gases are concerned. This is a direct attempt at slacking global warming.

Limit the Effects of Air Pollution

(a) Most communities have a system for air pollution alerts. Contact local or state air pollution control agency, the Environmental Protection Agency, a local hospital or your doctor for information. Local radio and television stations and newspapers also often report on air quality.

(b) Avoid outdoor physical activity or reduce the intensity and duration of outdoor exercise when an air quality alert has been issued.

(c) Avoid outdoor activity when pollution levels tend to be highest, which is often midday or afternoon. Exercising during rush hour also can expose you to higher amounts of pollution.

(d) Pollution levels are likely to be highest within 50 feet (15 meters) of a road. Urban environments and outdoor smoking areas also have higher pollution levels. If possible, avoid these kinds of areas when exercising.

(e) Vary routine with occasional indoor activities, especially on poor air quality days. Take a fitness class, check out a local gym or run laps on an indoor track.

Conclusion

World Health Organisation experts confirm that there is slight increased risk of some cancer types for some people who were exposed to the radiation. People can help protect health and the health of family, neighbours, and community from risk caused by air pollution, including the risk to your cardiovascular health. Compared to the inhalation of cigarette smoke during active or passive smoking, the gases and particles in ambient air pollution are relatively diluted, resulting in relatively small risk increases for reproductive and children's health outcomes. For the most part, the increased risks for pregnancy outcomes in more polluted versus less polluted areas range from 10 to 30 per cent for preterm birth and low birth weight, and between five and 20 per cent for infant mortality. Ambient (outdoor air pollution) in both cities and rural areas was estimated to cause 3.97 million premature deaths worldwide in 2013. In addition to outdoor air pollution, indoor smoke is a serious health risk for some three billion people who cook and heat their homes with biomass fuels and coal. You can help to reduce Air Pollution by driving good condition vehicles, walking wherever possible, bicycling, and using mass transit. Stop burning wastes, refusals and dry grass and leaves. Plant trees and avoid purchasing products un-friendly to environment. Support and follow Air Act / Laws. Let us help each other in making cleaner and healthier atmosphere where we live.

References

1. http://en.wikipedia.org/wiki/Air_pollution_in_India
2. http://www.conserve-energy-future.com/causes-effects-solutions-of-air-pollution.php
3. http://www.mass.gov/dep/air/aq/env_effects.htm
4. http://environment.nationalgeographic.com/environment/global-warming/pollution-overview
5. http://www.conserve-energy-future.com/causes-effects-solutions-of-air-pollution.php
6. http://www.ncbi.nlm.nih.gov/pmc/articles/PMC2698272/
7. http://archive-kz.com/kz/4/45minut.kz/2013-05-11_2058638_10/www_45minut_kz/
8. http://www.ncbi.nlm.nih.gov/pmc/articles/PMC3852930/
9. http://www.ukessays.com/essays/environmental-sciences/air-pollution-and-its-effect-on-asthma-environmental-sciences-essay.php
10. http://www.biomedcentral.com/1471-2458/13/891
11. http://windowsonmaine.library.umaine.edu/similar.aspx?objectid=7-326&page=4
12. http://www.biomedcentral.com/content/pdf/1471-2458-13-891.pdf
13. www.ncbi.nlm.nih.gov/pmc/articles/
14. www.ncbi.nlm.nih.gov/pubmed/
15. www.biomedcentral.com
16. www.ukessays.com
17. windowsonmaine.library.umaine.edu
18. windowsonmaine.library.umaine.edu/similar.aspx?objectid=...
19. Read more at http://www.brainyquote.com/quotes/keywords/natural_2.html#QXL8WMSZPxyc3xSc.99

19

Natural Resources for Tribal Women Empowerment: A Study in India

Prof D. Pulla Rao

"Women are, in my view, natural peacemakers. As givers and nurturers of life, through their focus on human relationships and their engagement with the demanding work of raising children and protecting family life, they develop a deep sense of empathy that cuts through to underlying human realities."

—Daisaku Ikeda

Introduction

It is widely accepted, basing on the scriptural evidences of the early Vedic period, that women had enjoyed respectable and the most dignified life on par with men. Women were honoured in the courts of the kings as Advisers, Teachers of Vedas etc, and thus influenced the affairs of the state. They had also participated in the yajna performed by the kings and thus enjoyed religious status on par with men. But with the introduction of the Law of Manu, Indian women were discriminated, marginalised and excluded. They were forcibly and systematically stripped off all their social, economic, and political rights and were denied access to resources that would re-empower them besides; they were subjected to several evils like, *sati* and child marriages and forced to work as a servant in the family kitchen/

vocation/occupation. Since woman was treated as a servant, slave, and a serf, she was not permitted to rule men folk; it was treated as a sin even to dream about it.

The British government had tried to amend the situation particularly after the 'sepoy mutiny' it was confined to legislation and localised reformation activities of the progressive ideologists like Raja Ram Mohan Roy, Ishwar Chandra Vidyasagar, Savitribai Phule, Pandita Ramabai, Jyotirao Phule, etc. Therefore, after independence, there arose a need to 'empower' women with social, economic, and the political rights and also provide access to the resources to enjoy a happy life on par with men. However, up to 1974, women welfare was not given special importance; they were clubbed with the general welfare measures. And from the fifth plan onwards government of India had started initiating special programmes for women to better their lives and thereby establish 'gender parity' in the society. For clarity of presentation, this paper is divided into three parts namely, Part I: Women empowerment policies and legislations of the government of India, Part II: Women empowerment programmes of the government of India, and Part III: Summary and conclusions

Part I:
Women Empowerment Policies and Legislations of the Government of India

In this section we will make a brief but critical assessment of various policies of the government of India aimed at upliftment of the social, economic, and political status of women in India. For better presentation, this part is divided into three sections, i.e., (a) Constitutional Provisions, (b) Legislative measures, and (c) Women empowerment policies in the five year plans.

(a) *Constitutional Provisions*

Indian Constitution, had purposefully incorporated the following articles to protect the social, economic, and political interests of the Indian women and thereby laid the path to 'gender parity' in the country.

1. Article 14 - Men and women to have equal rights and opportunities in the political economic and social spheres.

2. Article 15 – The State shall not discriminate against any citizen——Nothing in this article prevents the State from making any special provision for women and children.
3. Article 15(1) - Prohibits discrimination against any citizen on the grounds of religion, race, caste, sex etc.
4. Article 15(3) - Special provision enabling the State to make affirmative discriminations in favour of women.
5. Article 16 - Equality of opportunities in matter of public appointments for all citizens (without any kind of discrimination).
6. Article 39(a) - The State shall direct its policy towards securing all citizens men and women, equally, the right to means of livelihood.
7. Article 39(d) – Equal pay for equal work for both men and women.
8. Article 39(e) enjoins the State to ensure that the health and strength of workers, men and women and the tender age of children are not abused and that the citizens are not forced by economic necessity to enter avocations unsuited to their age or strength.
9. Article 42 - The State to make provision for ensuring just and humane conditions of work and maternity relief.
10. Article 51 (A) (e) –To renounce the practices derogatory to the dignity of women.
11. 73rd and 74th Amendments to the Constitution of India, 1993: seeking special quota of 33 per cent of seats for women in the Panchayati Raj Institutions.
12. The Women Reservation Bill to amend Article 243D to provide 33 per cent reservation for women in Parliament is still pending in the Lok Sabha since 1996.

(b) *Legislative Measures*

This section is divided into two categories i.e., (i) the legislations that are exclusively addressing the women problems, and (ii) general legislations by which women also will gain on par with men.

1. Exclusively Women Legislations

Special Marriage Act,1954; Hindu Marriage Act,1955; The Immoral Traffic Prevention Act 1956; The Maternity

Benefit Act,1961; (e) Dowry Prohibition Act, 1961 and Indian Divorce Act, 1969; The Medical Termination of Pregnancy Act 1971; Equal Remuneration Act, 1976; Family Courts Act, 1984; The Commission of Sati (Prevention) Act,1987; Constitution (Seventythird Amendment) Act, 1992; The Constitution (Seventy-fourth Amendment) Act, 1992; The Pre-Natal Diagnostic Technique (Regulation and Prevention of Misuse) Act, 1994; Protection of Women from DomesticViolence Act, 2005; Prohibition of Child Marriage Act, 2007; The Bill to amend Article 243D to provide 50 per cent reservation for women in seats and also offices of Chairpersons in all 3 tiers of Panchayats.

2. Women Inclusive Legislations

There are about 41 laws that deal with several fields that protect women also along with men. The most important laws relating to economic activities are listed: Factories Act 1948; Minimum Wages Act 1948; Employees' State Insurance Act, 1948; The Plantation Labour Act, 1951, The Bonded Labour System (Abolition) Act 1976.

(c) Women Empowerment Policies in the Five Year Plans

The government of India was blind to women exclusive plans for about three decades. Only and after receiving criticism from several quarters about its failure, it woke up and started doing something to better the lot of women in India. Let us have a brief but analytical review of the main focus of our Five Year Plans:

1. First Five Year Plan (1951-56): Establishment of the Central Social Welfare Board, organisation of Mahila Mandals/ Women's Clubs and the Community Development Programmes.
2. Second Five-Year Plan (1956-61): Intensive agricultural development programmes, equal pay for equal work, protected from injurious work, maternity benefits and crèches etc.
3. Third Five-Year Plan (1961-66): Women education, health, nutrition, family planning.
4. Fourth Five-Year Plan (1969-74): Stress on infant and maternal mortality rates, immunisation.

5. Fifth Five-Year Plan (1974-79): Women employment and income generation, functional literacy programmes, Report of the Committee on the Status of Women in India (1974), Women's Welfare and Development Bureau under the Ministry of Social Welfare (1976) to coordinate policies and programmes for the development of women, IRDP, ICSSR's Committee on Women's Studies on 'Critical Issues on the Status of Women' (1977), The Working Group on Employment of Women', (1977-78), etc.
6. Sixth Five-Year Plan (1980-85): Shift from welfare to development, National Committee on Role and Participation of Women in Agriculture and Rural Development (1979-80), 33 per cent quota in TRYSEM, and DWCRA as an all women programme.
7. Seventh Plan (1986-91): Gender equity and empowerment emphasised, National Policy on Education (1986), United Nations Decade for Women, a minimum of 30 per cent women beneficiaries under all anti-poverty programmes, National Commission on Self-Employed Women1987, Report, Shram Shakti, National Perspective Plan for Women' (1988-2000) etc.
8. Eighth Five-Year Plan (1992-97): Political empowerment of women through 33 per cent special quota in Panchayati Raj institutions, National Commission for Women (1992).
9. Ninth Five Year Plan (1995-2000): Women's Component Plan (WCP) allocated 30 per cent of funds/ benefits to women-specific programmes.
10. Tenth Plan (2002-07): National Policy for Empowerment of women (2001) to ensure survival, protection and development of Women and Children.
11. Eleventh Five Year Plan (2007-12): 'Gender Equity' sub plan was initiated, violence against women was addressed through the network of NYKS clubs and PRIs.
12. Twelfth Five Year Plan (2012-17): The broad vision and aspiration is simultaneous achievement of faster, sustainable, and more inclusive growth. Inclusiveness embraces Scheduled Castes, Scheduled Tribes, Other Backward Classes, Minorities, the differently abled and other marginalised

groups. Women can also be viewed as a disadvantaged group for this purpose. Ending of gender based inequities, discrimination and all forms of violence against girls and women is being accorded overriding priority in the Twelfth Plan. This is fundamental to enabling women to participate fully in the development process, and in fulfilling their social, economic, civil and political rights.

Part II: Women Empowerment Programmes of the Government of India

India is known for its widest net of poverty alleviation programmes targeting the marginalised categories. From the 7th Plan (1986-91) onwards, the government had considered 'women' also a 'target group' and had started separate programmes for their empowerment. The Ministry of Rural Development has been undertaking several poverty alleviation programmes for all categories of rural poor with 30 per cent special component plan for women. On 30th January, 2006, the government of India had converted the department of women and child development as the Ministry of Women and Child Development to take care of the 'women exclusive' programmes. It is also entrusted with the responsibility of monitoring the preparation of gender budgets by all the departments that are implementing women empowerment programmes in their respective fields. Therefore, let us examine the budgetary allocations in Part A; the programmes and achievements of the Ministry of Women and Child Development in Part B; and the programmes and achievements of the Ministry of Rural Development in Part C.

Gender Budgeting in India

Money matters first to undertake any 'women empowerment' programme. Gender budget was first introduced in 2005-06. It includes two parts i.e., Part A deals with the schemes in which 100 per cent provision is meant for women while Part B deals with the schemes in which the allocations for women constitute at least 30 per cent of the total provision. Let us have a look at the pattern of budgetary allocation made under this head as presented in Table-1.

Table-1: Statement of Gender Budget in India

Sl. No.	*Year*	*No. of Participating Dept.*	*No. of Demands*	*Total Magnitude of Gender Budget (BE) (in Rs. Crores)*	*% to Total Budget*
1.	2005-06	9	10	14,378.68	2.79
2.	2006-07	18	24	28,736.53	5.09
3.	2007-08	27	33	31,177.96	4.50
4.	2008-09	27	33	27,661.67	3.68
5.	2009-10	28	33	56,857.61	5.57
6.	2010-11	28	33	67,749.80	6.11
7.	2011-12	29	34	78,251.02	6.22
8.	2012-13	29	34	88,142.80	5.91
9.	2013-14	30	35	97,133.70	5.83

Source: Ministry of Women and Child Development, Govt. of India, Annual Report, 20012-13, page 81.

Programmes of the Ministry of Women and Child Development

The Ministry of Women and Child Development is presently running the following nine major schemes:

1. *ICDS*: Integrated Child Development Services which contained two components namely, nutrition and preschool education.
2. *Sabla:* Rajiv Gandhi Scheme for Empowerment of Adolescent Girls.
3. *IGMSY:* Indira Gandhi Matritva Sahayog Yojana.
4. *ICPS:* Integrated Child Protection Scheme.
5. *Family Counseling:* To address issues of violence against women.
6. *RGNCS*: Rajiv Gandhi National Crèche Scheme- for the children of working mothers.
7. *STEP:* Support to Training and Employment Programme for Women.
8. *ISWE:* Integrated Scheme for Women's Empowerment-for the North East.

9. *RMK*: Rashtriya Mahila Kosh- national credit fund for women

Now let us examine the budgetary implications and the achievements of the above nine schemes as presented in the Table-2.

Table -2: Ministry of Women and Child Development: Outlays and Achievements

Programme	*Funds released / utilised*	*No. of Persons benefitted*
ICDS (Nutrition)	5756.63	9,27,65,522
ICDS (Pre-school)	8794.63	3,46,65,683
Sabla	477.47	88,76,975
IGMSY	75.21	4,16,685
ICPS	253.84	5,94,625
Family Counseling	16.20	3,03,508
RGNCS	51.08	5,94,025
STEP	8.33	29,650
ISWE	1.51	378
RMK	229.31	7,17,434
TOTAL	**15664.21**	**13,89,64,485**

Source: Ministry of Women and Child Development, Government of India, Annual Report 2012-13.

Programmes of the Ministry of Rural Development

The Ministry of Rural Development has got two departments, viz., the Department of Rural Development and the Department of Land Resources. The ministry is presently running about six major schemes. The total budget of the Department of Rural Development for the year 2012-13 is Rs 73175 crore. In addition, a sum of Rs 25422.58 crore was also available as unspent balance as on 1.4.2012. Similarly, the total budget of the Department of Land Resources is Rs 3201 crore. In addition, a sum of Rs 4133.11 crore unspent balances as on 1.4.2012 was also available which amounts a total of Rs 1,05,931.69 crore. The major Programmes of this ministry are:

1. *MGNREGA:* Mahatma Gandhi National Rural Employment Guarantee Act is to provide statutorily guaranteed wage employment to the rural poor.

Table -3: Ministry of Rural Development: Outlays and Achievements

(For the year 2011-12)

S. No.	*Programme*	*Outlay Rs. Crores*	*Total Physical Achievement*	*Women*	*Women as % to total*
1.	MGNREGA	31000.00	21634 lakh days	10380 lakh days	47.98
2.	IAY	10000.00	32.66 lakh houses	21.15 lakh houses	65.76
3.	Swarozgaris		16,77,117	11,03,553	65.80
4.	No. of SHGs		2,33,713	1,53,558	65.70
5.	IGOAPS			223 lakh persons	
6.	IGNWPS			42 lakh persons	
7.	IGNDPS			8 lakh persons	
8.	NFBS			2.91 lakh families	

2. *IAY:* Indira Awaas Yojana is to provide housing to the rural poor.
3. *NRLM: Aajeevika:* National Rural Livelihoods, Mission is to create and support self-employment opportunities to the rural poor.
4. *PMGSY:* Pradhan Mantri Gram Sadak Yojana is to establish all weather connectivity to the remote rural areas for overall improvement in transport of rural people and their products.
5. *NSAP:* National Social Assistance Programme is to provide monthly pension to the rural poor living in distress conditions; this programme is passed on to the state government.
6. *IGNPS:* Indira Gandhi National Pension Scheme like old age pension, widow pension, and disability pension schemes.
7. *NFBS:* National Family Benefit Scheme provide for death of a primary bread winner of the household.
8. *IWMP:* Integrated Watershed Management Programme is to create efficient water management systems to the farmers.

Since this study is mainly focussed on women empowerment we will examine only those schemes that contain gender-wise details of outlays/achievements. The details of budgetary allocations and the physical achievements under important heads are presented in Table-3.

India's Poor Ranking in Gender Parity

This scale measures how close women are to reaching parity with men. India stands at the extremely lower ends in respect of its gender gap ranking. The details are furnished in Table-4.

Table- 4: India's Gender Gap Index

Area of Gender Inequality	*India's Rank out of 136*	*India's Score*
Economic Participation and Opportunity	124	0.4465
Educational Attainment	120	0.8574
Health and Survival	135	0.9312
Political Empowerment	9	0.3852
Global Gender Gap Index	101	0.6551

Source: World Economic Forum 2013, The Global Gender Gap Report.

Conclusions

Indian women suffered severely under male chauvinism for centuries. They lead a miserable life bearing the grunt of famines and poverty of higher magnitude compared to their male counterparts. The Indian tradition that was based on the Law of Manu was the root cause for their sub-human life. The efforts of the British government were confined to legislation and localised reformation activities of the progressive ideologists like Raja Ram Mohan Roy, Ishwar Chandra Vidyasagar, Savitribai Phule, Pandita Ramabai, Jyotirao Phule, etc. After independence, the Government of India had started undertaking systematic efforts to improve the lot of women in India. Since, the government of India has been implementing several intervention policies and programmes for women empowerment over the last sixty six years.

It is found that the government of India has taken adequate care by nullifying all the 'anti-women' social, economic, and political promulgations of the Manu Smrithi at a single stretch through appropriate provisions in the constitution followed by suitable legislations five year plans. The Government of India had allocated separate gender budget and ordered every ministry/ department to specify their respective gender demands. The Ministry of Women and Child Development is made as the coordinating agency of the gender budget of the Union Govt. The Ministry of Rural Development spear heads in respect of economic empowerment while the Ministry of Women and Child Development is taking care of overall developmental aspects of women in India. Given the budgetary limitations, they are functioning satisfactorily; greater coverage requires greater budgetary allocations coverage. Strictly speaking gap is still much wider, only about 24 per cent of females are covered under some programme or the other leaving 76 per cent of women to fend for themselves. And without time bound commitment from the side of every stake holder, it might take another half a century or even more to achieve gender parity in India.

Major Suggestions

1. The Indian Parliament shall become gender sensitive and vote for higher gender budget.

2. It needs women to fight war of gender parity.
3. Higher judiciary powers required for the National Commission for Women to prosecute every irresponsible person/authority that fails to implement the women specific legislations.
4. Create 'women wing' in all administrative units down to the Village Panchayat level.
5. Appoint women IAS and IPS cadre as Additional District Collectors and Additional Superintendents of Police to create confidence and easy access to rural women particularly. And for this the Government of India shall undertake a special drive to recruit committed women to the top slots.
6. There shall be gender quota in all ministries and departments at the central and state levels.

References

1. Basham, A L., (1954) Wonder that was India, Sidgwick and Jackson, London, 1954
2. Deepti Agarwal (2001) m "Empowerment of Rural Women in India", *Social Welfare*, Vol. 48, No. 4, July 2001, New Delhi.
3. Lakshmipathi Raju. M and Venkateswarlu. V, (2007), "Women Empowerment – Challenges and Strategies", Regal Publications, New Delhi.
4. Mira Seth Women and Development – The Indian Experience, New Delhi, Sage Publications, 2001.
5. Nanda, B.R, Indian Women: From Purdah to Modernity, New Delhi, Vikas, 1976.
6. Pandey, A.K. "Emerging Issues in Empowerment of Women", New Delhi, Anmol Publications, 2002.
7. Sadiq Aahamad Jilani Syed (2004), "Women in India, Legal and Human Rights", Centre for Professional Development in Higher Education and Women's Studies and Development Centre, University of Delhi.
8. Sakuntala Narasimhan, Empowering Women – An Alternative Strategy From Rural India, Sage Publications, 1999.
9. Suguna, B (2002), "Strategies for Empowerment of Rural Women", in the *Journal of Social Welfare*, Vol. 49, No. 5, New Delhi.

10. The Laws of Manu, Translated by G. Buhler.
11. Read more at http://www.brainyquote.com/quotes/keywords/natural_2.html#QXL8WMSZPxyc3xSc.99

Bibliography

1. Abiodun Alao (2007), *Natural Resources and Conflict in Africa: The Tragedy of Endowment,* University Rochester Press.
2. Alan Randall (1987), *Resource Economics: An Economic Approach to Natural Resource and Environmental Policy,* Wiley.
3. Anne E. Maczulak (2010), *Biodiversity: Conserving Endangered Species,* Infobase Publishing.
4. Antonio H. Noblejas (1961), *Philippine law on natural resources,* Central Book Supply.
5. Asish Ghosh (2003), *Natural Resource Conservation and Environment Management,* APH Publishing.
6. B.W. Pandey (2005), *Natural Resource Management,* Mittal Publications.
7. Bruce Morgan Campbell, Jeffrey Sayer (2003), *Integrated Natural Resource Management: Linking Productivity, the Environment and Development*, CABI.
8. Charles R. Menzies (2006), *Traditional Ecological Knowledge and Natural Resource Management*, U of Nebraska Press.
9. Christo Fabricius (2004), *Rights, Resources and Rural Development: Community-based Natural Resource Management in Southern Africa*, Earthscan.
10. David William Pearce (1994), *The Economic Value of Biodiversity,* Earthscan.
11. Donald Grebner, Pete Bettinger, and Jacek Siry (2013), *Introduction to Forestry and Natural Resources,* Academic Press.

12. Douglas M. Knudson, Ted T. Cable, Larry Beck (2003), *Interpretation of cultural and natural resources,* Venture Pub.
13. Edward B. Barbier (2007), *Natural Resources and Economic Development,* Cambridge University Press.
14. Ian Nuberg, Brendan Hugh George, Rowan Reid (2009), *Agroforestry for Natural Resource Management*, Csiro Publishing.
15. John I. Spicer (2009), *Biodiversity*, The Rosen Publishing Group.
16. Kevin H. Deal (2002), *Wildlife and Natural Resource Management*, Thomson/Delmar Learning.
17. Miguel A. Altieri (1994), *Biodiversity and Pest Management in Agroecosystems*, Food Products Press.
18. Mike J. Jeffries (2006), *Biodiversity and Conservation,* Routledge.
19. Nico Schrijver (2008), *Sovereignty Over Natural Resources: Balancing Rights and Duties,* Cambridge University Press.
20. Richard L. Knight, Sarah F. Bates (1995), *A New Century for Natural Resources Management*, Island Press.
21. Roger Perman (2003), *Natural Resource and Environmental Economics,* Pearson Education.
22. Roger Stern (2004), *Good Statistical Practice for Natural Resources Research,* CABI Pub.
23. Sharad Singh Negi (2001), *Participatory Natural Resource Management,* Indus Publishing.
24. Takuya Abe, Simon A. Levin, Masahiko Higashi (1996), *Biodiversity: An Ecological Perspective,* Springer New York.
25. Tanya M. Shenk, Alan B. Franklin (2001), *Modeling in Natural Resource Management: Development, Interpretation, and Application*, Island Press.
26. Thomas B. Daugherty (2000), *Managing Our Natural Resources*, Delmar Cengage Learning.
27. Thomas E. Lovejoy, Lee Jay Hannah (2005), *Climate Change and Biodiversity,* Yale University Press.
28. Thomas Sterner (2003), *Policy Instruments for Environmental and Natural Resource Management*, Resources for the Future.

29. Timothy C. Haab, Kenneth E. McConnell (2003), *Valuing Environmental and Natural Resources: The Econometrics of Non-market Valuation*, Edward Elgar.
30. Tony Prato (1999), *Natural Resource and Environmental Economics,* Wiley.
31. Vandana Shiva (1991), *Biodiversity: Social and Ecological Perspectives*, Zed Books.
32. Washington Odongo Ochola, P. C. Sanginga, Isaac Bekalo (2010), *Managing Natural Resources for Development in Africa: A Resource Book*, IDRC.
33. William E. Grant, Sandra L. Marín (1997), *Ecology and Natural Resource Management: Systems Analysis and Simulation,* John Wiley & Sons.
34. William G. Camp (1997), *Managing Our Natural Resources*, Delmar.

Index

I

J

K

L

M

N